THE DREAM AFTER A CENTURY

Committee of
Psychoanalytic Psychotherapeutic
Publications and Organizations

Monograph 2

Arnold D. Richards, M.D.

Book Series Editor

THE DREAM AFTER A CENTURY

SYMPOSIUM 2000 ON DREAMS

Edited by

Melvin Lansky, M.D.

International Universities Press, Inc.
Madison • Connecticut

Library of Congress Cataloging-in-Publication Data

The dream after a century : symposium 2000 on dreams / edited by Melvin R. Lansky.
p. cm.
Includes bibliographical references and index.
ISBN 0–8236–1422–0
1. Dream interpretation—Congresses. 2. Dreams—Therapeutic use—Congresses. 3. Psychoanalysis—Congresses. 4. Psychotherapy—Congresses.I. Lansky, Melvin R.

BF1078.D68 2008
154.6′3—dc22

2003067627

Manufactured in the United States of America

To Karen, Madeleine, and Joshua

Table of Contents

Acknowledgments

I would like to express my gratitude to Dr. Arnold Richards, Editor of *The Journal of the American Psychoanalytic Association* and general editor of the Symposium series, and to Dr. Arnold Rothstein, who organized Symposium 2000, for inviting me to edit the papers and discussions of this splendid symposium, and for their support and encouragement of my editorial labors. I also thank Dr. Margaret Emery of International Universities Press for her help and support.

Contributors

Mark J. Blechner is Training and Supervising Analyst at the William Alanson White Institute of Psychoanalysis and is also on the faculties of New York University and the Manhattan Institute for Psychoanalysis. He is a member of the editorial board of *Contemporary Psychoanalysis* and is in private practice in New York City. He is the author of *The Dream Frontier.*

Philip M. Bromberg is a Training and Supervising Analyst and Faculty Member, William Alanson White Institute, and Clinical Professor of Psychology at the New York University Postdoctoral Program. Dr. Bromberg is an Associate Editor of *Psychoanalytic Dialogues* and *Contemporary Psychoanalysis,* and on the editorial boards of *Psychoanalytic Inquiry* and *The Journal of the American Academy of Psychoanalysis.* He is author of *Standing in the Spaces: Essays on Clinical Process, Trauma, and Dissociation.*

Steven Ellman is Training and Supervising Analyst and President-Elect, Institute for Psychoanalytic Training and Research, New

York; President of the Independent Psychoanalytic Societies of the United States. He is the author (with James Antrobus) of *The Mind in Sleep* and the editor (with Michael Moskowitz) of *Freud's Technique Papers: Toward a New Approach to the Therapeutic Relationship.*

Elsa First is Associate Clinical Professor of Psychology, New York University Postdoctoral Program in Psychotherapy and Psychoanalysis.

James L. Fosshage is Clinical Professor of Psychology, New York University; Cofounder and Board Director, National Institute for the Psychotherapies, New York; and founding faculty member, Institute for the Psychoanalytic Study of Subjectivity, New York. He has coauthored (with Clemens Loew) *Dream Interpretation: A Comparative Study, Revised Edition* and (with Joseph Lichtenberg) *A Spirit of Inquiry.*

Robert D. Gillman is Training and Supervising Analyst, Baltimore–Washington Psychoanalytic Institute and the New York Freudian Society; a Supervising Child Analyst at the Cleveland Psychoanalytic Institute. He has written on children's dreams, dreams of pregnancy, and defenses in dreams.

Marianne Goldberger is Training and Supervising Analyst, New York University Psychoanalytic Institute; Professor of Clinical Psychiatry, New York University Medical Center. She is on the editorial board of the *Psychoanalytic Quarterly.*

Ruth Imber is Training and Supervising Analyst, faculty member, and fellow at the William Alanson White Institute. She is on the editorial board of *Contemporary Psychoanalysis.*

Ernest Kafka is Training and Supervising Analyst, New York Psychoanalytic Institute, Associate Clinical Professor, Cornell–New York Hospital. He has published papers on examination dreams and dyslexia in clinical analytic work.

Melvin R. Lansky is Volume Editor, Symposium 2000; Training and Supervising Analyst, Los Angeles Psychoanalytic Institute; Clinical Professor, UCLA School of Medicine, Department of Psychiatry. He is the author (with Carol Bley) of *Posttraumatic Nightmares: Psychoanalytic Explorations* and the editor of *Essential Papers on Dreams.*

Paul Lippmann is Training and Supervising Psychoanalyst, William Alanson White Psychoanalytic Institute, New York; faculty member, New York University Postdoctoral Program in Psychotherapy and Psychoanalysis; Director of *Nocturnes: On Listening to Dreams.* He is in private practice in Stockbridge, Massachusetts.

Edward Nersessian is Training and Supervising Analyst, New York Psychoanalytic Institute, Clinical Associate Professor, Weill Cornell Medical College. He is coeditor of *Neuro-Psychoanalysis.*

Edna O'Shaughnessy is Training Analyst, British Psychoanalytical Society; Supervisor for Child and Family, Tavistock Clinic, London.

Mervyn M. Peskin is a faculty member, New York Psychoanalytic Institute; Clinical Associate Professor at the Weill Cornell Medical Center.

Sydney Pulver is Training and Supervising Analyst, Psychoanalytic Center of Philadelphia; Clinical Professor of Psychiatry, University of Pennsylvania School of Medicine.

Ellen Rees is Training and Supervising Analyst, Columbia Center for Psychoanalytic Training and Research; Clinical Associate Professor of Psychiatry, New York Weill Cornell Medical Center. She is on the editorial board of the *Journal of the American Psychoanalytic Association.*

Morton Reiser is the Albert E. Kent Professor of Psychiatry Emeritus, Yale University School of Medicine; Training and Supervising

Analyst, Western New England Institute of Psychoanalysis. He is the author of *Mind, Brain, Body: Toward a Convergence of Psychoanalysis and Neurobiology* and *Memory in Mind and Brain: What Dream Imagery Reveals.*

Owen Renik is Training and Supervising Analyst, San Francisco Psychoanalytic Institute; Editor-in-Chief of the *Psychoanalytic Quarterly;* and Program Chair, American Psychoanalytic Association.

Howard Shevrin is Professor of Psychology, Departments of Psychiatry and Psychology at the University of Michigan; a member of the Michigan Psychoanalytic Society. His research has mainly been devoted to the investigation of unconscious processes employing psychodynamic, cognitive, and neurophysiologic methods.

Mark Solms is editor and translator, *Complete Neuroscientific Works of Sigmund Freud* (4 volumes) and also the revised *Standard Edition of the Complete Psychological Works of Sigmund Freud* (24 volumes). He is author of the *Neuropsychology of Dreams* and Coeditor of the journal *Neuro-Psychoanalysis*, an interdisciplinary journal for psychoanalysis and the neurosciences. He is an associate member of the British Psychoanalytical Society and honorary member of the New York Psychoanalytic Society; Lecturer in neurosurgery at Saint Bartholomew's Hospital and the Royal London Hospital.

Introduction: *The Interpretation of Dreams* after a Century—Where Are We on the Royal Road?

Melvin R. Lansky

Symposium 2000 was held on the hundredth anniversary of the publication of *The Interpretation of Dreams*, the book that declared the dream to be the royal road to an understanding of the unconscious mind—hence the title of the symposium. To set the conference in perspective, I will begin by looking at some legacies of *The Interpretation of Dreams*. These legacies—still powerful in their impact both on those who affirm and those who reject their foundational importance—include the overarching and now controversial question of the status of the psychoanalytic theory of how the mind works and of the relation of clinical practice to that theory of the mind. For many decades, the theory of the mind and its workings, as put forward in chapter 7, was presumed to be foundational for psychoanalysts' clinical handling of dreams, but there is by no means universal agreement that it remains so today. If, in fact, the text is foundational, it challenges us to ask in what way it is so. If *The Interpretation of Dreams* is not foundational, we are faced with further questions: Do we need theoretical foundations, and, if so, what if anything can be presumed to be foundational in our psychoanalytic handling of dreams? These questions move us into the even deeper questions that face us in an age of pluralism: What is theory? What is the relation of psychological, neurological, or cognitive theory to what we do in the consulting room?

The papers that follow take a wide range of stands toward these questions. First and foremost, they are intended to be clinical papers, each illustrating the author's technical stance toward dreams in the context of that author's own clinical evidence. Yet the choices in the handling of the dream made by each clinician reveal, implicitly or explicitly, the position that clinician takes toward theory and its relation to clinical work. Each paper focuses primarily on the clinical material, supplying the minimal background on the author's assumptions and clinical foundations. This format is unusual in psychoanalytic conferences, most of which allow distinguished clinicians to discuss the work of others without presenting their own work. The present format allows the reader access to what distinguished practitioners of different psychoanalytic persuasions actually do, and also allows for an interchange between the authors themselves and the audience at the Symposium about the implications of their clinical presentations.

THE INTERPRETATION OF DREAMS AND ITS LEGACY: A SELECTIVE OVERVIEW

In *The Interpretation of Dreams* (1900), we are given the account of Freud's attempts to apply what he had learned about the *disturbing memory* which was both expressed and defended against by *symptoms* in his study of psychoneurotic adults, hysterics (psychiatrically symptomatic adults who had been sexually abused as children), to another type of ideation, *dreams*, which he believed both to reveal and to hide another type of upsetting ideation, the *disturbing wish*, which he believed underlay the manifest dream and drove that dream into being.

It is important to realize that the term *psychoneurosis* had a much more specific connotation than is commonly realized today, and that Freud's nosology of psychoneurotic symptoms included only irrational ideas: Conversions were ideas about bodily dysfunction not corresponding to known patterns of innervation. Phobias were ideas about irrationally feared objects. Obsessions were, for the most part, ideas about feared impulses. Compulsions were ideas about acts felt to be obligatory. Delusions were ideas about feared objects. In the case of psychoneurotic symptoms, Freud hoped to analyze the pathological manifest ideation so as to arrive at an underlying pathogenic idea, a painful memory. With the dream, he hoped to do the same for the underlying wish that was painful to acknowledge.

Freud's scientific ambitions were, to some extent, therapeutic, but for the most part he sought to place the dream, which had been more the province of poets and oneiromancers than of scientists, under the aegis of scientific understanding. He was strongly in the tradition of Charles Darwin (1859), whose works on evolution he studied itensively; of Franz von Brentano (1874), whose lectures on philosophy Freud attended, and who emphasized the study of "that which is presented to consciousness"; of the scientist and philosopher Helmholtz (1995); and of the philosophy of John Stuart Mill (1843), whose attempt to found a science of human nature on the laws of association of ideas was also well known to Freud. This very sweeping intellectual agenda is far from limited to the therapeutic arena of relieving neurotic suffering. *The Interpretation of Dreams* was first published at a time very early in the history of psychotherapy as we now understand it. It dates from the prepsychoanalytic era of dream analysis and self-analysis, in which Freud was the only practitioner of psychoanalysis, and thus antedates psychoanalysis proper, which can be said to originate in anything like its present form only with the first glimmerings of the significance of the transference for psychoanalytic treatment in 1899. Both the grand intellectual sweep and the relative therapeutic naivete accompanying the investigations that went into the book should be appreciated when its legacy is considered.

What about *The Interpretation of Dreams* remains relevant today, what is its legacy? What are the central issues, and what do they mean to today's clinicians? The Symposium is, of course, not so much about the legacy of *The Interpretation of Dreams*, as it is about the present-day clinical handling of dreams in psychoanalytic practice.

As background for this agenda, I will examine the text of *The Interpretation of Dreams*, emphasizing some major themes that, positively and negatively, still raise pertinent questions. These themes include: psychodynamics, particularly those centered around the concept of incompatibility with conscience, first put forward by Freud in *Studies on Hysteria* (Breuer and Freud, 1893–1895); with fulfillment and the relation of wish fulfillment to both meaning and function and to the nature of dream instigation; self-deception inherent in the notion of the dream as representing, in disguised form, the fulfillment of a wish; and the integration of the clinical handling of dreams with the theory of how the mind or how the brain works.

Let us note at the outset the mistranslation, an important one in my view, of Freud's title into English. *Traumdeutung* does not mean *interpretation of dreams* so much as *meaning of dreams,* and the difference is significant. *The Interpretation of Dreams* is, in fact, much more a treatise on the meaning, formation, and function of dreams than it is a treatise on clinical dream interpretation. It is a serious error, and one that is often made, to regard *The Interpretation of Dreams* as a book about the clinical handling of dreams in psychoanalysis. Freud intended to demonstrate his ideas about dreams and analysis in a work to be called *Dreams and Hysteria.* That work became "Fragment of the Analysis of a Case of Hysteria" (1905), the so-called Dora case, and changed course and purpose when Freud, in examining the reasons for Dora's sudden interruption of treatment on the last day of the century after twelve weeks of analysis, appreciated for the first time the significance of the transference. I shall not, in this introduction to the Symposium, discuss Freud's views on the clinical handling of dreams that were set out in his later writings about clinical dream interpretation.

AN OVERVIEW OF *THE INTERPRETATION OF DREAMS*

Chapter 1: The Overture

Though the bulk of the text of *The Interpretation of Dreams,* chapters 2 through 7, was completed by 1896, chapter 1, the introduction, was written in 1899 just before the publication of the book. Chapter 1, the often neglected "overture" to the work, is not simply a review of the literature on dreams. If the reader is not unduly distracted by the copious references to now-forgotten early contributors to the study of the dream, chapter 1 provides a critical dimension to the understanding of the massive project of synthesis and empirical demonstration accomplished in the subsequent six chapters. It is an exploration, through the voices of previous contributors, of the array of theses and antitheses from which the book emerges as a grand synthesis. Regrettably, chapter 1 is ignored in most psychoanalytic training curricula today. To get a sense of its centrality to the book as a whole, the reader is well advised to consider the book's table of contents. Freud introduces topics in chapter 1 that are covered empirically in chapter 5 and theoretically in chapter 7: Are dreams made up of recent sensory or very remote early components? What is the role of somatic contributions? Does thinking go on in dreams? What about the moral sense of dreams? The topic outlines in chapter 1, repeated in chapters 5 and 7, reveal much about the major thrust of the text.

The Empirical Chapters (2–6)

In chapter 2, the reader is plunged into Freud's methodology for studying dreams by using the associative method and radically eschewing the use of allegory or fable as the model for dream interpretation. The method involves reducing the dream to its elements and, by associating exhaustively to each element, arriving at the latent meaning of the dream.

The radical associationalism put forth in chapter 2 becomes less consistent as the text progresses. Freud seems at times to exempt certain kinds of dream material from exclusive and radical reliance on the associative method: We are told later in the book about typical dreams, but never what the status of a "typical" dream is or how it is recognizable as "typical." The same is true of symbols. We are told that symbols are (quite idiosyncratically) defined as dream elements that do not arise from recent sensory impressions, and that symbols may be interpreted directly without use of associations. Yet the epistemology of symbolic meaning is never completely clarified. Later in Freud's writings (1920, 1933), we learn of traumatic, repetitive dreams, a lasting problem for the theory of wish fulfillment. My own view is that what Freud has said about typical dreams and about symbols refers, in fact, to empirical generalizations, not true exceptions to the use of the associative method.

In chapter 2, Freud's clinical material, specifically, the Irma dream, gives the first of many vivid descriptions of the instigation of dreams, but Freud never quite develops a theory of instigation that takes into account the full complexity of his clinical examples of instigation. Since the process of instigation links happenings in the dreamer's life to his or her internal world, the issue of instigation is an important theoretical one. But, in his theoretical treatment of instigation, Freud omits theoretical attention to the disturbances in narcissistic equilibrium, which are sensitively detailed in almost every one of his dreams, and instead treats instigation theoretically by using the metaphor of the capitalist (the unconscious wish) and entrepreneur (the preconscious worry), discussed briefly in chapter 7.

Chapter 3 embarks upon the topic of wish fulfillment by consideration of wishes that are obviously and on the surface fulfillments of wishes: dreams of convenience and children's dreams, dreams that, in an obvious way, set themselves to solving a problem. The instigating circumstance becomes the "question," so to speak, to which the latent dream content is the "answer." In this sense, wish is an obvious psychological desire. Thirsty because he had eaten anchovies before retiring, Freud dreams of drinking a glass of water. This dream of convenience offsets the physiological signals of thirst sufficiently for him to stay asleep. Inherent in this simplest type of dream are the very complex notions of the dream as an attempt to solve a problem (drinking water being the answer to the problem posed by thirst) and of self-deception—the dream per se does not solve the problem of thirst, but only deceives the dreamer temporarily into thinking that the problem has been solved.

The notion of wish expands in complexity very rapidly in chapter 4, "Distortion in Dreams," which addresses the issue of dreams where the underlying wishes are not obvious. Chapter 4 may be considered the dramatic point of entry of dynamic thinking regarding the dream as a product of the mind. Distortion and disguise conceal the wish from view. Furthermore, dreams have not simply meaning, but also function. They solve a problem posed by the instigating circumstance, and yet another problem caused by anxiety regarding the conscience, here called the *censor.*

Freud's investigatory posture often led him to emphasize the defensive aspect of dream formation at the expense of the expressive aspect, but the expressive was always important. His strong mistrust of the manifest content expressed in this chapter would seem excessive to most contemporary clinicians (Pulver, 1987). In chapter 4, the notion of defense is introduced into our thinking about the dream, and continues Freud's thinking about defense in general as introduced in *Studies on Hysteria* (Breuer and Freud, 1893–1895). It likens the structure of the dream as a replacement in consciousness for the disturbing awareness of an underlying forbidden wish to the structure of the symptom as expression of and defense against an underlying disturbing memory.

In thinking about hysterical symptoms, Janet emphasized the weakened psyche, Breuer emphasized trauma, and Freud reconciled the two by positing incompatibility with conscience as an accompaniment of trauma. Memory is banished from consciousness (repressed) because of painful affects that ensue when the memory is incompatible with the dictates of conscience. In chapter 4, Freud extended the same line of thinking to dreams: the wish is banished from consciousness by distortion or disguise when awareness of it threatens disturbance because of the wish's incompatibility with conscience, the censor.

All of the considerations regarding defense, distortion, and disguise introduced in this chapter are in the service of better understanding the overarching premise of the entire text. First, that the meaning and function of the dream are inevitably intertwined, that this commingling of meaning and function can only be understood in terms of the wish-fulfilling function of dreams, and second, that all distortion and disguise is aimed (by the workings of the censor) at keeping the painful awareness of the disturbing wish from entering consciousness.

Chapter 5, ''Material and Sources of Dreams,'' originated from Freud's own meticulous self-analytic work. Such exploratory detail, oblivious as it is to the prevailing psychoanalytic process, would be rare in clinical psychoanalytic practice today. Freud, continuing from his observations in chapter 1, noted that dreams were often constructed from recent sensory impressions and indifferent material. Recent material was used because of the way that memory works in the psychic apparatus—it was recent material that was available as raw material from which to construct a dream. Indifferent material was deployed by what was soon to be referred to as the *dream work,* because disturbing material is kept from consciousness by displacement onto material that is less charged and less disturbing. One of the functions of the dream is to dampen intensity that might otherwise threaten sleep.

The next section of the chapter, ''Infantile Material as Sources,'' is in many ways the centerpiece of the book. Freud, through the discussion of the magnificently analyzed Count Thun dream, introduced the infantile unconscious. Freud's analysis of his own dream unearthed two powerful infantile memories, which in turn cast light on the instigation of the dream by events at the train station on the dream day. This astonishing and revolutionary section of the book is followed by a relatively bland section that concludes that somatic sources of the dream are mere day residue. Freud then discussed ''typical dreams,'' not so much typical dreams as a category qualitatively different from other dreams, but typical unconscious predicaments that show up in dreams: embarrassing dreams of being naked, death of persons of whom the dreamer is fond, and examination dreams.

Chapter 6, ''The Dream Work,'' concerns the topics of displacement, condensation, symbol formation, and secondary revision. Often unappreciated about this chapter is the fact that it conveys, more than any other of Freud's previous or subsequent works, an exhaustive empirical study of how the imagination works to produce imagery. The dream is, so to speak, pure imagination, hence the special status of the mental product that Freud called the royal road to the workings of the unconscious mind. Because of our contemporary tendency to give more and more emphasis to the persons and the actions in the dream scenario, a focus on who is doing what to whom, we sometimes forget to lift out and submit for the patient's associations specific elements in the dream, products of the imagination that were deployed toward some purpose. Reiser (1997), in the tradition of Isakower (1938), has reminded us that these details are crucial in the analysis of a dream and for our understanding of why it is that the dream had to be *dreamt*.

In this chapter, Freud introduced the problem posed by symbols. He defined a symbol, somewhat surprisingly, as a dream element that, on exhaustive analysis, is not found to originate from the sensory day residue. Empirical study of such elements reveals them to be small in number, to relate to predicaments in the childhood familial situation: parents, siblings, and processes internal and external that had caused consternation in childhood, such as eating, destroying, copulating, defecating, and the like. As Freud used the term, *symbols,* like their counterparts typical dreams, are not so much departures from the associative method, as they are empirical generalizations resulting from the study of these dream elements. Freud's views on symbol formation have been much elaborated and changed since his death (e.g., Segal, 1952).

The final topic of chapter 6 is *secondary revision,* that part of the dream added by the preconscious so that the final product will be more coherent than was the original experience of dreaming and also more distant and less obvious in terms of its disturbing meaning.

Wish Fulfillment and Self-Deception Seen Theoretically in Chapter 7: What Is the Mind Like, Such That It Can Make Up a Lie and Then Be Soothed by Believing It?

Chapter 7, "The Psychology of the Dream Processes," draws from the vast amount of clinical material presented in the preceding five chapters in an attempt to deal with the theoretical implications of Freud's empirical investigations for an understanding of how the mind works.

As he made clear at the beginning of that chapter, Freud's intent was not to propound doctrine, but rather to tentatively but systematically think through the implications of his empirical findings from chapters 2 through 6 in a disciplined way:

> But as soon as we endeavour to penetrate more deeply into the mental processes involved in dreaming, every path will end in darkness. There is no possibility of *explaining* dreams as psychical processes, since to explain a thing means to trace it back to something already known, and there is at the present time no established psychological knowledge under which we could subsume what the psychological examination enables us to infer as a basis for their explanation. On the contrary, we shall be obliged to set up a number of fresh hypotheses which touch tentatively upon the structure of the apparatus of the mind and upon the play of forces operating on it [Freud, 1900, p. 511].

My very brief comments on chapter 7 will be confined to the problems surrounding wish fulfillment and self-deception, problems that remain even though our knowledge of neuro- and cognitive science advances and changes. Chapter 7 details the ways in which we are equipped by our psychic apparatus to lie to ourselves as a means of tolerating the harshness of reality. The fundamental and horrifying view of the human psyche—as an apparatus that, in the dream and elsewhere, is so constituted that, without the conscious decision to do so, it makes up a soothing but untrue tale and (as audience of the dream) beholds and believes the tale for the purpose of lowering the impact of some impinging disturbance—does not become superseded as our knowledge of neuro- and cognitive sciences evolves and changes. I shall not, in this brief survey, present a summary or a critique of Freud's neuroscientific or physiologic assumptions in chapter 7.

The preamble to chapter 7 centers around the account of the moving dream of a father at the wake of his recently deceased son. The sleeping father, who, in sleep detected the odor of burning cloth that a fallen candle has ignited, incorporated this sensation into a dream of the still living, but gravely ill child saying, "Father, I'm burning." The dream, in addition to signaling the current danger of fire, revealed also the wish that the son was still alive. "Father, I'm burning" looks both backward to the illness and high fever that preceded the son's death and forward to the danger of fire from the overturned candle. That dream highlights the wish as attempting to solve a problem—in this case, one posed by the dreamer's grief and by the prescience of danger, and poignantly illustrates the fact that this solution to a problem, this wish-fulfilling aspect of the dream, takes place by a kind of self-deception.

The fact that self-deception is an inextricable part of the Freudian notion of wish fulfillment has not received sufficient theoretical attention. As we turn again to Freud's simplest of examples—the dream of convenience of his drinking a glass of water that was instigated by his thirst after eating anchovies—we see in this rather banal example of wish fulfillment a shocking aspect of wish fulfillment in our dreams: In our dreams, we (as authors) make up a calming, wishful lie and then we (as audiences) believe that lie to tone down the impact of an irritant that threatens sleep. We as dreamers make up a story, put it in visual form, then believe it so as better to mitigate the disruption caused by the irritant, so to speak, that instigates the dream. Continuing along this line of thinking, one might ask regarding the psychic apparatus generally: What is the mind like such that it can deceive itself in this manner? Freud's preamble provides the way for a systematic theoretical consideration of a shocking view of the psyche as centered around the avoidance of affective pain by (in the case of dreams) imagining a story, one which we invent, create as a visual experience, and in which we become immersed in order to deal with that irritant or instigating situation? That the problem posed by the function of dreams as wish fulfillments inevitably heads into a conceptualization of the mind such that it can and does deceive itself, may be seen as a major problematic of chapter 7 because such a conceptualization rests entirely on empirical observation, and not on theoretical preconceptions about the workings of the nervous system that have become or might become superseded by changing views on the basic tenets of neuroscience.

The Interpretation of Dreams is continuous with Freud's work as a whole up to 1900 in that the underlying wish, when unacceptable to the standards of conscience, is analogous to the repressed memory qua "incompatible idea" as expounded in *Studies on Hysteria.* Freud stated explicitly, however, that he did not intend to connect his explorations of dream as mental product with his work on repressed memory in the treatment of neurotics because he did not want the former dismissed as deriving from data from disturbed persons. The parallel, nonetheless, exists, and the similarity between the memory as an idea "incompatible" with the standards of conscience and the latent wish in the dream as an idea "incompatible" with the standards of the "censor" make it clear that the lines of investigation and theoretical presumptions are identical. The repressed wish, incompatible with the standards of conscience, is the ''incompatible idea'' applied not to symptoms, but to dreams.

Let us pause over this model briefly: the dynamic struggle is over awareness that generates painful affective response from the conscience. Freud says in *Studies on Hysteria* (Breuer and Freud, 1893–1895):

> [By] means of my psychical work, I have had to overcome a psychical force in the patients which was opposed to the pathogenic ideas becoming conscious (being remembered). . . . From these I recognized the universal characteristic of such ideas. They were all of a distressing nature calculated to arouse the affects of shame, of self-reproach and of psychical pain and the feeling of being harmed; they were all of a kind that one would prefer not to have experienced, that one would rather forget. From all this, there arose, as it were, automatically, the thought of *defense*. . . . The patient's ego had been approached by an idea which proved to be incompatible, which provoked on the part of the ego a repelling force of which the purpose was defense against this incompatible idea [Breuer and Freud, 1893–1895, pp. 268–269].

Defense, then, is always defense against awareness, that is, against consciousness incompatible with the conscience. Such ideas are banished from conscience (repressed) because they generate affect that is painful: either fear of the conscience (anxiety), or moral emotions emanating from the conscience (shame and guilt). Although drive and drive derivatives are in evidence and important, drive itself is not opposed by defense. Defense opposes awareness—of the actual or potential expression of drive—that awareness is banished from consciousness because of the anticipation of painful affect in response to that awareness, and is a very early conceptualization of the signal anxiety concept decades prior to its official entry into the psychoanalytic literature.

The model of the incompatible idea provides the basis for the distinction between that which is latent—the forbidden wish or the painful memory—and that which is manifest—the manifest dream or the symptom (conversion, phobia, delusion, obsession, compulsion). The basic model of the incompatible idea, this time with the repressed wish as that idea, constitutes Freud's notion of dream formation and the dynamics of defense and distortion in dreams. In dreams ''from below,'' the imagination (dream work) responding to an impinging irritant (the instigator) weaves a segment of nighttime ideation (the manifest dream) that both reveals and conceals the unconscious solution to the problem posed by the instigator (the wish). The centrality of wish and of wish fulfillment in relation to the conscience is the center of Freud's conceptualization of dreams.

The wish, however, is not merely a desire in any simple sense of that word. The operation of wish in a dream is highly nuanced and complex. To see this more clearly, let us consider a dream from *The Interpretation of Dreams*. In his discussion of disguised wish fulfillment in chapter 4, Freud cited the case of a young woman's report of a dream that, she protested, could not have been a wish. It was a dream of her nephew's death: ''I saw Karl lying before me dead. He was lying in his little coffin with his hands folded and with candles all round—in fact just like little Otto, whose death was such a blow to me'' (1900, p. 152). Otto, the brother of Karl, had died previously and had been the patient's favorite. They were her sister's sons. The dreamer had lived with this much older sister, but had moved out on her own after the sister had interfered in her romance with a literary man, the Professor, whom she had wanted to marry. The Professor, much to the dreamer's disappointment, did not come calling after that interference except on the occasion of Otto's funeral. The dreamer, still much attached to the Professor, attended his public presentations, and when she heard that he was to attend a concert, managed to attend also so as to get a glimpse of him. In fact, on the dream day, she had a ticket for a concert that the Professor was to attend. Freud says to her, ''If now, the other boy were to die, . . . you would spend the day with your sister and the Professor would be certain to come to offer his condolences, so that you would see him again under the same conditions as the other time. The dream means no more than your wish to see him once more, a wish which you are inwardly struggling against. I know you have a ticket for to-day's concert in your pocket'' (1900, p. 153).

Let us consider this dream from the point of view of the dreamer's wishes in relationship to her conscience. The dream scenario shows the little corpse with hands folded, so reminiscent of the situation with Otto's death. The dreamer, we can infer, is present at this funeral and looks on at the corpse with shock and grief. This is a picture of herself as suffering bereavement and reacting with appropriate grief, a view of herself very compatible with the standards of her conscience. Freud's remarks presume that this imagined scenario is simply a technique for seeing the Professor again. He calls the dream a "dream of impatience" (p. 153), since she is to see him in only a few hours. His line of thinking takes into account only her erotic attachment, not her shame at being the one who pursues the Professor who has stopped calling on her.

Let me consider the dreamer not only as the "actress" in the dream, the loving, grieving aunt at the funeral of a nephew, but also as the "author" of the dream and the "audience" who beholds the dream. The "audience," in beholding the dream, sees an adoring and grief stricken aunt bereft again of a loved nephew, and recalling with sadness and increased grief, the funeral of the first. To the "audience," this view of the dreamer is very favorable—very far from "incompatible." When, prompted by Freud's questions, the scenario expands, we find the dreamer assuming that the Professor will surely come calling as he did at Otto's funeral. One of the wishes in the dream, then, arranged in the circumstances by the dreamer as author of the dream, is to create a situation in which the Professor calls on her sister, and, thereby, also calls on her. This wish—to see him in circumstances under which he calls on her rather than in circumstances in which she pursues him—obviates the shame she feels at chasing the Professor (attending his lectures) with no reciprocation from him.

But there is a much darker side to the dream that Freud seems entirely to have overlooked. When we pursue the dream's meaning further in relation to the conscience, we come upon a very obvious meaning, found within the manifest content, that, it seems to me, must have been too upsetting for the patient to acknowledge and probably for Freud to consider. I am referring to the dreamer's rage and envy of her sister—rage elicited in response to the sister's destruction of the dreamer's chances to have a marriage and a family—which provokes the envious attack on the sister's family. The score is evened, as it were, by the choice of the author of the dream to take away the sister's remaining child. This envious wish for the death of the sister's remaining child is, we can presume, so discordant with the standards of the woman's conscience as to be utterly unacceptable. The fulfilled wish is not due to the agency of the dreamer as actress in the dream—the actress did not kill the nephew—but to the agency of the dreamer as author of the dream, who set the dream in circumstances surrounding the nephew's death. And so the dreamer as audience is spared the horror of confronting the destructive, spiteful, and envious wish.

The wish to see the Professor is an erotic wish. The dreamer's wish to have him call on her, rather than her pursuing him, is a defensive wish aimed at obviating the shame she felt at pursuing a man who had ceased to call on her. A more profound defensive need, hence a defensive wish, involves the wished-for revenge in the form of the death of the sister's remaining child enacted by the author, not the actress in the setting of the dream. The wishes, then, go far beyond the already acknowledged erotic desire that was emphasized by Freud. The defensive wishes, portrayed as circumstances of the dream rather than actions of the dreamer or others on stage, betoken a struggle with conscience that, a century after the text was written, psychoanalysts are better able to appreciate than did Freud in 1900.

But the wishes in this dream cannot be understood apart from an understanding of the dream's function in obviating intense affects of shame and guilt, moral emotions from the conscience, by the (unconsciously made) decision to bury the shame-producing agency for the libidinal and aggressive wishes in the circumstances of the dream. Unless we appreciate the activities of the author and the judgments of the audience, we miss something vital about the dynamics of the dreamer that have been forced to the surface by the tensions with her sister.

This vignette was presented as an example of counterwish dreams. The dreamer, Freud's patient in her sessions, protests to him—but also to herself, her conscience as audience of the dream—that the nephew's death could not have been her wish (p. 252). This protest, we may speculate, can be understood within the context of the transference as an envious attack on Freud by debunking his (explicitly proclaimed) wish-fulfillment theory. The self-deception in the dream scenario is, in the parlance of 1900, for the purpose of dampening disturbance, of guarding sleep. In the expanded view of defense that has evolved over the last century, the dream's purpose is to defend against anxiety.

These selected remarks on the text of *The Interpretation of Dreams* have stressed the centrality not only of meaning, but also of function, of the dream understood as an ideational product of the mind. The function of the dream is intimately connected with wishes, both expressive and defensive, that are responses to an instigating circumstance and which deploy the imagination (the dream work) to engage in self-deception by constructing a scenario that, in some important way, seems to solve the problem, and, hence, to reduce the disturbance posed by the instigating circumstances. In the century since the book's first publication, there has been enormous expansion of the agency that I have called the *author* of the dream, that is, the "organ of adaptation," the ego, as well as enormous expansion of what we know about incompatibility with what is acceptable to the audience (i.e., the censor or the conscience). There has been, in my view, much less expansion of the notions of wish, of the function of dreams, of instigation in dreams, of self-deception, and of empirical study of dream formation.

Just as the disturbing memory is the centerpiece of Freud's early conceptualizations of the psychopathology of neurotic symptoms, so the disturbing wish is the centerpiece of his overarching theory of dream formation. Such disturbances concern, for the most part, effective reactions involving the conscience that arise from awareness of the wish, not merely the sexual or aggressive wish in isolation. Unfortunately, some objections to the Freudian theory of the mind do not consider the concept of wish in all its complexity, or take sufficiently into account distressing affect as an aspect of conflict. That is to say, objections to what for decades has been the accepted mainstream view of dreams are not always based on a specific and nuanced understanding of wish and conflict in relation to conscience in that model.

CURRENT AGENDAS: PLURALISM AND INTEGRATION

The climate and agendas of psychoanalysis after a century is, of course, quite different from that in 1900. In the wake of *The Interpretation of Dreams* and its century of influence, we are no longer absorbed with the very large questions in the same way as were the great nineteenth-century thinkers—Mill, Darwin, Helmholtz, and Brentano—who had such a strong influence on Freud. What is more, our therapeutic discipline is not in a stage of infancy. We have a century of clinical experience and an astonishing legacy of literature. I shall confine my remarks on the contemporary agenda at the turn of the twenty-first century to the issues of pluralism and of integration with nonpsychoanalytic disciplines.

Pluralism and the Forking of the Royal Road

After a century, the royal road seems to have forked into many paths without an agreed upon decision procedure regarding the choice of any one of these paths as more psychoanalytically valid than any of the others. Contemporary pluralism refers to the diversity of assumptions and emphases in psychoanalytic schools. Irreducible disagreement as to what is and what is not basic and foundational in our theory and practice requires either some form of pluralism or domination of one outlook over the others for reasons other than agreed upon foundational principles.

Like it or not, we are faced at the beginning of our new century with a plurality of views that cannot be pushed prematurely into resolution without many feeling that the resolution is arbitrary and based on authority rather than convincing reason. At its best, such diversity reflects a freedom from domination by any one school of thought, a freedom that respects different approaches to flourish and develop without presuming a hegemony of received correctness concerning the basics of psychoanalytic theory and practice. At its worst, pluralism can result in an undisciplined motley of diverse views providing a venue for unchecked fragmentation without effective efforts to unify psychoanalysis into a respected discipline by respectful attempts to integrate the field and to justify to other disciplines and to the public what constitute the basic premises and assumptions of psychoanalysis.

Major disagreements exist among clinically prominent and theoretically productive psychoanalysts who have a strong psychoanalytic identity. These disagreements concern issues which, up to the last few decades of the twentieth century, were presumed to be agreed upon as the givens of psychoanalytic theory and technique. These issues include, but are not limited to, the importance of defense and disguise as a major aspect of dream formation or of clinical dream interpretation; the importance of the analyst's relative anonymity and nonparticipatory stance in analysis; the centrality of conflict in psychoanalytic work; the importance of oedipal conflict in analytic work; the importance of dissociation as opposed to repression in the dream; the centrality of acknowledging the repressed wish as central to the process of psychoanalytic progress; and the special place of the dream in psychoanalytic practice. The requirements for too close a tether to a unified theory risk, in the view of many, putting undue pressure on the formulation of clinical explorations and observations, especially if the pressure to use the language of the overall theory forces an unwieldy conceptual apparatus on the clinician that makes the capturing of clinical evidence difficult or impossible.

Many view today's pluralism, insofar as it reflects productive work of competent people who do not at the present time agree, as the flourishing of freedom of thought and practice in a way never experienced previously in psychoanalytic history. Wallerstein and Weinshel (1989) have celebrated the current pluralistic climate in psychoanalysis, arguing that we have become emancipated from a too close relationship of psychoanalytic practice and even psychoanalytic theory to the theoretical framework and the overarching view of the human mind as put forward in chapter 7 of *The Interpretation of Dreams*.

Some Perils of Pluralism and *Pars Pro Toto* Thinking

But pluralism runs the risk of going to extremes of factionalism that detract from the credibility and the productiveness of psychoanalysis. For the presentation of our discipline to the greater community of scientists and of healers, for the teaching of psychoanalysis, the advancing of its literature, and for the joining of psychoanalysis with other of the sciences concerned with the human mind and with human nature, some way must be found to resolve, in principle at least, the claims of each group within an overarching view of psychoanalysis.

Mark Solms, in this volume and elsewhere, has credibly asserted that we have a crisis posed by a multiplicity of theories, one that must be resolved. Rangell (1997 and elsewhere) has made a similar observation from another point of view, arguing convincingly for a total composite theory which synthesizes disparate contributions into a unitary model. The alternative to pluralism is neither stasis nor dogmatism, but integration. The major risk of pluralism, as Rangell has often pointed out, is the high likelihood that, in the excitement over new discoveries in psychoanalysis, what has been discovered will *replace* rather than *add* to the body of amply demonstrated knowledge and theory that we have acquired. The danger, then, is that each discovery will support fragmentation into a new radicalism, a *pars pro toto* overemphasis on one aspect of psychoanalysis at the expense of a balanced view of the new finding or findings.

The problem is not with what is new that diverse approaches add to psychoanalysis, it is with what they are at risk of leaving out. The issue concerns the confusion that is generated when excitement over the new, together with what the critic Harold Bloom (1997) has called "the anxiety of influence," the thrust of any current generation (in Bloom's argument, of poets—applied to our topic, psychoanalysts) is motivated to establish itself by a consistent and overdetermined misunderstanding of the tenets of the previous generation.

Examples abound of errors resulting from *pars pro toto* thinking. The almost exclusive emphasis on transference interpretation—as opposed to a balanced addition of a vastly increased understanding of the significance and of the subtleties of the analytic relationship to the whole composite of psychoanalytic thought—in some psychoanalytic schools, is an example of *pars pro toto* thinking that tends to *replace* the existing body of knowledge with the new rather than add new findings to our existing body of knowledge. Overly aggressive technique that focuses solely on the analytic relationship departs from optimal exploratory conduct of the treatment by taking the a priori stance that it is only the transference significance of clinical material that matters. Such a *pars pro toto* overemphasis on transference has the cumulative, unanalytic impact of dogged suggestions. Even if it is based on a heightened awareness and accurate perception of material referring to the analytic relationship in the patient's associations, such overemphasis risks a serious departure from an exploratory stance of technical neutrality in such a way as to make a true understanding of an unfolding transference impossible.

Exciting discoveries, ones with enduring value, concerning the nature of the conscience have resulted in a tendency to replace, rather than add to what we know, and have led to costly fragmentation of psychoanalytic thought over many decades. Expansion of our thinking about the conscience, for example, is replete with *pars pro toto* errors, starting with those made by Freud himself. Within a year after coining the term *superego* for the conscience in its entirety, Freud (1924, 1925) went on to refer to that part of the conscience that was the postoedipal "organ of prohibition" as the superego. The 1923 sense of the word *superego* included, in principle at least, preoedipal aspects and the postoedipal ego ideal as well. This position has been continued by some of Freud's followers who, by minimizing the difference between the ego ideal and the superego, conflate shame and guilt. Melanie Klein's (1933) discovery of the early, savage, projective conscience in the child has been referred to in Kleinian thought as the superego, and in the Kleinian context, has been taken to mean conscience in its entirety, not just the preoedipal aspect of conscience concerned with rage and the experience of retaliatory persecution in response to that rage. Kohut (1971, 1977), the major psychoanalytic thinker most appreciative of shame, specifically disavows the connection of shame to the ego ideal, the supposed "organ of aspiration," and hence divorces shame from the conscience and from the arena of conflict altogether. As a result of attempts to replace existing knowledge by what is new, rather than adding what is new to what knowledge we have, there is a babel of theoretical tongues speaking at cross-purposes, much to the detriment of our understanding of clinical phenomenology in relation to the conscience.

Another case in point, one that concerns the dream, is the tendency of some schools of psychoanalysis, especially those committed to a particular type of psychology, to hear the dream entirely within the framework of the psychological system being embraced (Reed, 1987). Such a posture toward the dream is not psychoanalysis in the open-ended, exploratory sense of the word, so much as it is making use of the dream as allegory or parable instantiating the particular psychology being privileged.

The adoption of a specific point of view regarding human nature or of psychopathology, constitutes a major departure from the exploratory nature and the technical neutrality that have characterized psychoanalysis from the beginning. Adoption of a favored point of view or attitude toward an aspect of human nature has always remained a countertransference risk (i.e., the pleading of a special type of psychology or theory of an aspect of human nature rather than the nonjudgmental and compassionate exploration of how the individual's mind works).

I am in no way presuming that newer findings may not appropriately challenge previously received theoretical and clinical tenets. An example regarding the dream concerns the tendency of psychoanalysts of almost any current persuasion to regard the manifest content of the dream with much less dismissal and suspicion than did Freud. Another example concerns the notion of psychoanalytic interpretation in *The Interpretation of Dreams*—it is hard to imagine any agreement currently with Freud's original notion of dream interpretation as taking the reverse of the pathway involved in dream synthesis, that is to say, in traversing backward the pathway used in the formation of the dream.

It will be for the reader to decide on both the merits and the disadvantages of the theoretical and clinical diversity reflected in the papers in the Symposium.

Integration with Nonpsychoanalytic Disciplines

Psychoanalysis today includes the thrust to integrate conclusions obtained using the psychoanalytic method with those obtained using the methodology of the neuro- and cognitive sciences. In part this thrust comes from the maturity of our discipline, confident enough in its own methods and results to be able to profit from a joining of inquiry with other disciplines related to the mind and the amelioration of psychological distress. On the other hand, the pressure to do so comes from both an overidealization of the methods and the respectability of the so-called replicable sciences as well as the recognition that it is not in our best interest to maintain the insularity of psychoanalysis. A good deal of energy is devoted to integration of findings and the establishment of dialogue between disciplines. We have things to learn from other methods of study. As Mark Blechner suggests in chapter 1, we also have a responsibility to assume a portion of the leadership role in the sciences of the brain, the mind, and human nature.

We will certainly be required to revise some of our tenets based on the perspectives of other disciplines. One basic revision concerns the very notion of what a dream is. Psychoanalysis has regarded the dream to be (the narrative of) a predominantly visual experience during sleep, remembered well enough to be told to the analyst. Informed by findings from the sleep laboratory, our definition must expand. For a sleeping subject in a sleep laboratory who is awakened during REM sleep and asked if she or he were just dreaming, the realm of dream recall is much, much greater than it is for those who remember dreams after awakening. Most dreams are forgotten, and most remembered dreams seem to have been dreamt near the time of awakening. Freud's discussion of the forgetting of dreams in section A of chapter 7 addresses itself only to the experience of remembering that one has dreamt without being able to recall the specific dream. Overattention to this very small set of the totality of dream experiences that are forgotten, places too much emphasis on the role of repression and other defenses in the forgetting of dreams generally.

We have much to discover from the neuro- and cognitive sciences, but our present-day zeal is not, as yet, accompanied by significant tangible evidence of the value of integration for clinical practice. All too often, findings from the neuro- and cognitive sciences are adduced after the fact to justify the synthesizer's preestablished, and usually oversimplified, conclusions about psychoanalysis, which frequently leave out substantial and important sectors of the psyche that concern the darker (and more unpleasant to acknowledge) side of human nature: self-sabotage, self-deception, envy, and spite, to list only a few of the many topics usually unillumined by syntheses of psychoanalytic and neuroscientific data. In such cases, we might say of the present push toward integration with nonpsychoanalytic disciplines what years ago was said disparagingly of metaphysics (i.e., that it is the finding of bad reasons for what we intend to believe anyway). Efforts at integration curiously, to me at least, seem more likely to concentrate on the neurosciences and cognitive sciences than on general psychiatry and psychopharmacology.

Psychoanalysis and indeed interdisciplinary studies of many kinds, are in need of a separate discipline, a philosophy of science that emphasizes the principles of integration per se. Absent a methodology and a reliable epistemology for the task of integration, we are left with an undisciplined, scissors-and-paste, arbitrary type of synthesis that does not begin with a methodology for establishing, prior to a synthetic effort, what sort of data would, in principle, answer the question at hand. In my view, Hobson's (1988, see especially chapter 9) critique of psychoanalytic dream theory is a clear example of the use of a premature and poorly thought out extrapolation from laboratory findings to construct an arbitrary and scientifically flimsy basis for criticism of psychoanalysis, one that has since been discredited (Solms, 1995; Kaplan-Solms and Solms, 2000).

We do have an excellent model of successful integration of psychoanalysis with a nonpsychoanalytic discipline. A synthetic endeavor which has grown, gone to some excesses, and now achieved maturity is the union of integration of data from the analytic session with data from the observation of child development. The blending of data from sessions with observations of human natural history has had a long and distinguished course in the history of psychoanalysis. It includes Anna Freud's (1965) concept of developmental lines; Melanie Klein's (1933) work; Mahler's (1968) observations on the stages of separation and individuation; the work of Spitz (1965), Emde (1981), Stern (1985), and the founders of and the numerous contributors to *The Psychoanalytic Study of the Child*—to name only a few of the distinguished contributors to the field. But the road to balanced and productive synthesis has also included serious overstatements and *pars pro toto* errors. Mahler's theories of pathological fixation at stages of separation and individuation received a good deal of unbalanced and poorly thought out clinical application in the 1970s when those theories underwent a vogue of explanatory authority that, in retrospect, had only tentative validity as one factor among many. The same may be said of the popularity of Stern's work fifteen years later.

We are now at a more mature stage of harvest from the synthesis of psychoanalytic data with those from child observation and from child psychotherapy and child psychoanalysis, and much can be learned from considering the actual history of the maturizing process of this integrative effort. Notwithstanding all the present zeal for synthesis, we have, at the present time, very little in the way of tangible results that are useful theoretically or clinically from the synthesis of psychoanalysis and neuro- and cognitive science. Suppose we ask, for example, what, in principle, would have helped us understand, more than Freud did at the time, the significance of his patient's dream of the dead nephew discussed above? We might point to the fact that

Freud attempted to explain the dream solely in terms of the patient's erotic attachment to the Professor, failing to take into account the dreamer's shame at pursuing the Professor, her destructive envy directed at the family of her sister, and her presumably mortifying shame and guilt were her envy to be exposed to herself or to others. That is to say, we are aware that there is more to know more clinically—about shame, guilt, envy, and defenses against them that are now obvious to us in the dream's manifest content—than Freud seems to have appreciated at the time. We would also want to be free of captivation by the theoretical models (overemphasis on simple erotic attachment in a *pars pro toto* manner) that seemed to have held Freud captive. When we ask, concerning this dream, what, in principle, might the neuro- and cognitive sciences have to contribute to our understanding of it, we can, at this early point, only speculate.

WHAT IS THE STATUS OF THE PSYCHOANALYTIC STUDY OF THE DREAM TODAY?

The question of the status of the psychoanalytic study of the dream today should be kept in mind when reading the papers and discussions from Symposium 2000. Part I is devoted to theory and research in dreams. Morton Reiser introduces two presentations by distinguished psychoanalysts who have contributed greatly to the topic of synthesis of psychoanalysis and neuro- and cognitive sciences, Steven Ellman and Mark Blechner. Mark Solms discusses the papers, and audience discussion follows.

Part II is devoted to clinical dream interpretation. It consists of three panels, each consisting of three presentations by distinguished clinicians of very different persuasions. The presentations are followed by discussion among the presenters and with the audience. The first panel, chaired by Ellen Rees, includes presentations by James Fosshage, Edward Nersessian, and Edna O'Shaughnessy. The second panel, chaired by Ernest Kafka, includes papers by Elsa First, Paul Lippmann, and Robert Gillman. The third panel, chaired by Ruth Imber, includes papers by Philip Bromberg, Marianne Goldberger, and Mervyn Peskin.

Part III consists of commentary and rejoinder. Owen Renik chaired that session, which began with brief overview commentaries by Sydney Pulver and Howard Shevrin, followed by a lengthy discussion including commentators, presenters, and audience participants.

REFERENCES

Bloom, H. (1997), *The Anxiety of Influence: A Theory of Poetry,* 2nd ed. Oxford: Oxford University Press.

Brentano, F. (1874), *Psychology from an Empirical Standpoint,* ed. D. Kraus. New York: Routledge, 1995.

Breuer, J., & Freud, S. (1893–1895), Studies on Hysteria. *Standard Edition,* 2. London: Hogarth Press, 1955.

Darwin, C. (1859), *The Origin of Species.* New York: Prometheus Books, 1991.

Emde, R. (1981), Changing models of infancy and the nature of early development: Remodeling the foundations. *J. Amer. Psychoanal. Assn.,* 29:179–219.

Freud, A. (1965), *Normality and Pathology in Childhood: Assessments of Development.* New York: International Universities Press.

Freud, S. (1900), The Interpretation of Dreams. *Standard Edition,* 4&5. London: Hogarth Press, 1953.

——— (1905), Fragment of an analysis of a case of hysteria. *Standard Edition,* 7:1–122. London: Hogarth Press, 1953.

——— (1920), Beyond the Pleasure Principle. *Standard Edition,* 18:1–64. London: Hogarth Press, 1955.

——— (1923), The Ego and the Id. *Standard Edition,* 19:1–66. London: Hogarth Press, 1961.

——— (1924), The dissolution of the Oedipus complex. *Standard Edition,* 19:171–179. London: Hogarth Press, 1961.

——— (1925), Some psychical consequences of the anatomical distinction between the sexes. *Standard Edition,* 19:241–258. London: Hogarth Press, 1961.

——— (1933), New Introductory Lectures on Psycho-Analysis. *Standard Edition,* 22:1–182. London: Hogarth Press, 1964.

Helmholtz, H. (1995), *Science and Culture: Popular and Philosophical Essays,* ed. D. Cahan. Chicago: University of Chicago Press.

Hobson, J. A. (1988), *The Dreaming Brain.* New York: Basic Books.

Isakower, O. (1938), Contributions to the patho-psychology of phenomena associated with falling asleep. *Internat. J. Psycho-Anal.,* 19:331–345.

Kaplan-Solms, K., & Solms, M. (2000), *Studies in Neuropsychoanalysis.* London: Karnac.

Klein, M. (1933), The early development of conscience in the child. In: *Psychoanalysis Today,* ed. S. Lorando. New York: Covici-Friede, pp. 149–162.

Kohut, H. (1971), *The Analysis of the Self.* New York: International Universities Press.

——— (1971), *The Restoration of the Self.* New York: International Universities Press.

Mahler, M. (1968), *On Human Symbiosis and the Vicissitudes of Individuation,* Vol. 1. New York: International Universities Press.

Mill, J. S. (1843), On the Logic of the Moral Sciences (Book VI). *A System of Logic,* Vol. 4. New York: Bobbs-Merrill, 1965.

Pulver, S. (1987), The manifest dream in psychoanalysis: A clarification. *J. Amer. Psychoanal. Assn.,* 35:99–118.

Rangell, L. (1997), At century's end: A unitary theory of psychoanalysis. *J. Clin. Psychoanal.,* 6:465–484.

Reed, G. (1987), Rules of clinical understanding in classical psychoanalysis and in self-psychology: A comparison. *J. Amer. Psychoanal. Assn.,* 35:421–446.

Reiser, M. (1997), The art and science of dream interpretation: Isakower revisited. *J. Amer. Psychoanal. Assn.,* 45:891–905.

Segal, H. (1952), A psychoanalytic approach to aesthetics. *Internat. J. Psycho-Anal.,* 33:196–207.

Solms, M. (1995), New findings on the neurological organization of dreaming: Implications for psychoanalysis. *Psychoanal. Quart.,* 64:43–67.

Spitz, R. (1965), *The First Year of Life: A Psychoanalytic Study of Normal and Deviant Development of Object Relations.* New York: International Universities Press.

Stern, D. (1985), *The Interpersonal World of the Infant.* New York: Basic Books.

Wallerstein, R., & Weinshel, E. (1989), The future of psychoanalysis. *Psychoanal. Quart.,* 58:341–373.

Part I:

PSYCHOANALYTIC THEORIES OF DREAMS AND DREAMING

Chair, Morton Reiser

1

Proposals for the Next Century of Psychoanalytic Dream Studies

Mark J. Blechner

In the year 2000, we marked the hundredth anniversary of the publication of Freud's scientific masterpiece, *The Interpretation of Dreams.* I believe that we can best do homage to Freud's great work by reexamining his theories in light of one hundred years of new findings from clinical psychoanalysis, clinical neurology, and the laboratories of cognitive science. This is the task I have undertaken in my book *The Dream Frontier* (Blechner, 2001), and I would like to summarize some of my main ideas here.

There were many important landmarks in this century of dream study. Psychoanalysts were initially very taken by the dream, and saw in it the most direct route to studying the unconscious. By midcentury, many psychoanalysts were disenchanted with the dream and were seeing it as only one among many ways of understanding unconscious process (Waldhorn, 1967). But then there was a backlash to the backlash, led by Robert Fliess (1953), Ralph Greenson (1970), James Hillman (1979), and others, claiming that dreams still had a special and privileged place in our understanding of mental life. Meanwhile, other psychoanalysts sought to expand our conception of the role of dreams—such as by seeing them not only as expressions of the unconscious, but also, when told, as having communicative functions, being especially useful within the psychoanalytic relationship. These analysts included Edward Tauber (1952), Mark Kanzer (1955), Martin Bergmann (1966), John Schimel (1969), Edgar Levenson (1983), and myself (Blechner, 1995).

The renewed interest in the dream came in the face of challenges from neurobiologists about the meaningfulness of dreams. Allan Hobson and Robert McCarley (1977) claimed that dreams are relatively meaningless (although they later backed off from that position somewhat), and Francis Crick and Graeme Mitchison (1983) went even further, claiming that dreams are waste products of the mind, and that it was potentially harmful to attend to them.

As clinicians, many of us today are fully aware of the tremendous potential in dreams to depict a patient's mental functioning in a vivid and personally affecting way. And yet, even among psychoanalysts, there is much less focal interest in dreams than there used to be. I think that the reduced interest in dreams has several reasons: First, analysis of dreams has become less rigorous, with too much attention to metaphoric elaboration of dreams and too little attention to the specificity and directness of dreams; there is a tendency among psychoanalysts to translate dreams too quickly into latent content, rather than retaining the details of manifest content as evolving sources of clinical insight. Also, the primary psychoanalytic theory of dreams has not been adequately revised, even though there is evidence to suggest the need for substantial revisions.

The first area I would like to address is the distinction between manifest and latent content. Freud (1900) argued, and here I quote him, that in proper dream interpretation, we should "disregard the apparent coherence between a dream's constituents as an unessential illusion, and that we should trace back the origin of each of its elements on its own account" (p. 449).

Freud is arguing that the overall narrative structure of the manifest dream is not relevant to deciphering the underlying dream thoughts. Instead, we should analyze the dream elements individually, via free association, which I call the ''rebus technique of dream interpretation.''

Unlike Freud, I would not dismiss the coherence of elements in the manifest dream narrative. On the contrary, I think that the best dream interpretations use piecemeal analysis as a means of clarifying the entirety of the manifest dream. I would go further, and suggest, that if you analyze a dream piece by piece, and you arrive at an interpretation of the dream that fits into the totality of the manifest dream narrative, you are on the right track. If the associations contradict the manifest dream narrative or seem irrelevant to it, then they have not led you closer to the meaning of the dream. Associations can clarify the dream, but they also can lead you astray from the dream.

I am stressing the truth of the manifest dream content. In my view, dreams are our most honest communications, perhaps the only human communication in which we cannot lie. We can lie *about* our dreams, but not *in* our dreams. In light of Freud's theory that dreams disguise the underlying latent dream thought, it may seem a bit ironic for me to claim that dreams never lie, but I believe it to be so. Dreams are not crafted to disguise. They are also not crafted to be readily understood. Dreams show us the mind creating meaning without attempting to be understandable. As the composer Ned Rorem (1994) has written: ''Dreams are dreams, with their own integrity, not symbols designed to keep us asleep. Like music, whose sense and strength and very reason-for-being can never be explained by mere intelligence, the meaning of dreams forever evades us, not because that meaning is too vague for words but because it is too precise for words'' (p. 517).

In *The Dream Frontier*, I have proposed that good dream interpreters are able to set up the context of the dream, which, when you know it, makes the manifest dream text understandable. Dream interpretation may thus be like the game *Jeopardy!,* in which you are provided with the answer, and you have to come up with the right question. In dream interpretation, if you provide the right question, the dream image will function as the answer. If you set up the right context, then the seeming nonsense will make sense. Too often today, dream interpretation seeks to transform the dream image instead of contextualizing it. Such work with dreams then tends to be less precise and more fanciful, a tendency that has robbed dreams of their importance in clinical psychoanalysis.

This leads into my second area of focus—the distinction between concrete and metaphoric approaches to dreams. For heuristic purposes, I am exaggerating the differences between these two approaches. According to the metaphoric approach, the dream creates a metaphor for something in the patient's experience or thought. According to the concrete approach, the dream portrays important information directly, although in a language that is not designed to be communicable.

In contemporary dream interpretation, so far as I can tell from recent publications and from case conferences, there is an overemphasis on metaphoric interpretation and an undervaluation of the concrete implications of the dream. Each school of psychoanalysis has developed its preferred metaphors. Relational psychoanalysts, from Otto Rank (1926) to the present day, have emphasized how dreams can be a metaphoric representation of the analytic relationship. Freudian psychoanalysts have emphasized how the dream images can be a metaphor for bodily experience, especially having to do with the oral, anal, and genital zones.

While the analysis of metaphor is essential to good dream interpretation, it allows the analyst and patient great flexibility and often a chance to move away from the most precise, anxiety-filled aspects of the dream. In my view, the concrete images of the dream will have validity, even when a metaphoric interpretation also seems valid. Of course, in working with dreams, balance is important. If the dreamer is too concrete, then the psychoanalyst may balance that concreteness with metaphoric interpretations. If you pursue both avenues of dream interpretation and integrate them, your work with dreams will be that much richer.

Very often, patients who cannot or will not share critical information with their psychoanalyst may provide such information with their dreams. In some cases, the dreams are a few months or even a few years ahead of the material that is discussed openly in the treatment. If the patient denies being aware of any connection between the concrete kinds of experience portrayed in the dream, just wait. In time, the truth of the dream will come out. I have experienced this phenomenon with so many patients that it almost seems like a rule of thumb.

For instance, a patient told me three dreams in her second session. The first one went as follows: "I'm standing on the bed, trying to fix the ceiling fan (that my father and I, in reality, installed in my bedroom). The fan starts up. The fan catches my hair. It's getting wound around blades pulling out my hair, my scalp. It's out of control. I'm yelling for help. I realize there is a chain, I pull it, and it turns off."

The patient was extremely afraid of analysis. Before the session, she had told the dream to a close friend, who was also in analysis and had obviously learned how to interpret dreams within the transference. He told her that the dream was about her fear that I would pull things out of her head and damage her mind. This transference interpretation was certainly valid, and we could have stopped there.

In the second dream she had that night, she was swimming underwater in a pool, and banged her head on the side of the pool. Her friend interpreted that dream as her fear that if she went into the depths of her mind, she would also be damaged.

I think her friend's transference interpretations were valid. But I also noted that in each of her dreams, she sustained a head injury. And so, as is my way, I asked, "Have you ever had a head injury?" She said, "No, nothing."

The next session she returned, and said, "I can't believe I thought I had never had a head injury. After our last session, I remembered that I was once working as a waitress, and another waitress carrying a tray full of dishes rammed the tray into my head, fracturing the bone around my eye."

Two years later, we discovered yet another concrete referent of the dream. The patient came from a physically abusive family. There would be violent fights at home, and she tended to hide under the dinner table. She remembered that during these fights, her mother would periodically slap her head, which was extremely painful.

The fact that the concrete meaning of the manifest dream usually pans out does not invalidate the more metaphoric interpretation of the dream. This woman was truly afraid of what analysis would do to her head. The concrete and the metaphoric can both be true. But many psychoanalysts, finding the metaphoric interpretation more acceptable to the patient (and perhaps being proud of their creativity when they are the source of the metaphoric interpretation) may not go further. Ironically, the most powerful and anxiety-laden meaning of the dream may be right in the surface. Oscar Wilde once said, ''Only superficial people look below the surface.'' While psychoanalysis is known as a ''depth psychology,'' I think we do our best clinical work not by looking *below* the surface, but by looking as closely as possible *at* the surface.

Patients can even use metaphoric interpretations of a dream as a defense against a more concrete but conflict-ridden interpretation. For example, a woman dreamt that she was a burglar.

> The place I was burgling was a business building downtown. It had a marble lobby, brass elevators, and a guard. I had an accomplice, a man my age, I don't know who. It had a teenage quality. He and I are ''hanging'' in the building. I know there is money in the basement. I will come back and steal it. We come there after midnight. I go down an elevator shaft. It is square. I climb down it, like a cat-burglar. I get the money and I put it in my pocket and I don't get caught. I try to go back and do it again. I want to improve my technique. I have a flashlight around my neck, so I won't have to turn on the light. I take some more money. Like an idiot, I hang out there the next day. The guard notices and suspects me.

In the session in which she tells me the dream, she associates me to the accomplice and her husband to the guard. She then develops three metaphoric interpretations to the dream. She has the dream just after increasing the number of her sessions. She wonders: Is she guilty about spending the extra money? Has she fully disclosed her decision to increase the number of sessions to her husband? Is she implicitly burgling money from him?

She also suggests a sexual interpretation of the dream. The flashlight is phallic, the elevator shaft is vaginal. The combination of the two, both in her control, could be about getting masturbatory satisfaction. Finally, she connects the business building of the dream to a building in which she recently did some professional work in the building's basement, where the level of her ''professional technique'' was exposed. The building had a marble lobby, a brass elevator, and a guard, although so does the building in which I have my office. She is extremely ambitious within her profession and competitive with me in that area.

All of these interpretations seemed valid. Yet I was struck by the burglary aspect of the dream, and, in my characteristic approach to dreams, I asked her if she had ever committed a burglary. She told me of two instances from her adolescence, in which she had shoplifted, which fit in with the detail of the dream having a ''teenage quality.'' She then reassured me emphatically, ''I have never stolen anything since.''

She entered the next session with an embarrassed look on her face.

> I have to confess something, and I know it will be hard to do, but I might as well just get to it. It has to do with my cat-burglar dream. You asked me if I had ever stolen something. Well, last summer, you made an error in my bill. In July, I sent you a check for May. It was the same amount as my bill for June. You must have thought that check was for the June sessions, and so your bill for the June sessions indicated that I had paid for them, when I knew I hadn't. I thought a lot about it, and I justified it to myself, that you made the mistake, so why should I pay it? But after the dream, I realized that the burglary was my burglary, and I decided to tell you, so here is a check for that amount.

So the concrete approach to dreams may pay off, literally.

Now I would like to turn to my third area of focus: the question of why we dream. A person who remembers almost none of his dreams and who never tells them to anybody still dreams. Our theory must incorporate the fact, which Freud did not know, that most of our dreams are never remembered, let alone told or analyzed. Our explanation of why we dream would have to include a reason for these dreams, which in fact never achieve conscious awareness and are never interpreted. What use does our mind-brain make of these dreams? Do they have a function in our mental life, and if so, what? From an evolutionary standpoint, if something as complicated as dreaming has evolved in mammals, it probably has helped the organism survive. What is the dream's contribution to the survival of human beings?

I think our theory of dreams also has to take account of the bizarreness of some dreams. Freud saw bizarreness as a result of the dreamwork's disguising operations on the latent dream thoughts. Hobson and McCarley (1977) saw bizarreness as a failure of the cortex to synthesize coherent material from a randomly generated image—in their words, bizarreness is a sign of the cortex ''making the best of a bad job.'' Thus, for Freud and for Hobson and McCarley, dream bizarreness is an epiphenomenon of the process of dream creation. An alternative viewpoint, my viewpoint, is that the bizarreness of dreams has a function of its own, a function that is integral to our mental life. In my view, one of the greatest accomplishments of the dream is that it allows us to entertain startling ideas which would not be allowed in waking thought, ideas that go beyond our traditional rules of categorization and concept formation. Freud's great chapter on condensation outlined some of the processes by which this occurs.

The greatest forms of condensation are the kinds of dream formations in which there is an object, an idea, or a feeling which falls somewhere between two relatively familiar prototypes. For example, a patient of Donald Meltzer (1984) dreamt of "something between a phonograph and a balance." Try to imagine that. What is this thing between a phonograph and a balance? What does it look like? What does it mean? Allan Hobson dreamt of "something between a paint-frozen hinge and a lock." Bert States dreamt of "something between a swimming pool and an aqueduct." Freud called these kinds of dream formations "intermediate and composite structures." I would prefer to call them by the new term *interobjects.*

These interobjects are the most precious of dream formations, truly new things that cannot exist in the waking world, but can exist in the dream world. The dreamer must write them down, for otherwise they will likely be transformed into something more familiar and acceptable.

It is my view that such dream creations are fundamental to the question of why we dream. I propose that one of the reasons we dream is to create new ideas, new objects, and new experiences, which can then be retained if judged useful.

I call this the theory of oneiric Darwinism (*oneiros* is the Greek word for *dream*; Darwinism refers to Darwin's model of mutation and selection). Dreams introduce variations into psychic life and internal narratives. They produce "thought mutations." Our minds can then select among these mutations and variations to produce new kinds of thought, imagination, and self-awareness.

Oneiric Darwinism accounts for the value of dream bizarreness and unconscious dreaming: New ideas and experiences can be generated in dreams that we never remember. If they are retained as useful, we may "rediscover" them while awake and never recognize their original source in our dreams. Sometimes, we may retain an inkling of their source with a sense of déjà-vu; we feel we have encountered these things before, but we cannot recollect where.

The theory of oneiric Darwinism conflicts with a cherished axiom of psychoanalysis—the axiom of psychic determinism. As Freud (1901) put it: "Nothing in the mind is arbitrary or undetermined" (p. 242). There is grandeur to such a theory, but it might not tell the whole story. One of the great contributions of psychoanalysis to psychology is the view that many seemingly senseless or puzzling human actions betray an underlying, unconscious motivation. That great insight will not be weakened by adding that other psychological mechanisms, including some chance processes, are also involved, especially in dream formation. Our theory will be strengthened if we shift from absolute psychic determinism to acknowledging some role of chance processes in the sound functioning of an adaptive and creative mind.

Finally, I would like to turn our attention to my fourth point: the potential of clinical work with dreams to provide data on the structure and operation of the brain. Freud's book *The Interpretation of Dreams* was not just about dreams, it was an attempt to develop a model of how the mind works. Freud used dream phenomena as evidence for the functions and structure of the mind. He looked at the forgetting of dreams and developed the concept of repression. He looked at the imagery of dreams and developed the idea of regression. Now, one hundred years later, armed with more clinical experience and greater knowledge of the brain, we need to extend Freud's studies, with closer examination of the phenomenology of dreams in relation to brain function.

Freud's model of regression in dreaming implied a one-directional flow of information while we are awake—from sensory contact with the world through the perceptual system and into the memory system. Freud felt that in dreaming, this is reversed. Input from the sensory system is blocked, and the flow of information between the perceptual and memory systems is reversed. The perceptual system receives *input* from images stored in memory.

Freud's proposal was brilliant in its time, but it needs to be revised today in light of new information about the brain-mind. We know that the transformation of raw sensory data into percepts is more complex than Freud thought. It occurs in many stages, and information of differing complexity is processed in different parts of the brain. The thinking today, among many scientists, is that mental functioning is best described by a model of parallel distributed processing (PDP). This means that information does not flow only in one pathway; instead there are multiple pathways for information that can shift independently.

For example, in vision, the information enters the eye, but it is divided along several pathways that lead to different parts of the brain. One part of the brain may analyze certain kinds of features, while another part of the brain analyzes the image for a different kind of information. In addition, there are many recurrent feedback loops along the way that feed the partially processed information back into the system.

So Freud's proposal that, in dreaming, the flow of information is reversed, probably needs to be revised. How can you simply reverse a process with multiple lines of information flow and with recurrent feedback loops? But we can modify Freud's idea and propose that in dreaming, the flow of information, if not simply reversed, is *changed.* But how is it changed? That is a great research project still to be done, although we already have some fascinating early results, from brain-imaging studies (e.g., Braun et al., 1998).

But, in my view, it is not only up to neuroscientists to explore this issue. We practicing psychoanalysts must study dreams themselves closely, for the varieties of experience that occur in dreams and the implications of these dream phenomena for understanding the organization of the brain. We are in a unique position to do so. Most of us hear and analyze dreams in extraordinary detail, every day of our working lives. We are immersed in the phenomenology of dreams more than anyone else in our society. And if we listen to dreams with neurobiological questions in mind, we may be able to outline some neurological processes based on the phenomenology of dreaming. We can identify and catalogue the kinds of cognitions that are common in dream life and relatively absent from waking life. Then, we can take these observations and formulate proposals about the kinds of processing of information and emotion that differentiate dreams from waking mental life. Such proposals could then help guide neurophysiologists about where to look, about which mental functions may be functionally and neurologically separable from one another, and how, in sleep, these mental functions are reorganized. The power of such theory will be strengthened if the data from the phenomenology of dreams converge with data from other sources, including neuropathology and experimental studies of intact brain function.

Let me give just one example that may illustrate how I am thinking. Consider the following bizarre dream formation. A dreamer says, "I knew she was my mother, although she didn't look like her." Any clinician who hears dreams regularly knows that such statements are not at all uncommon.

It surprises me that this is not usually surprising to people. Many people, when reporting a bizarre experience in a dream, will prepare the listener by saying, "It was the strangest thing. . . ." or "I don't really understand how this could happen, and yet. . . ." But when people see someone in a dream whose identity doesn't match their appearance, they usually don't use a qualifying preface to describe the experience—at least my patients don't. They take it for granted that I will know what they mean. It is a commonplace bizarreness of dream life.

The dreamer recognizes a character's identity, even though a person's appearance does not match the identity. There is a disjunction between appearance and identity. In waking life, most sane people would assume that they mis-saw or mis-identified the person, and correct for it; but not necessarily in dreams.

This is just one example of what I call "disjunctive cognitions." Two aspects of cognition do not match each other; the dreamer is aware of the disjunction, yet that does not prevent it from remaining.

The global hypothesis, and I wish to emphasize, this is just a hypothesis, which I suggest we explore is as follows: Wherever disjunctive cognitions occur, the two aspects of cognition that are disjunctive are handled in different brain areas whose mutual integration is suppressed or shifted during sleep. Thus, the specifics of bizarre dream experiences may clarify what are the different stages of perceptual processing. As these are clarified, we can update Freud's regression model, and spell out how different modules of perceptual processing can interact and provide input to create the dream.

We also will want to pay attention to which disjunctive cognitions do *not* occur. For example, although it is common to dream, "I knew it was my mother even though it did not look like her,'' the converse dream is not common: ''I knew it was not my mother, even though it looked like her.'' In fact, in all of my records of my patients' dreams and my own over twenty-five years, I don't have a single dream like that. If anyone has a verbatim record of a dream like that, I would be very interested to hear of it. If such dreams do not occur or are very rare, that will also be important for our theory.

Now, clinicians usually think of disjunctive cognitions in terms of their psychodynamic meaning. Fosshage and Loew's (1987) book on dream interpretation, presented one patient's dreams to six clinicians from different schools of thought for interpretation. The first dream included the following disjunctive cognition: ''My mother was in there going through my purse. She didn't look like my mother'' (p. 11).

Most of the clinicians, regardless of their school of thought, agreed that the person who does not look like who she is represents not the person herself but the internal object, the internalized mother. The focus among these analysts was not the division of the brain function, but the division between actual people in the outer world and internalized ''people,'' the internal object representations, that we all carry in us.

But here we face an intriguing possibility. The fact that we can divide our perceptions between internal and external object representations must have a mechanism in the brain. What is the brain basis for internal object representations? Is the neural anatomy that allows internal object representations related to the separate brain areas involved in feature perception and identity perception? For anyone interested in a neurally grounded psychoanalytic science, this seems to be an essential question, even though we may not yet have definitive answers, given our current neurological knowledge.

We may ask, isn't it odd to feel so certain about the identity of the person, in the face of contradictory physical evidence? What does this division tell us? It suggests that the processes of seeing the physical attributes of a person are not identical, perhaps not even isomorphic, with the recognition of the identity of that person. But is there any other evidence that those processes are separate in our minds?

Indeed, there is. Let us first look to the field of neuropsychology. We find that some people who have suffered strokes or other brain damage have a syndrome known as prosopagnosia. A prosopagnosic man may look at his wife of fifty years, see all of her features clearly, and yet not recognize who she is. In such people, the process of seeing is intact, but the process of facial identity recognition is not (Bodamer, 1947).

We also have the phenomenon of Capgras's syndrome, in which a person may feel that a close relative is actually an impostor. The features are recognizable, but the person's identity is not. Then there is Frégoli's syndrome, in which a person may mistakenly identify strangers as people that he actually knows.

We also can find relevant data from research on visual perception in animals and humans. Scientists are identifying the parts of the brain that are responsible for different aspects of face recognition (Mesulam, 1998). Gorno Tempini et al. (1998) found that in humans, identifying unfamiliar faces activates unimodal visual association areas in the fusiform region while the recognition of familiar faces also activates transnodal nodes, including those in the lateral midtemporal cortext. Also, a similar division of function was found by Perrett, Rolls, and Caan (1982) in macaque monkeys. From such findings, we have come to recognize that the process of facial recognition is indeed very complex and may be achieved by a part of the brain that is different from the brain areas involved in general visual analysis.

Thus we have several kinds of data converging on a single phenomenon; we have data from human neuropathology, from experimental brain research with humans and animals, and from dreams, all showing that the processes of feature perception and identity recognition are separated. In normal waking consciousness, the two work in tandem. That may be one of the reasons it is hard in analysis for people to become aware of their "internal objects." But perhaps the person-recognizing module of the brain can see mother even when the physical features show "not mother." In dreams, psychosis, neuropathological syndromes, and very intense transference states, this division shows up more clearly than in normal waking consciousness.

Psychoanalysts, I think, should be excited by this. It suggests a manifestation in dreams of two fundamental concepts of psychoanalysis; namely, transference and object representations, and holds out the possibility of identifying the neurobiological mechanisms of these phenomena.

The study of disjunctive cognitions in relation to neuropathological syndromes, which I am describing, is related to what Freud (1933) called *endopsychic perception.* Freud meant by this term that psychopathological symptoms like hallucinations and delusions also have a positive value for researchers, in that they may suggest how the human mind is organized and structured (Blechner, 2002). For example, delusions of being watched may be considered a projected "endopsychic perception" of the superego. Freud wrote (1933):

> [Psychotics] have turned away from external reality, but for that very reason they know more about internal, psychical reality and can reveal a number of things to us that would otherwise be inaccessible to us.
>
> We describe one group of these patients as suffering from delusions of being observed. They complain to us that perpetually, and down to their most intimate actions, they are being molested by the observation of unknown powers—presumably persons—and that in hallucinations they hear these persons reporting the outcome of their observation: "now he's going to say this, now he's dressing to go out" and so on. Observation of this sort is not yet the same thing as persecution, but it is not far from it; it presupposes that people distrust them, and expect to catch them carrying out forbidden actions for which they would be punished. How would it be if these insane people were right, if in each of us there is present in his ego an agency like this which observes and threatens to punish, and *which in them has merely become sharply divided from their ego and mistakenly displaced into external reality*? [p. 59; emphasis added].

In this fascinating discussion, Freud is suggesting that the delusions of madmen reflect an insight into the organization of the mind. The delusion of being judged is an "endopsychic perception" of the morally judging aspect of the personality; the internal psychic agency, the punitive superego, is perceived as being outside the self. But the delusion itself may be evidence of the existence of the internal psychic agency.

I suggest that we expand Freud's conception of "endopsychic perception" into what I call "endoneuropsychic perception." By this I mean that certain psychological phenomena may represent an insight into the organization of the brain. The brain may be observing its own psychoneural activity and portraying it either metaphorically or directly in dream formations. I have already suggested (Blechner,

2001, pp. 269–294) that dreams offer us endoneuropsychic perception of brain processes regarding perception of pain, color, and time, as well as memory, reality monitoring, and other forms of metacognition. If we carefully examine the pattern of disjunctive cognitions in our patients' dreams, we can provide essential data to cognitive neuroscience, and we may help formulate many new hypotheses about the structure of the human mind-brain.

REFERENCES

Bergmann, M. (1966), The intrapsychic and communicative aspects of the dream. *Internat. J. Psycho-Anal.,* 47:356–363.

Blechner, M. J. (1983), Changes in the dreams of borderline patients. *Contemp. Psychoanal.,* 19:485–498.

——— (1995), The patient's dreams and the countertransference. *Psychoanal. Dial.,* 5:1–25.

——— (2001), *The Dream Frontier.* Hillsdale, NJ: Analytic Press.

——— (2002), Hallucinations and delusions. In: *The Freud Encyclopedia,* ed. E. Erwin. New York: Routledge, pp. 141–142, 251–252.

Bodamer, J. (1947), Die Prosopagnosie. *Archiv Psychiatrische Nervenkrankheiten,* 179:6–54.

Braun, A., Balkin, T., Wesensten, N., Gwadry, F., Carson, R., Varga, M., Baldwin, P., Belenky, G., & Herscovitch, P. (1998), Dissociated pattern of activity in visual cortices and their projections during human rapid eye movement sleep. *Science,* 279:91–95.

Crick, F., & Mitchison, G. (1983), The function of dream sleep. *Nature,* 304:111–114.

Fliess, R. (1953), *The Revival of Interest in the Dream.* New York: International Universities Press.

Fosshage, J., & Loew, C., Eds. (1987), *Dream Interpretation: A Comparative Study,* rev. ed. New York: PMA.

Freud, S. (1900), The Interpretation of Dreams. *Standard Edition,* 4&5. London: Hogarth Press, 1953.

——— (1901), The Psychology of Everyday Life. *Standard Edition,* 6. London: Hogarth Press, 1960.

——— (1933), New Introductory Lectures on Psycho-Analysis. *Standard Edition,* 22:1–182. London: Hogarth Press, 1964.

Gitelson, M. (1952), The emotional position of the analyst in the psychoanalytic situation. *Internat. J . Psycho-Anal.,* 33:1–10.

Gorno-Tempini, M., Price, C., Josephs, O., Vandenberghe, R., Cappa, C., Kapur, N., & Frackowiak, R. (1998), The neural systems sustaining face and proper-name processing. *Brain,* 121:2103–2118.

Greenson, R. (1970), The exceptional place of the dream in psychoanalytic practice. *Psychoanal. Quart.,* 39:519–549.

Hillman, J. (1979), *The Dream and the Underworld.* New York: Harper & Row.

Hobson, J., & McCarley, R. (1977), The brain as a dream state generator: An activation-synthesis of the dream process. *Amer. J. Psychiatry,* 134:1335–1348.

Kanzer, M. (1955), The communicative function of the dream. *Internat. J. Psycho-Anal.,* 36:260–266.

Levenson, E. (1983), *The Ambiguity of Change.* New York: Basic Books.

Meltzer, D. (1984), *Dream-Life.* Strathclyde, Scotland: Clunie Press.

Mesulam, M.-M. (1998), From sensation to cognition. *Brain,* 121:1013–1052.

Perrett, D., Rolls, E., & Caan, W. (1982), Visual neurones responsive to faces in the monkey temporal cortex. *Experiment. Brain Res.,* 47:329–342.

Rank, O. (1926), Die analytische Situation. In: *Die Technik der Psychoanalyse,* Vol. 1. Vienna: Deuticke.

Rorem, N. (1994), *Knowing When to Stop.* New York: Simon & Schuster.

Schimel, J. (1969), Dreams as transaction: An exercise in interpersonal theory. *Contemp. Psychoanal.,* 6:31–38.

Segal, H. (1950), Some aspects of the analysis of a schizophrenic. *Internat. J. Psycho-Anal.,* 31:268–278.

Tauber, E. (1952), Exploring the therapeutic use of countertransference data. *Psychiatric,* 17:331–336.

Waldhorn, H. (1967), *Indications for Psychoanalysis: The Place of the Dream in Clinical Psychoanalysis.* Monograph 2, Kris Study Group of the New York Psychoanalytic Institute, ed. E. Joseph. New York: International Universities Press.

2

Dreaming, Endogenous Stimulation, and Development

Steven Ellman

BRIEF SUMMARY OF TOPICS FROM CHAPTER 7

Although Freud initially presented a complex model of dreaming, the emphasis of this model was on the wish. The wish[1] (derived from chapter 7 in *The Interpretation of Dreams*), to paraphrase Freud, is the capital needed to fuel the dream and Freud and those that followed him have focused heavily on the capital in the business of dreaming. Freud maintained that dreams are instigated by unconscious wishes. After making this assertion in chapter 7, Freud frequently reminds us of Socrates helping his listeners search for the meaning of the good and the beautiful. The skeptic might ask whether all dreams are instigated by a wish, what about anxiety dreams or dreams that feel horrific

[1] The wish in this volume is pleasurable in that it reduces the amount of endogenous or internal excitation (Freud, 1900, p. 598).

and typically are called nightmares? Freud answered these queries, and his answers led him to consider a realm of experience that up to that point had been largely unexplored, the earlier and deepest recesses of human experience. He defined an unconscious wish as a pleasure[2] that has its source in early childhood. It is a pleasure that if activated shows the mind in conflict since what is pleasurable at one level (unconscious) will cause anxiety on another level (pcs-conscious).[3] This conflict is mediated by the censorship (which serves a defensive function) and these two levels of awareness are *primarily* governed by different modes of cognitive (primary vs. secondary process).

Why does a dream occur? Here Freud posited that sleep is both a condition for regression and during sleep the censorship is weakened. Thus the emergence (representation) of a wish (which was activated during the previous day) can more easily occur during sleep. The censorship that is still active provides the impetus for a compromise formation, which consists of the transformation of the wish into sensory form[4] that is sufficiently disguised to allow the person to dream and stay asleep. Anxiety dreams in Freud's theory signal the failure of the dream process and dreamwork to adequately disguise and deal with the wish. In the dream book Freud theorized about how different systems communicate, and it is this communication that he labeled as transference.[5] It is via the dream that Freud gives theoretical definition to this concept that will gradually change the way he conceptualizes the treatment situation. As a last point in this brief summary, Freud attempts to show the similarities between dream formation, symptom formation, and during the same period a variety of other phenomena (momentary forgetting, slips of tongue, etc.; Freud, 1901). In short, chapter 7 is unparalleled in psychoanalytic thought in that Freud attempts the most general theory that has been put forth probably up to the present time. Despite this heroic attempt, Freud will find various

[2] To quote Freud, a wish is "a diminution of excitation and was felt as pleasure" (Freud, 1900, p. 598).

[3] Here we are using Freud's model in *The Interpretation of Dreams*. When he puts forth the structural model both defense and wish are unconscious.

[4] The movement from motor activity (and thought) to sensory experience is Freud's first definition of regression.

[5] Freud says specifically that "an unconscious idea is as such quite incapable of entering the preconscious and that it can only exercise any effect there by establishing a connection with an idea which already belongs to the preconscious, by transferring its intensity on to it and by getting itself 'covered' by it" (1900, p. 562).

difficulties with his theoretical structure and certainly others will find even greater difficulty.

RELATED THEORETICAL ISSUES

When Freud wrote the dream book he was just beginning (or about to begin) to develop a drive theory.[6] His first drive theory contrasted the drive or tendency toward survival of the self with survival of the species. There were a number of contrasting tendencies that emerged from this conceptualization, ego (self) libido and object (other) libido were translated into issues that involved narcissism and object love. During the period when Freud utilized this drive theory he developed his most sophisticated (or at least most varied) points of fixation. This period is what we (Bergmann and Ellman, 1985) have called Freud's object relations era.[7]

In part it was traumatic dreams that led to Freud's change in his drive theory. After World War I, Freud and other clinicians encountered an increase of cases where trauma was present. There were cases where soldiers had repeated dreams in which they re-lived threatening circumstances over and over again. Freud reasoned that these dreams (as well as the symptoms and people's life circumstances) were beyond the pleasure principle (1920). He could not see how traumatic deaths were motivated by an unconscious wish.[8] This led to a change in his theory of drives where he postulated that there was one drive, thanatos (destructive in nature), that was beyond the pleasure principle, and one drive eros, (Freud, 1920), that combined sexuality and survival instincts (Bibring, 1941). Traumatic dreams and other experiences

---

[6] I am using the term *drive*, although Freud did not explicitly distinguish *instinct* from *drive*. By *instinct* one ordinarily is referring to behaviors that are closer to what ethologists call *fixed action patterns* (Lorenz, 1981). Imprinting is an example of this type of behavior. Freud's use of the term *instinct* most frequently refers to a constant internal signal where the behavior is more flexible than a fixed action pattern and the object of the behavior is also more flexible. I have labeled drive as *endogenous stimulation* and will use *drive* and *endogenous stimulation* as interchangeable terms.

[7] Titling this era Freud's *object relations era* is not intended to mean that it was the only era during which Freud was interested in object relations. Nor should it be construed that this was his only interest during this period.

[8] Certainly Freud vacillated about this issue, but in the final analysis he reasoned that to stay within the original pleasure principle was not tenable in the light of traumatic dreams and other aspects of trauma that affected people's behavior.

(e.g., certain types of masochism) were considered to be under the sway of thanatos. Freud began to understand dreams that were expressions of unconscious guilt (another new concept[9]) and these dreams also were of a somewhat different character. At the end of this period Freud's view of the dream was not totally reconciled with his new theory of instincts.[10]

THEORETICAL STATEMENT

I am presenting research that has been done in my laboratory from 1970 to 1991. In this research I was trying to find the holy grail, or perhaps more accurately I was trying to operationalize Freud's ideas about dreaming and drive or what I will call *endogenous (internally) generated stimulation.* Since dreaming was related to REM sleep it is not surprising that, along with a variety of analysts, psychologists, and psychiatrists, I was intrigued by the discovery of REM sleep. I will only mention three things about REM:

1. The brain is extremely active during REM (as active as in active waking) even though the organism (typically a mammal) is asleep.
2. Dreaming is found in REM sleep. Or more accurately the most vivid sleep mentation is found in REM sleep. Various authors have called other stages of mentation, dreams, but I will limit the term *dreams* or *dreaming* to REM sleep mentation (Ellman and Weinstein, 1991; Ellman, 1992).
3. If one deprives a mammal of REM then there will be increased REM in subsequent sleep periods; this is called REM rebound.

Following Freud, I have assumed that there is at least one, or two counting the ascending reticular activating system (ARAS), neurophysiological system(s) that provide mammals with endogenous stimulation. Freud saw the dream as a type of safety valve; we asked what

[9] Although one could infer from Freud (1916) that unconscious guilt was present in his essays.

[10] By this I mean that if Freud continued to believe that formation of dreams was instigated by a wish then this did not fit in with his new ideas about traumatic dreams. If he believed that dreams were instigated by any type of unconscious derivative (i.e., derived from eros or thanatos) then he would have to emend his dream theory.

could that mean in terms of modern psychobiology. The closest I could come to his ideas was to think about the REM state as a type of regulator for what he called drive or unconscious phantasy. Before we describe the regulation function of REM sleep, I should spell out another assumption about REM mechanisms. REM in our view is a manifestation of what Kleitman (1963) called the basic rest–activity cycle (BRAC). In Kleitman's view, the twenty-four-hour or circadian cycle is a series of alternating states of resting and activity. In our theory, REM mechanisms fire periodically to create activity in mammals (and avian predators).[11] This activity is a manifestation of drive mechanisms where thresholds for centers that are crucial to the animal's survival are lowered. Thus, during this activity phase the animal is primed to perform crucial behaviors involved in the animal's or group's survival (e.g., food seeking, courting, nest building). REM sleep is part of BRAC and is an activity period during sleep. This activation allows for an unbroken period of sleep while also allowing for periodic activation of survival mechanisms in case the animal encounters an emergency (e.g., a predator). REM sleep also changes waking thresholds; if, for example, waking thresholds are high for drive behaviors (as in depression) there will tend to be less REM sleep or less discharge during sleep in an attempt to lower waking thresholds. In this way one can view REM sleep as performing a regulatory function or alternatively one can say that REM sleep is part of the basic rest–activity cycle and is affected by waking thresholds and experiences. Implied in these statements is the idea that the same mechanisms that fire during REM sleep are also activated periodically during wakefulness (Ellman and Weinstein, 1991).[12]

In attempting to operationalize Freud, we reasoned that if one had more drive (higher drive discharge) during the day (without introducing an external threat) then there would be less of a need for REM sleep. Conversely, if one had less REM sleep there would be more drive behavior or lower thresholds for various drive behaviors during wakefulness.[13] Dement had used a similar logic when he conducted

[11] In an elongated view of this theory, avian predators who need a more flexible drive system will also have REM as adults. This is not true of birds who are not predators.

[12] During REM sleep there is a difference in that the animal (including humans) is prevented from movement by an active inhibition that occurs at the pontine and spinal cord levels. By *active inhibition* I mean that motor output is blocked.

[13] In this respect we differed from Freud in that we see drive levels as reaching optimal levels (homeostatic model) rather than reinforcement (pleasure) occurring with the lowest levels of stimulation (hydraulic model).

his REM deprivation studies (1960). He assumed that if one eliminated REM sleep then there would be extreme psychological effects on his human subjects. He hypothesized that if REM sleep was eliminated there would be psychoticlike effects during the period of REM deprivation (REMD). We thought, however, that the increased drive (endogenous stimulation) would not have the type of universal effect on humans that Dement had sought in his experiments.[14] Instead we went to another aspect of Freud's theorizing and noted that Freud was attempting to talk about the pleasure–unpleasure sequence in human experience. It was his view that pleasure and unpleasure were basic building blocks of human experience and so we attempted to find a physiological mechanism that corresponded to this Freudian concept.

To satisfy this quest we turn to the research of the pioneering physiologist–psychologist James Olds (1962), who found that there were sites (and later pathways) that were what he called *pleasure centers*. When given a chance, animals would work (press a bar or give some alternative response) to receive electrical stimulation to these sites. The phenomenon is called self-stimulation or intracranial self-stimulation (ICSS). Most of the sites that Olds explored were in the limbic system or in areas that were deemed to be part of the basic motivational system located in the midbrain. In our first experiments (Ellman and Steiner, 1971; Steiner and Ellman, 1972) we defined drive as stimulation from an ICSS site. We had a pre–post experiment (with appropriate controls) and we found that REMD both increases ICSS rates and lowers the threshold for ICSS. In our first study we looked at the effect of REMD on ICSS and found that there were lowered thresholds and increased rates of responding following REMD. In our second study we found that REM rebound was greatly reduced by allowing ninety minutes of ICSS during waking. We concluded that there was a reciprocal relationship between REM and ICSS; if one eliminated REM then there would be more waking ICSS behavior; if one allowed ICSS during wakefulness then there would be less REM sleep.

We ran a more stringent test in a subsequent experiment where we allowed subjects as much ICSS as they desire (bilateral ICSS in

---

[14] We also of course had the benefit of Dement already having conducted his experiments.

the locus coereleus).[15] When animals were allowed ICSS they pressed for almost seventeen hours in a row (with time off for rest and non-REM sleep but no REM sleep). Over a four-day period, animals obtained a great deal of non-REM sleep, virtually no REM sleep, and during the four-day recovery period there was no REM rebound. REM sleep was entirely replaced by ICSS from the pons (Spielman, Elman, and Steiner, 1991). We concluded that REM sleep is an ICSS system. When REM mechanisms are activated, ICSS pathways are activated. It is beyond the scope of the present discussion, but in a large series of experiments we attempted to delineate these ICSS pathways. I will state three conclusions that we feel are supported by a reasonable amount of evidence: (1) We do not know the precise locus (or loci) of REM sleep. (2) We have demonstrated an ICSS pathway that includes pontine sites and courses through the midbrain to the cortex. We have strong evidence that this pathway is activated during REM sleep (as shown by our studies and subsequent studies); Ellman, Ackermann, Farber, Mattiace, and Steiner, 1974; Ellman, Bodnar Ackerman, and Steiner, 1975; Bodnar, Ellman, Coons, Ackermann, and Steiner, 1978, 1979). (3) We have shown a reciprocal relationship between ICSS and REM sleep and from this we have concluded that they are the same neural system (Steiner and Ellman, 1972).

What is the function of activating ICSS pathways in REM sleep? In our theory REM activates pleasure (ICSS) pathways or neural networks that are intimately tied to basic behavioral functioning. In the rat (to pick a species with a good deal in common with humans), what I have called basic behaviors might include nest building, food seeking, courting behaviors, and most fundamentally aggression. Whenever a mammal goes into REM sleep the ICSS or pleasure pathways are activated and in turn are a factor in regulating these behavioral areas. Memories associated with these areas are also stimulated. It is important to remember that in this theory, pleasure centers include those areas responsible for aggressive behaviors. All centers where aggression can be elicited are also ICSS sites.

One might ask how this theory can be applied to primates, or more specifically to humans. We are assuming that REM mechanisms

[15] Locus coereleus is an area in the pons that our laboratory discovered to be an ICSS site (Ellman, Bodnar, Ackermann, and Steiner, 1975).

function in humans as they do in other mammals. In humans frequently the activation of ICSS pathways activates memory systems that involve conflict, and most typically the dream or the mentation present in REM sleep contains material about issues that are most relevant or threatening to the individual at any given point. This is not necessarily always true; one might dream about an unconflicted pleasurable situation, but in our view, for most adults (and most children) the most important situations in their lives involve some conflict. Under optimal circumstances, the dream provides some way of resolving the conflict, and if this is the case, the dream is forgotten. At times intense pleasurable dreams will be remembered (usually by people who are good dream recallers) but this is unusual. Traumatic dreams are ones where the dreamer cannot envision a pain-free resolution. The dreamer has a dream where he or she can only envision an outcome that would result in injury or death. Traumatic dreams are ones that are frequently repeated.

One might ask how the present theory relates to Freud's concept of wish fulfillment. Freud considered that the dream was instigated by an infantile wish. As a result of a defensive process, the infantile wish was one that was unconscious. In this formulation an infantile wish might gain expression in the dream formation, but the motivation for the dream is not based on a regressive aim (satisfaction of an unconscious wish) but rather the dream is seen as presenting important issues that are related to survival of the individual. Here it is important to realize that survival can have many meanings to an adult: success in a business, a promotion at work, or the well-being of one's family. These are all derivatives of survival issues. In this formulation, the dream is seen as having an adaptive function, but clearly under many circumstances regressive themes will appear and predominate. Usually in a dream, as in life, unconscious wishes will play a part and the part they play will depend on the defensive balance in a given individual. This formulation, however, implicitly challenges Freud's concept of primary process. It implies that the primary motivation of early strivings is toward attachment to obtain pleasure from an external object. Thus, survival mechanisms in early and later development are geared toward reality; however, at times of conflict, reality may be unbearable or the individual may be so conflicted as to not be able to comprehend reality.

DREAM STUDIES

Let me mention one type of dream study that we have performed. In our dream studies we have tried to look at the structure of the dream and how it is influenced by the underlying physiology of REM sleep. We have presented evidence that self and object representations are influenced by the intensity of REM phenomena. Thus, if one wakes up a subject during an intense REMP, more eye ion and self-reflection will tend to be absent. At a less intense physiological point, REM mentation looks more like non-REM or waking mentation. It is less sensory, less intense, with a higher probability of self-reflection being present. The mentation from these two states is readily discriminable by raters. However, not all subjects initially demonstrate differences in their mentation during these two states. Subjects who tend not to recall dreams (and are not psychologically minded as shown on the California inventory) tend to have less vivid dreams and even during intense REM bursts self-reflection is present. However, if REM sleep is made more active through REMD, then these nonrecallers look like the other subjects after one or two nights of REMD (Weinstein, Schwartz, and Ellman, 1988, 1991).

In the human studies we have tried to look at quantitative factors and to show that these factors influence self and object representations. In addition, we have concluded that nonrecallers defend against actively being engaged in dream mentation, and since they are also repressors (on the sensitizer–repressor scale) this defensive style is present in their dream life as well. We know that it is not a function of reporting since following REMD we assume there is a change in the dynamic balance, and at that point defensive attempts are less successful and their dream reports become more vivid and significantly less self-reflective.

Let me continue this brief exegesis by repeating a difference in the present theory as compared to Freud's theoretical structure. In my opinion Freud's view of the ontogeny of primary process is a biological–psychological impossibility; how could an organism that survives, begin life by turning away from reality with a hallucinated wish? From our perspective (a view articulated before attachment research began), REM sleep is designed to facilitate a mutual gratifying interplay between infant and mother. The REM state in this conceptualization is thought to facilitate those mechanisms that would aid the possibility of the organism's survival. In different species these obviously would be different behavioral sequences, but in the human infant it would be those behaviors that facilitated pleasurable interactions with the mother as well as those behaviors that clearly signaled distress. Thus, the early abundance of REM sleep[16] may be thought of as facilitating those motor pathways that would be interpreted by the mother as signaling needs for food. After memory traces are laid down they are re-created to facilitate the occurrence of behaviors that have led to gratification.

From my perspective this theoretical view that I am presenting is wholly consistent with what I have called Freud's object relations period (Bergmann and Ellman, 1985; Ellman, 1991). Between 1908 and 1917 Freud presented his views on object love, and his psychosexual stages consisted of the relationship of self to object in terms of the child's representational world. His drive theory presented the duality of survival of the self and survival of the species. Conflict was seen as deriving from tendencies induced by these two drives. Clinically we could say that he was describing the conflicts involved in narcissistic disorders[17] and the difficulties involved in achieving the capacity for object love. During this period his fixation points did not simply reside in the oedipal period but rather he had a more fully developed array of fixation periods. (Obsessive compulsives fixated at the point of object choice, hysterics at object love, while melancholics, paranoids, and schizophrenic or paraphrenics were fixated at different points in the period of narcissism [Freud, 1911a, 1913, 1915]).[18] While Freud did not present us with a full theory of development the scaffolding that he developed during this point of theorizing is in my view the

[16] One-day-old infants may spend from ten to fourteen hours in REM sleep (Ellman and Antrobus, 1991).

[17] It is important to realize that Freud's concept of narcissism is not derived from the instinct of survival of the self. Rather it is the first time that there is a libidinal (sexual) cathexis and this libidinal cathexis is of the self. Nevertheless the libidinal cathexis is combined with the instinct of survival of the self. Thus, there is a combination of drives. For a longer discussion of this see Bergmann and Ellman (1985).

[18] Here one might quarrel with a distinction between fixation and regression. Freud is clear, however, when he says that "The difference between narcissistic and hysterical identification may be seen in this; that whereas in the former the object-cathexis is abandoned, in the latter it persists and manifests its influence, though this is usually confined to certain isolated actions" (Freud, 1915, p. 250). Here Freud is maintaining that in hysteria the fixation point is in the oedipal stage (or object love) and this fixation point does not suffer a complete regression.

best point of origin for a new theory of development. If we were to stay consistent with Freud's notion of survival of the self then we have to remember that he maintained that this was the primary drive and motivational current at the beginning of life. In his attempt to be Darwinian (although he never quite understood Darwin's work), he missed the essential idea that the first activities of the infant are designed to bind the infant and mother. What is primary in that interaction is that when that interaction fails, what Freud called *wishes* are created. Even in that event one should not miss, as Rapaport and Gill (1959) stressed, the adaptive aspect of a wish (to repeat: in the earliest phases of life to keep life-sustaining contact with the mother).

THE TREATMENT SITUATION

In what has preceded this section it must be clear to the reader that we view REM sleep and REM mentation as extremely important in the lives of human beings. The dream in 1900 was the royal road to understanding of the unconscious. Freud was hopeful that this road would replace hypnosis and the pressure technique in allowing him quick access to the patient's pathological memories and phantasies. His first published attempt (Freud, 1905) at venturing down this road was a therapeutic failure; Freud published two of Dora's dreams. Although Freud ostensibly encouraged Dora to free associate, free association was far from the point in the interrogation of Dora; rather Freud wanted to prove that the dream indeed could bring one directly to unconscious ideation. Why was this so important to Freud? Here the answer seems clear, Freud wanted to prove the importance of the dream in uncovering unconscious dynamics, even if the patient discontinued the treatment. The dream would be as direct a pathway to the unconscious as hypnosis and the pressure technique were thought to be in terms of the patient's pathogenic memories. However, one must speculate that Freud could have published dreams from other patients where the results of the treatment were more successful. It is my view (Ellman, 1991) that Freud eventually published the Dora case to include the postscript that involved his renewed contact with Dora, his reconsideration of their treatment, and indeed his reconceptualization of the treatment situation in general.

In fact Dora was the end of an era. After his experience with her, Freud's conceptualization of the treatment situation would never be the same. Before the publication of his paper on Dora the transference was largely something to be avoided. Freud wrote that transference was a nuisance and he at first "was greatly annoyed" with it until he "noticed that transference . . . brought about no great addition to what I had to do" (Breuer and Freud, 1893–1895, p. 304). Of course what he had to do was help patients remember by pressuring them into trying to remember crucial experiences. It was in the postscript of the Dora case that the transference in the clinical situation first began to be seen as an essential curative component of the psychoanalytic situation. After Dora, Freud maintained that, "it becomes evident that transference is an inevitable necessity. . . . [though] This happens to be by far the hardest part of the whole task" (Freud, 1905, p. 116). Why mention this when we are discussing the dream? When using hypnosis or the pressure technique Freud tried to maintain that recovering the memory was automatic in terms of a curative factor. Freud found that a number of factors (e.g., resistance, transference) intervened in both treatment methods (hypnosis and pressure) and so the dream was the next logical candidate that would allow the analyst to automatically effect a cure and bypass transference.

Freud's new emphasis on transference proved to be incompatible with his view of the dream as the royal road to an understanding of the unconscious. Freud (1911b) wrote "The Handling of Dream-Interpretation in Psycho-Analysis" and it publicly marked a significant shift in his ideas about treatment. In his dream interpretation paper he opposed virtually everything he had done in the Dora case. He said clearly that nothing should interfere with an analysis and an analyst who is overly interested in dreams could deflect a treatment from its optimal therapeutic benefits. This is a far different stance from one that he had taken previously, but he now was much more interested (at least in theory) in hearing where the patient is and starting from the surface of the patient's mind (from their conscious experience). His interest during this period had now firmly shifted to the analysis of transference and it was during the same period that he wrote his three transference papers. More importantly, Freud's focus was now on the interaction between analyst and analysand even though he would find it difficult to hold onto these concepts in his own clinical practice.

In his last paper on dream interpretation, Freud (1923) further changed his emphasis and yet paradoxically and simultaneously retreated to an earlier position. In this paper Freud raised several distinctions that have become popular among some analysts. He presented the concept of dreams from above and below. Here Freud was again placing the dream inside the context of the therapeutic situation and recognizing that frequently the patient's associations broaden instead of deepen. Freud had now seen a number of patients (as opposed to Dora in 1900 who was one of his first patients) and recognized that when the patient had not yet developed trust in the analyst or the analytic process their reactions to dream material would be quite different from another (usually a later) point in the analysis.

After Freud there was a distinct division in the psychoanalytic community about how to handle dreams in the clinical situation. This division is perhaps best illustrated by the Kris Study Group monograph (1967). Here we see one group in this monograph state that:

> The dream is a definably unique product of mental functioning, being formed in an altered ego state, which is unlike altered ego states to be observed in other conditions which favor regression. . . . In addition to the dream's capacity to register the impression and experience of recent and current events in a particularly sensitive way, the patient also seems to have a special capacity for the recollection of experiences of childhood [pp. 97–98].

Here we have an updated version of Freud's position on the dream where the adherents of this position maintained that the dream is an exceptional mental event sensitive to current communications and perhaps uniquely able to facilitate a certain type of emotive recall. Dr. Waldhorn spoke for the other group in the Kris Study Report and maintained that the dream is:

> Clinically speaking a communication in the course of the analysis similar to all others with which we, as analysts, work. One obvious proposition implicit in such an understanding is that "we analyze the patient, not the dream." The manifest dream reported is, after all, the patient's first set of associations to the dream experience, and, as such, can be treated as any other set of associations. . . . This regression (involved in dreaming) in the direction of infantile (primary process) mental functioning

> with its reliance on visual imagery is not unique for sleep. It appears as well in other temporary regressions (daydreams, reverie, fatigue, inattention, excitement, etc.) including those related to jokes, art, and other "regressions in the service of the ego" [p. 100].[19]

For Waldhorn (writing for the group) the dream is not an exceptional event, particularly since the dream we receive in analysis is characterized as the patient's first association to the dream. Thus to this faction of the Kris Study Group the dream had no special status in analysis or as a mental event.

Clearly if one believes that an analyst can achieve neutrality, focusing on any aspect of the treatment situation (including a dream) is problematic. From my point of view all interpretive efforts are in one way or another selective and the concept of neutrality in unachievable ideal. The central issue in an analytic treatment is the extent to which the analyst can facilitate the transference in interpretable form. Since my theory states that transference is a ubiquitous phenomenon, the question for me is not whether one will destroy the transference but rather whether the analytic dyad will be in a position to experience and interpret transference–countertransference sequences. It is my intention in the remainder of the paper to try to show how this position is compatible with the dream still occupying an exceptional position.

DREAMS IN THE CLINICAL SITUATION

It is possible to misinterpret our theory as being only biological in emphasis. Biology is one influence on an individual's functioning and this influence can be interpreted in several different ways. If one views the dream in the clinical situation as one way for the patient to communicate to the analyst, then the biological underpinnings of the dream are deemphasized. How then do we view dreams in the clinical situation? In many ways it depends on what point in the treatment a dream

[19] There clearly were two different groups that reported in this volume of the Kris Study Group. The present quote was from the Brenner group that maintained that dreams have no special access to primary process or memories and should be treated as any material in the course of an analysis. The other group argued for a (guarded) special status of the dream in analysis. They recognized the danger of overvaluing the dream but also felt that the Brenner group (as exemplified by Waldhorn) was undervaluing the dream.

is reported. Frequently, in the early stages of treatment, a dream is the easiest way a patient has to relate important feelings and thoughts without completely owning these feelings. The dream is viewed as coming from "outside influences" despite the fact that the patient usually knows that the dream is theirs.[20] Later on in a treatment, what is of primary interest to me is how the dream is used in the treatment situation. Since in my view the dream always contains transference elements later in the treatment, a crucial question is how the transference is responded to in the patient's associations to the dream. Is the occasion of a dream report a way to combine early memories with the ongoing transference, or is it a way to separate these memories from the transference? In other terms, is the dream loved as a creation or can be it utilized as part of the self? If taken as part of the self, the dream will not only include the ongoing transference but also lead to the inclusion of new elements of the defended or vulnerable self. I have only stated two dichotomized ways of viewing the dream, but obviously there are many other possibilities (as many as any other aspect of the treatment), and one frequent occurrence is the dream as a statement of the position of analyst and patient in the treatment.

Let me cite an example: After almost two years in treatment a patient told me that her father had sexually molested her when she was 11 years old and this continued until she was 12. This patient had been in a previous analysis but despite this she felt uncomfortable lying on the couch. When she told me that she had been sexually abused I wondered about her continuing on the couch, given her difficulties in constantly needing to know where I was, what I was thinking, what I was doing. Gradually she told me that this issue (the sexual abuse) did not come up in her previous treatments. This seemed strange to me but not as strange as one might think. It is my view that we underestimate the things that patients do not comment on that are consciously available to them.

Her telling me about the sexual abuse led to a period of provocation where her response was to consistently denigrate our analysis; emotionally I felt betrayed. I was surprised by this feeling but I shortly came to realize that I felt that I had provided the type of holding

[20] Freud in a similar vein wrote, "Thus the dreaming experience appears as something alien inserted between two sections of life" (Freud, 1900, p. 10).

environment that allowed her to tell me what had happened to her and she was devaluing what I had to offer to her. I clearly was not yet in a position to deal with the transference. I was acting as if the trust that she had placed in me was my accomplishment and she should display gratitude for what I had offered her. This was my initial reaction instead of realizing that her response to the abuse was the development of a sadomasochistic structure where all pleasure (and trust is a type of pleasure) had to be destroyed because one could not depend on it or anyone who offered her a stable environment.

In a subsequent session she related how difficult it was to get to my office so early in the morning. She related that "it shouldn't matter to me anyway since my treatment is meaningless to me—this treatment doesn't work—I'm feeling worse not better and the only thing that helps is exercise" (I respond by saying, "You can only be helped by yourself").

At the next session, she said, "Have you noticed that I never tell you any dreams or phantasies? I gather from your lack of response that you haven't noticed—I feel so foolish, why is this bothering me, I just want to laugh at the whole thing—we can't undo what happened—insight is the booby prize." I said that it seemed as though she was struggling with something that she wanted to tell me but it was quite difficult for her to do. So she went on: "You're interested in what I'm thinking about? It should be obvious that I've had a dream—I'm going to say it quickly":

> There were a lot of acres of prairie, and Jerry (her lover) and John (her husband) were out in a pickup truck helping me move stuff out of this house. I thought isn't it great that these guys are moving stuff and I don't have to fight with them and they are not antagonistic. It felt good and relieving. Then I was driving, you were in the car. I was driving fast—it felt very scary, familiar in some way, but it was scary primeval, frightening, not fairy tale frightening (she laughed nervously). I was driving fast and around a lot of curves—it was distinctly not the prairie—I do drive fast in reality but I have bad night vision and it was dark, perhaps twilight, and we went up this really steep slope. It is impossible, but it seemed as if it was 90 degrees. At the top of the road somehow the road disappeared and you took over the driving—the next is too embarrassing but I bet you're loving this. [I said, "You imagine that I am enjoying your difficulty as a way of turning your terror into a more manageable torture." She shuddered a bit and said] We went into a café, we were

> having an affair—it wasn't really a café but a redneck bar—not the kind of place that you went to as a kid, but I did at times—nice Jewish boys don't go into a redneck bar—we ordered beer, John loves beer. You wouldn't want beer, you'd want white wine. We started making out and you told me that I was the most fascinating woman you knew. You then mentioned a word that I didn't know, *earthenment.* I don't know what it was supposed to mean but I thought about earth, and then children, I assume you have children. How much of me can you see back there—here I can't see anything of you—of course I hate to look at you when I come into the office (you often look away). It's nice to know that you noticed—it's interesting, I can't stay on the sarcastic edge, the dream is still with me, it felt that what I was doing was so dangerous.

The telling of this dream signaled the beginning of an interpretable transference. At this point in the treatment the patient was able to symbolize her transference to me and to tolerate this symbolization in the treatment situation. In Winnicott's terms we can say, "Everything eventually comes under ego-control, and thus becomes related to secondary processes. The patient is not helped if the analyst says 'your father really seduced you'. . . . Changes come in an analysis when the traumatic factors enter the psycho-analytic material in the patient's own way, and within the patient's omnipotence" (Winnicott, 1960, p. 37). In this way trauma is turned into material that the patient can own and where the material will not overwhelm the patient. In theoretical terms that we have introduced, the analyst's job is to sense the patient's threshold for tolerating the pleasure–unpleasure sequence that will unfold once the transference is in interpretable form. When a patient presents an interpretable dream then the patient can tolerate the pain that this dream represents. The patient is offering material that is crucial to his or her survival (or self-esteem, all survival derivates) and is willing to face this material. The patient I have briefly presented was willing to deal with issues that threatened the survival of some aspects of her self and her functioning in a love relationship. She was able in the dream to tolerate transference elements with memories that overtly go back to her college and medical school days and where her associations take her back to her earliest memories (3 to 4 years old). She was also in the dream able to see John her husband in a new light that highlighted some of the benefits that had derived from the analysis. (She was doing something with him and not arguing.)

Then the sexuality that is so threatening and disruptive to her came up in a way that we shared, and despite the fact that she was defensive in relating the dream she was able to tolerate her active sexual phantasies without having to either completely hide them or attempt to unconsciously re-create the traumatic events that she had endured. I believe (as opposed to the Kris Study Group) that the dream in the therapeutic situation is unique in combining these elements in a single product.

REFERENCES

Bergmann, A., & Ellman, S. J. (1985), Margaret S. Mahler: Symbiosis and separation-individuation. In: *Beyond Freud*, ed. J. Reppen. Hillsdale, NJ: Analytic Press, pp. 195–216.

Bibring, E. (1941), The development and problems of the theory of instincts. *Internat. J. Psycho-Anal.,* 22:102–130.

Bodnar, R. J., Ellman, S. J., Coons, E. E., Ackermann, R. F., & Steiner, S. S. (1978), Monophasic pulse pair analysis of intracranial self-stimulation loci. *Physiolog. Psychol.,* 6:48–52.

——— ——— ——— ——— ——— (1979), Differential locus coereleus and hypothalamic self stimulation interactions. *Physiolog. Psychol.,* 7:269–277.

Breuer, J., & Freud, S. (1893–1895), Studies on Hysteria. *Standard Edition,* 2. London: Hogarth Press, 1955.

Dement, W. C. (1960), The effects of dream deprivation. *Science,* 131:1705–1707.

Ellman, S. J. (1991), *Freud's Technique Papers: A Contemporary Perspective.* Northvale, NJ: Jason Aronson.

——— (1992), Psychoanalytic theory, dream formation and REM sleep. In: *Interface of Psychoanalysis and Psychology,* ed. J. Barron, M. Eagle, & D. Wolitzky. Washington, DC: American Psychological Association pp. 357–374.

——— Ackermann, R. F., Farber, J., Mattiace, L., & Steiner, S. S. (1974), Relationship between dorsal brainstem sleep sites and intracranial self-stimulation. *Physiol. & Behavior,* 2(1):31–34.

——— Antrobus, J. S. (1991), *The Mind in Sleep.* New York: Wiley.

——— Bodnar, R. J., Ackermann, R. F., & Steiner, S. S. (1975), Comparisons of behavior elicited by electrical brain stimulation in dorsal brainstem and hypothalamus in rats. *J. Compar. & Physiolog. Psychol.,* 88:816–828.

——— Steiner, S. S. (1971), Relation of REM sleep and intracranial self-stimulation. *Brain Res.,* 19(2):290–296.

——— Weinstein, L. N. (1991), REM sleep and dream formation: A theoretical integration. In: *The Mind in Sleep,* ed. S. J. Ellman & J. S. Antrobus. New York: Wiley, pp. 466–488.

Freud, S. (1900), The Interpretation of Dreams. *Standard Edition,* 5. London: Hogarth Press, 1953.

——— (1901), The Psychopathology of Everyday Life. *Standard Edition,* 6. London: Hogarth Press, 1957.

——— (1905), Fragment of an analysis of a case of hysteria. *Standard Edition,* 7:1–122. London: Hogarth Press, 1953.

——— (1911a), Psycho-analytic notes on an autobiographical account of a case of paranoia (dementia paranoides). *Standard Edition,* 12:1–82. London: Hogarth Press, 1958.

——— (1911b), The handling of dream-interpretation in psycho-analysis. *Standard Edition,* 12:89–96. London: Hogarth Press, 1958.

——— (1913), The disposition to obsessional neurosis. *Standard Edition,* 12:317–326. London: Hogarth Press, 1958.

——— (1915), Instincts and their vicissitudes. *Standard Edition,* 14:109–140. London: Hogarth Press, 1957.

——— (1916), Some character-types met with in psycho-analytic work. *Standard Edition,* 14:309–333. London: Hogarth Press, 1957.

——— (1917), Mourning and melancholia. *Standard Edition,* 14:237–258. London: Hogarth Press, 1957.

——— (1920), Beyond the pleasure principle. *Standard Edition,* 18:1–64. London: Hogarth Press, 1955.

——— (1923), Remarks upon the theory and practice of dream-interpretation. *Standard Edition,* 19:107–121. London: Hogarth Press, 1961.

Kleitman, N. (1963), *Sleep and Wakefulness,* 2nd. ed. Chicago: University of Chicago Press.

Kris Study Group of the New York Psychoanalytic Institute (1967), *The Place of the Dream in Clinical Psychoanalysis,* Monogr. 2. New York: International Universities Press.

Lorenz, K. (1981), *The Foundations of Ethology.* New York: Harcourt Brace and World.

Olds, J. (1962), Hypothalamic substances of reward. *Physiolog. Rev.,* 42:554–604.

Rapaport, D., & Gill, M. M. (1959), The points of view and assumptions of metapsychology. *Internat. J. Psycho-Anal.,* 40:153–162.

Spielman, A. J., Ellman, S., & Steiner, S. S. (1974), The effects of varying amounts of electrical self-stimulation of the ''normal'' sleep cycle of the rat. *Sleep Res.,* 2:38–40.

Steiner, S. S., & Ellman, S. J. (1972), Relationship between REM sleep and intracranial self-stimulation. *Science,* 177:1122–1124.

Weinstein, L. N., Schwartz, D. G., & Ellman, S. J. (1988), The development of scales to measure the experience of self-participation in sleep mentation. *Sleep,* 11:437–447.

——— ——— ———(1991), Sleep mentation as affected by REM deprivation. In: *The Mind in Sleep,* ed. S. J. Ellman & J. S. Antrobus. New York: Wiley, pp. 377–395.

Winnicott, D. W. (1960), The theory of the parent–infant relationship. In: *The Maturational Processes and the Facilitating Environment.* New York: International Universities Press, pp. 37–55.

Discussion

Chair, Morton Reiser
Discussants, Mark Solms, Mark J. Blechner, Steven Ellman, and Audience Members

Mark Solms: Mark Blechner in his chapter (1) said the following: "'Freud's book *The Interpretation of Dreams* (1900) was not just about dreams, it was an attempt to develop a model about how the mind works. Freud used dream phenomena as evidence for the function and structure of the mind'' (p. 37). I agree with this statement. In fact, I think this is why psychoanalysis is so important. What distinguishes it from the myriad schools of psychotherapy that sprang up during the century that followed the publication of Freud's book is that psychoanalysis is not merely a therapeutic procedure. It is a source of knowledge about how the mind works. It was in fact the first serious attempt to make a scientific theory of human mental activity, of what makes us tick, of what makes us who we are.

Few tasks could be more important, and its importance was certainly the basis of my own interest in psychoanalysis and what brought me into this field, and I am sure that applies to many analysts. I don't mean to undervalue the importance of psychoanalysis as a therapeutic procedure, but our therapy rests heavily on our theory. We are only able to reliably help people to the extent that we understand them, and the aggregate of that understanding is our theory.

Like any scientific theory, ours rests upon the systematic application of a method of investigation. We have heard a little from Blechner and Ellman (chapters 1 and 2) about that method and what place dream interpretation occupies in relation to it. But this is where our problems start. Freud devised the method of free association, and as Steven Ellman emphasized, dream analysis occupied pride of place, at least initially, as the paradigmatic example of how this method can be used to reach new insights about the structure and function of the mind. Later, as Ellman also pointed out, this paradigm was extended to incorporate the discovery of the importance of transference, and to a large extent transference analysis eventually replaced dream analysis as the royal road to a deeper understanding of the mind.

Nevertheless, the basic clinical method of free association (coupled with the evenly suspended attention of the analyst, leading to gradual formulation of hypotheses in the analyst's mind, which are then tested by putting them in the form of interpretations to the patient), this in a nutshell is the experimental method of psychoanalysis still in use today. It has served us very well, but like any other scientific method, this method has both strengths and limitations. Today, more than a hundred years after it was first applied, the limitations of the psychoanalytic method are painfully obvious for us all to see. Those limitations have led us to what I would call the "crisis situation" which Mark Blechner alluded to casually, when he said to quote him again, that "in contemporary dream interpretation. . . . Each school of psychoanalysis has developed its preferred metaphors" (p. 32). The plurality of theories reflected by this plurality of preferred metaphors represents for me an untenable situation. The very existence of different schools in contemporary psychoanalysis is highly problematical. Different schools, different theories, they simply can't all be right. I think that we have to admit it is a nettle that we have to grasp at this point in the development of our field.

In a small way, something of these limitations of our method and the serious implications for our science in operation are apparent in Blechner's and Ellman's chapters. To cite just one example, Mark

Blechner tells us that he doesn't agree with Freud's theory of censorship and disguise. He tells us that this systematic application of Freud's method has led him to conclude that, to quote him, ''Dreams are not crafted to disguise'' (p. 31). Therefore in dream interpretation the analyst should seek not to translate the manifest dream image to a latent dream thought, but rather to contextualize it, in relation to other manifest content, currently disconnected content. This conclusion quickly suggests a whole new theory of technique and ultimately translates into an entirely different theory of the structure and functions of the mind. Similarly, Ellman has told us about ways in which he disagrees with the conclusions that Freud reached by an application of the same basic method. I could easily multiply the examples.

This is the problem that we as a discipline are faced with. These problems of dream interpretation writ large are the problems of psychoanalysis as a whole today. Freud's method of free association and evenly suspended attention is very good for generating hypotheses about how the mind works, but his interpretation technique is not an adequate method for testing the validity of those hypotheses and reliably distinguishing the true ones from the false. Maybe ideally the method can perform this task; Freud certainly seemed to believe it could, but in practice, at least today, it does not. This is how we have arrived at the current crisis.

So what should we as a discipline be doing about this problem? There is a weakness in our basic method: How do we decide between the various, competing, mutually contradictory theories, or partial theories, that have gradually replaced and fragmented the coherent theoretical legacy that Freud bequeathed us? How do we differentiate between the competing hypotheses? What I think is that we have to grasp the nettle and admit: not by the psychoanalytic method alone. Both Blechner and Ellman have begun to point us in the direction that I believe we should go.

One of Freud's most basic hypotheses was that consciousness has two perceptual surfaces, indeed that consciousness comprises data derived from two different perceptual surfaces facing in two different directions. One of these surfaces points inwards and registers events occurring within us in the form of mental experiences, feelings, desires, fantasies, dreams, and the like. The other surface (in this model) faces outwards and registers events going on outside of us, in the form of material objects, the data of our external sensory organs.

Psychoanalysis is a science of the mind that studies the mind from the viewpoint of its inner surface, from the point of view of the data that are generated on the inwardly directed surface of consciousness. The neurosciences study the human mind from the point of view of what can be observed about it on the outer surface of consciousness, the mind as it is materialized in an organ, a physical object.

If you point, as it were, the inner surface of consciousness toward other people, toward the outer world of objects, it still generates only inner sensations, the phenomenon that we conceptualize, at least in Britain under the heading of *countertransference* and in the United States perhaps under the heading of *empathy.* But the inner surface can only generate feelings, desires, fantasies, states of mind; no matter what it is registering, it always registers it in that form. These are the data of psychoanalysis. The neurosciences, when observing precisely the same thing, the human mind, register this data in the objective form of a physical organ; and the experiments that one can perform on this physical organ offer numerous advantages from the point of view of scientific methodology over what one can do in relation to the inner surface of consciousness. The important point is that these two surfaces of consciousness, these two methods derived from them, or these two disciplines derived from a systematic scrutiny of what one can learn from these two different points of view, are ultimately attempts to study the same thing.

Now, if one accepts this basic metapsychological formulation, which as I say is pretty fundamental to our whole discipline, then it adds the possibility of using this duality, this fact that the same thing can be studied in these two different ways, as providing an opportunity to correct viewpoint-dependent errors. When problems have arisen where our method is unable by itself to solve theoretical questions, we might be able to apply this other perspective to these same questions, and take advantage of the correcting influence that a different metapsychological perspective might bring to hear. Neuroscientific methods are of course not infallible. Each method has its own strengths and limitations. This is precisely the rationale for using multiple methods rather than relying simply on a single one.

Mark Blechner suggested the method of clinical disassociation (or double disassociation, as it is called in neuropsychology), referring to the fact that in abnormal states the mind fractures along lines of functional cleavage. So in pathological states or in abnormal states of mind one is able to discern the functional components—parts of the mind separate out in ways that enable us to discern what those functional components are. He referred to how Freud used this method quite self-consciously, which in turn, as it happens, reflects the origins of the psychoanalytic clinical method in a certain school of neurology, in Charcot's method and the method of syndrome analysis, which relied also fundamentally on this method of detection of disassociations in clinical neuropathological states.

The implicit point in what Mark Blechner was saying is that we should be able to use these neuropsychological or behavioral–neurological applications of the same basic clinical approach, of trying to find the functional lines of cleavage, the distinctions that make up the different component parts of the mind, by studying it in psychopathological states. By using also the range of neuropsychological and neurological applications of this method, we might come to more reliable conclusions about what the true component parts of the mind are, or what the theoretically most coherent component parts are, and thereby to a model of what the structure of the mind might be. It must be possible to reconcile these two different points of view, and it can only be to the advantage of both.

But Ellman, for his part, suggested the use of experimental neurophysiological methods, for example, the sleep-deprivation paradigm. I was fascinated to hear his conclusions, to the effect that dreaming arises from the endogenous activation of what Olds (1997) calls "pleasure or self-stimulation pathways in the basal forebrain." In my own neuroscientific research, I have been led independently to exactly the same conclusion by the application of a completely different method; that is, the clinico-anatomical method, used in human cases with focal brain lesions (Solms, 1997). Nofzinger et al. (1997), Maquet et al. (1996), and Braun et al. (1997) have all reached the same conclusion too, in the past few years by the application of yet another method, functional imaging of regional cerebral blood flow and metabolism.

The implications of all this for a scientific reappraisal of Freud's dream formula are obvious. Following Freud's hypothesis that dreams are fundamentally driven by the activation of instinctually rooted wishes, Ellman has begun to outline a revised drive theory that might enable us to accommodate these implications. I find much to recommend in what he said. I would also argue that we must remember that these new theoretical possibilities suggested by neuroscientific methods need always to be taken back to the primary psychoanalytical laboratory of the clinical situation, where they can be evaluated afresh with the method by means of which all our basic theoretical concepts are operationalized. Proceeding in this way, I firmly believe that we can get past the current theoretical impasse that we face and reinvigorate our method to serve a new scientific purpose. Meanwhile, Blechner reminded us that this collaboration between psychoanalysis and neuroscience needs to be a two-way process. It is not only a matter of how psychoanalysis can benefit from this sort of dialogue, but also what psychoanalysis might be able to offer to the neurosciences, and he made some suggestions as to how this might be possible.

I think that this is very important. We must never forget that each method has its strengths and its limitations. There are things that one can see about the mind by studying it from the viewpoint of subjective experience that one simply can't see by looking at it as an organ. Psychoanalysis, if it occupies its proper place in relation to other disciplines in mental science, has something enormously important to offer them. Eric Kandel (1998) is perhaps the perfect example of a leading neuroscientist who has called for exactly this sort of cooperation precisely for that reason: what psychoanalysis has to offer the neurosciences today. What is required, therefore, now, is a sustained, systematic dialogue and scientific collaboration between psychoanalysis and the neurosciences.

Mark Blechner: I basically agree with virtually everything Mark Solms said in his discussion. On one point, however, he made a point about plurality of metaphor—I did say that, but I don't think it represents a crisis for psychoanalysis. There is a plurality of metaphors but that doesn't necessarily mean that we are not talking about similar things. In Fosshage and Loew (1987), you have six different clinicians, each of whom takes the dream and interprets it within his or her own metaphor and yet somehow their clinical conclusions are remarkably similar for certain aspects of the dream. In some ways they are very different and those differences really are important, but whether people take the dream and interpret it through a bodily metaphor, or an interpersonal metaphor, or the Jungian taking it into some kind of collective unconscious or mythological metaphor, doesn't necessarily mean that they come to different clinical conclusions. So I don't think it is a crisis that we have so many different metaphors working in psychoanalysis. I do think that those kinds of projects where people from different schools are brought together help us really understand that we have in common and what the bedrock is that underlies the metaphor. To my mind, that isn't a crisis, but rather a project for modern psychoanalysts to identify the bedrock, but that doesn't mean that we have to abandon the metaphors that we find useful.

First, I really appreciated Steven Ellman's discussion of the Dora case, but although Freud considered it a failure and a lot of people agree, I see it as a terrific therapeutic success and I think if every one of my cases worked out as well as the Dora case I would be delighted. Even though Dora supposedly fled the treatment—she didn't accept Freud's interpretations—part of her problem was this terrible family system that she was living in. Out of the confrontation with Freud she then confronted the people in her family and basically resolved these terrible ongoing family crises. Second, in regard to Ellman's patient: What really interested me was his use of that word *earthenment*—the creation of that word. I would have loved to have heard what happened with that. If she were my patient I would really want to dwell on that. What has got into that word? It probably would become a code word for some very private but very basic experience that she was having.

Steven Ellman: I wouldn't want to go back and debate about Dora. She didn't consider the treatment of much use when she was actually interviewed and perhaps Ball's analyst who interviewed her later on felt that she was a difficult, very troubled person. But my guess is that Mark Blechner does a good deal better with his patients. I think he is being quite modest about that. But in any case, I think that my point really wasn't whether Freud was successful or not—how he began to recognize the transference–countertransference aspects of the case and how important that was in changing the focus of the treatment. That was really the point I was making, and I tried to show through certain historical records that in fact it took him three or four years to come up with the idea of transference in a clinical situation. It had taken him a reasonable amount of time. In fact if you read his psychotherapy papers in 1903 and 1904, transference is not mentioned at all in those papers and some historical records have now been found to show the kind of struggle that he was having to really capture the notion of transference.[1] I felt that was the more important aspect of the Dora case. Dr. Solms's very interesting discussion encouraged me to describe my understanding of the idea of endogenous stimulation in the clinical situation which is a major focus of my writing just now. This particularly circled around one anorexic woman I saw when she was about 70 pounds (she was 5 foot 8 inches) and how the intensity of what I regard as her internal structure would allow a certain kind of oedipal dynamics to be traumatic for her whereas most anorexic patients that I had seen had quite different dynamics. I can't do it justice now, but I am trying to sketch out the idea of how something that I think came from Freud, the whole idea of intensity, one could put it in terms of intensity of affect, how that manifests itself in the clinical situation and how it is particularly important. It is also something which we tried to capture in a variety of our dream studies, where we tried to show that when there is particularly intense central nervous system firing, various things happen to self and object representation. So, we are trying now to use some of these stories to look at clinical dream reports.

Mark Solms: I would just like to clarify: There is nothing wrong with plurality of metaphors. The emphasis in the quotation from Mark Blechner's paper was on the schools of thought, the schools of psychoanalysis that have developed their own preferred metaphors. I said that the plurality of feelings that are reflected in the plurality of metaphors is the crisis. Of course it is inevitable, it is in the nature of what psychoanalysis is, that there is going to be a plurality of metaphors. The unconscious is unconscious and we have to develop a figurative

[1] Freud's initial recognition of transference came in the postscript to the Dora case. He published this in 1905, and in 1903 and 1904 he had published two papers on treatment where he did not mention transference at all. In Ellman (1991) the author tries to show that it took Freud this time to recognize the importance of transference. Gradually, from 1905 to 1915, Freud became more at home with the implications of transference and wrote his three transference papers (Ellman 1991).

language to try to describe what we, as it were, see there. But we don't really see anything, so we have to invent figurative terms to try to capture, to use as vehicles, to convey something of the psychical reality that we become aware of by the psychoanalytical method. The plurality of figurative languages is, as I say, an inevitable consequence of the unconsciousness of the unconscious. That's not a problem, but it does create complications when we try to communicate from one school to another if we have different metaphors, different figurative languages. It might appear that we are saying something different when in fact we are saying one and the same thing. That is a complication and this is what Mark Blechner is saying is not a problem. The problem goes far deeper than that. It is not just a matter of different metaphors. We have fundamentally different theories in psychoanalysis today and all of them are called psychoanalysis. What I am saying is that this is a product of our method, which has created this problem. You can't have a whole lot of different theories about the same thing and each of them be correct. The psychoanalytic method, for all of its strengths, doesn't seem to enable analysts to decide between these different theoretical points of view. All the different schools of psychoanalysis apply basically the same method, which is this method of free association, evenly suspended attention, full relations arising in the analyst's mind, and the analyst puts them to the patient, and this is meant to be the testing of the hypothesis. But somehow it veers off in one of these different directions and we end up with these different aggregate conclusions about how the mind works. Our method doesn't seem able to solve that problem. I think that the way we all privately solve it is that we know that our theory is right and the others are all completely wrong.

Steven Ellman: I don't think we all do use the same method, the methods are really quite different. Even the suspended attention, which I find to be an important concept, in many methods it is not important at all. It is partly the different methods that we use that have led to some of the different metaphors that we are faced with. A systematic view of theories and really spelling out what one's theoretical assumptions are would be useful because it is very often not clear what different theories are even saying, besides the fact that the techniques vary.

A question from the audience was, did I say that activation of pleasure centers involves the activation of conflict. From my perspective, these pleasure center pathways serve as regulators, and that is something we have been trying to map, for aggression, say. When you start to activate what I call basic behavioral areas, from my perspective, in human beings that always involves conflict. It is hard for me to imagine that there wouldn't always be conflict. One might wonder about aggression being linked to pleasure centers. In any place that you can elicit aggression in the brain, that place is also a pleasure center. So that, from my perspective, aggression is really built into the organism as part of survival mechanisms and is a necessary part of the behavioral repertoire.

Audience member: There are two points I would like to raise. They both derive from Mark Solms's discussion. The first point has to do with the issue as to what if anything is testable within the clinical situation. For example, Mark Blechner raised the point that you have both to deal with the metaphor and the concrete aspects of the dream, and that will be better, by some set of criteria. That seems to me to be a testable clinical hypothesis which I don't think that neuroscience has addressed to any degree. One of the problems we have is how to distinguish between those hypotheses that are testable within the clinical situation, to determine differences in theory, and those which are not testable. Rubenstein and Rapaport have written about this point.

The second point is a more clinical one that I will direct toward Steven Ellman and Mark Solms. Ellman's findings, which point to a very close relationship between the activation of the pleasure center, the reward, the motivational center, and REM sleep, is not a position that Solms has taken in a recent paper of his, in which he dissociates dreaming from REM sleep and considers motivation to be a separate instigator of dreams. Now, this is a very interesting empirical difference or a very good general approach in which neuroscience and psychoanalytic concepts converge. It is a very rich and rewarding method but I wonder about its validity because Steven Ellman found a very close relationship between motive, drive strength, REM sleep and, I believe, also primary process thinking or mentation, whereas Mark Solms's research points to a division between these, at least as I have thus far understood it.

Mark Solms: I will take the second point first. Steven Ellman must speak for himself, but my understanding is that he is not in disagreement with me that REM sleep is not the basis for dreaming. In other words, that dreams occur in REM and non-REM sleep. This is one of the instances of that sort of functional dissociation which I was talking about earlier that is such a useful paradigm for us. We are demonstrating pathological cases, that REM sleep can occur without dreaming and dreaming can occur without REM sleep, and when REMs generate in parts of the brain that are damaged you still have dreams. This shows you that these two different things normally occur together, and here is where the problem arises. Because they normally occur together it appears as if the dream phenomena, that is, *pleasure, reward*—there are different words that different people use for those motivational pathways of the basal forebrain—because those pathways are activated in REM sleep it might give the appearance that those can *only* be activated during sleep by REM. We have gone as far as we can with that process and we are left with big theoretical questions which divide us fundamentally and those questions are apparently unanswerable by that method. So do we have fifty different psychoanalyses existing side by side or do we try to resolve those differences? If we are going to resolve those differences, I think we need to look to other methods. So it is not a matter of psychoanalysis as a method being unable to test any hypothesis, far from it, and certainly the closer you get to the surface and the more you are dealing with the individual case, the more the method comes into its own.

Steven Ellman: I don't think we have gone nearly as far as we can in studying psychoanalysis. I would agree with the question, or at least with what I understand the implications of the question to be. There are many testable hypotheses that were neurophysiological and the neurosciences really can't answer the questions nearly as well as we could from a psychoanalytic qualitative way of looking at things. So whether Mark Blechner's idea is better or worse, I think first you have to define what you mean by better *within* the theory and what kind of results you are looking at.

The second point, I really do agree with: If those mechanisms are firing, which we extend from our perspective, from the locus coereleus coursing through the midbrain to the cortex, if those things are firing, they can fire outside of REM sleep and still fire dreamlike phenomena. I suspect, though, that the mentation looks quite different. A patient of mine just went off an old-fashioned tricyclic antidepressant which is a complete REM suppressant, and when she would report a dream she would say that it didn't feel like a dream, it was some thought she had during sleep. And gradually during treatment she went off the antidepressant and now she's dreaming in technicolor. There is quite a difference when you have the whole phenomena of REM sleep coming together with the sensory and motivational components, but certainly it can occur outside of REM sleep. Our REM deprivation studies have shown that. It can spill over both into non-REM and into waking states.

Mark Blechner: We need to find the significance of our differences, but some of the apparent differences between schools of psychoanalysis are more in the language of the way we speak than what we actually do. I used to teach a course on working with schizophrenics and my training in that area is mainly the work of Harry Stack Sullivan. I came across a paper by Hanna Segal in which she describes her work with a schizophrenic patient. The language of her theory is so completely different from Harry Stack Sullivan, but, if you look at the work that she does, her approach is so similar it is just astonishing, even though I think she may feel she is from a completely different school.

Morton Reiser: First of all, psychoanalysis is not simply an effort to have a theory of the mind and how the mind works. There is a very important element in this, namely, an attempt to understand the interrelationship between the developing person and the context in which he or she develops a variety of special idiosyncratic characteristics in dealing with the world, which they are capable of perceiving through their own mental processes, as they go through life. In addition, there is the explanation of that developmental arrangement and its capacity to be reinterpreted according to a different set of sensory or cognitive possibilities, which complicates the matter very greatly. The significance for the practicing analyst or for psychologists is in the way in which the mind works and how things are processed, where they are stored, and so forth, but this is not the whole story. Then, there are such individual variations when one talks about communication and language. I think it is important to take into account that there is a problem first of all that we all have in translating our inner experience into any kind of language that is satisfactory to us so far as explaining what we are experiencing, and that secondarily, to put it in some form which makes it comprehensible to somebody else. So that there is an inner communication problem, particularly since we seem to think in more than verbal forms. It is not only the metaphors that we are talking about; it is the capacity to construct metaphors which we also have to talk about. So, I think everybody should look at Arden Rothstein's book about mental disability–dyslexia, which is another approach to the problem. How do people sequence? How do they make connections and relationships between entities? Do they use similar kinds of arrangements and ways of thinking and how is that communicated to other people?

Mark Solms: I don't think the problem is one of figurative languages, which is inevitable. With Morton Reiser's first point about the mind and development and the environment, when I say psychoanalysis is about the mind, I don't mean the mind in a box, I mean the mind which develops and the mind which interacts with other minds. One of the strengths of psychoanalysis that it contributes in this dialogue with other disciplines is that it has always seen the mind in this dynamic complexity.

Audience member: At the beginning of your discussion, you posed the question: Why do we dream? I got excited. Then I thought, well this is easy, every human being dreams, almost every night. But then at the end of the lecture I still didn't know, *why* do we dream? Maybe that's part of the problem. It's like a patient who writes, "You know, I am having a great time, tell me why." Maybe we have to pinpoint our comments a little closer to direct research. For instance, I did some research on dreaming. I studied women on the third day postpartum. That's when the milk comes in and they had very special dreams when the milk came in. I looked at it as a releasing phenomenon. And that was the hormonal root. You apparently were going through the brain root. But there are many ways of approaching dreams and timing of dreams. So we have to be more specific than asking why do we dream?

Steven Ellman: My notion is that we dream when there is an activation of the pathways that I have talked about and there is an absence of external stimulation. My assumption is that those pathways fire during waking and sleeping and so we are trying to replicate Kripke and Sonnenschein's (1973) study of sensory isolation where you have REM-like phantasies every 70 to 90 minutes. During sleep you dream when these pathways are activated and this begins to stir up the kinds of memory systems that I have talked about.

REFERENCES

Braun, A., Balkin, T., Wesensten, N., Carson, R., Varga, M., Baldwin, P., Selbie, S., Belenky, G., & Herscovitch, P. (1997), Regional cerebral blood flow throughout the sleep–wake cycle. *Brain,* 120:1173–1197.

Ellman, S. J. (1991), *Freud's Technique Papers: A Contemporary Perspective.* Northvale, NJ: Jason Aronson.

Fosshage, J. & Loew, C., Eds. (1987), *Dream Interpretation: A Comparative Study,* rev. ed. Costa Mesa, CA: PMA.

Freud, S. (1900), The Interpretation of Dreams. *Standard Edition,* 4&5. London: Hogarth Press, 1953.

——— (1904), Freud's psycho-analytic procedure. *Standard Edition,* 7:247–254. London: Hogarth Press, 1953.

Kandel, E. (1998), A new intellectual framework for psychiatry. *Amer. J. Psychiatry,* 155:457–469.

Kripke, D., & Sonnenschein, D. (1973), A 90 minute day-dream cycle. *Sleep Res.,* 18:187–191.

Maquet, P., Peters, J., Aerts, J., Delfiore, G., Degueldre, C., Luxen, A., & Franck, A. (1996), Functional neuroanatomy of human REM sleep and dreaming. *Nature,* 383:163–166.

Nofzinger, E., Mintun, M., Wiserman, M., Kupfer, D., & Moore, R. (1997), Forebrain activation in REM sleep: An FDG PET study. *Brain Res.,* 770:192–201.

Olds, J. (1977), *Drives and Reinforcements: Behavioral Studies of Hypothalamic Function.* New York: Raven Press.

Solms, M. (1997), *The Neuropsychology of Dreams.* Mahwah, NJ: Erlbaum.

Part II

Dreams in Clinical Work

Clinical Panel 1

Chair, Ellen Rees

3

The Organizing Functions of Dreaming: A Contemporary Psychoanalytic Model

James L. Fosshage

Dream mentation, a process that occurs during sleep, centrally functions, as waking mentation does, to process information and regulate affect in keeping with motivational priorities. When we dream, we variably use, as Freud (1900) suggested, dual modes of cognition. In contrast to Freud's energy-based conceptualizations involving the mobility of cathexes, however, we now view the dual modes essentially as the imagistic, sensory-dominated primary process mode and the linguistically anchored, secondary process mode (Noy, 1969, 1979; McLaughlin, 1978; McKinnon, 1979; Fosshage, 1983, 1987a,b; Lichtenberg, 1983; Bucci, 1985, 1994). These modes appear in dreams in the form of sensory images and spoken and unspoken words. Just as words are placed in a logical, coherent order to shape meaning and cognitive focus, so too are images sequentially ordered to express meaning and to further affective–cognitive processing (Fosshage, 1983). Sensory images tend to evoke more affect (see Epstein, 1994, for a review), which clarifies why dreams (especially REM dreams, which are more imagistically dominated as compared to non-REM dreams) can be so emotionally powerful. Although contemporary dream models differ, the view of dreams as centrally organizing information and regulating affect in keeping with shifting needs and motivational priorities is, I believe, an increasingly convergent perspective evolving out of dream and neuroscientific research, contemporary psychoanalytic theory, cognitive psychology, and clinical work.

I refer to my particular model as the *organization model of dreams* because the core process and function of dreaming is to organize data. I posit, more specifically, that dream mentation, like waking mentation, develops, maintains, and restores psychological organization and regulates affect in keeping with motivational priorities (Fosshage, 1983, 1987b, 1997). In its variable use of imagistic and linguistic modes of mentation during REM and non-REM cycles, dreaming, like waking mentation, ranges from elemental cognition (e.g., momentary replay of an event) to the most highly complex forms of mentation (e.g., efforts at complex emotional as well as intellectual problem solving).

I will briefly delineate this model as well as the model-derived guidelines for working with dreams, and conclude with several clinical illustrations. Elaborations of this model, including presentations of research evidence and ample clinical illustrations, can be found in a number of publications (Fosshage, 1983, 1987a,b, 1988, 1989, 1997; Fosshage and Loew, 1987; Lichtenberg, Lachmann, and Fosshage, 1996).

DREAM FUNCTIONS

Dream mentation, like waking mentation, can contribute to the *development* of psychological organization (e.g., the establishment of categories and expectancies) and the consolidation of memory that involves a wide range of affective experience. Dreams can contribute to the consolidation of *negative* or *positive* self-percepts that have emerged out of relational experience and to memories of *traumatic* or *vitalizing* events. Research amply demonstrates that REM sleep and dreams contribute to learning (see Fosshage [1997], for a review), aspects of what I call the developmental function of dreams. Extrapolating from the neurophysiological research findings that REM quantitatively decreases during our life span, Meissner (1968), Breger (1977), and Reiser (1990) posit that dreaming fosters structuralization of the nervous system.

In addition, dream mentation, in keeping with a posited overarching motivation to develop or "self-right" (Lichtenberg, Lachman, and Fosshage, 1992, 1996), can contribute to the *development* of newly emergent psychic configurations that are developmental advances. In contributing to development, new perceptual angles, new percepts of self and other are achieved, and new ways of behaving are imagistically portrayed. Dream mentation often continues the unconscious and conscious waking efforts at conflict resolution or problem solving—through restoring a previous state, using defensive processes, or creating a new solution. For example, the dreamer can experience new moments of vitalizing expansiveness, overcoming previous prohibitions.[1] Summarizing the research with regard to problem solving in dreams, Kramer (1993) notes: "A successful night's dreaming, which occurs about 60 percent of the time, is the result of a progressive-sequential, figurative problem solving occurring across the night" (p. 187).

Dream mentation, like waking mentation, can serve to *maintain and restore* psychological organization and self-cohesion. Maintenance and restoration are closely related functions and cannot always

---

[1] Considerable evidence suggests an overall motivation to develop, what I and my coauthors, Lichtenberg and Lachmann (1992, 1996), have referred to as self-righting. Kohut (1984) likewise assumed a fundamental striving "to realize the nuclear self and its program of action." Dream, like waking mentation in my view can contribute to development. This developmental function is probably the most unrecognized dream function in psychoanalysis today, primarily due to the dominant influence of the classical model and the view that dreaming is a regressive and, therefore, primitive process. Jung (1916) was the first to suggest otherwise in positing compensatory and prospective functions. When "ego consciousness" deviates too sharply from the self (the central guiding principle of personality), the dream provides a "compensatory" function, that is, the dream attempts to get the person back on track—what we call self-righting. The dream's foreshadowing of possible actualities to emerge in the near future Jung calls the *prospective function.* In my view, dreaming does not just foreshadow future developments but is actively engaged in bringing about those internal changes. Moreover, the posited dichotomy between ego consciousness and the unconscious self, in my judgment, positions Jungians to look to the dream all too much for serving as the "true" guide for development which can potentially disempower conscious waking efforts. I believe an individual struggles in both dreaming and waking mentation to find his or her way and either at any particular moment may be in the forefront in these efforts.

be distinguished. *Maintenance* refers to the modulation and continuation of ongoing psychological organization, whereas *restoration* addresses a more severe state of psychological disorganization. Regulation of affect in these dreams is central (Kramer, 1993). When we have insufficiently expressed our anger and aversiveness in reaction to a perceived threat during the day, for example, we may attempt to set the situation right (self-righting) in our dreams through expression of anger (regulating affect) and restoration of self-equilibrium. Kohut's (1977) self-state dream addresses the dreamer's efforts at restoration when the dreamer's self is in the threat of fragmentation or dissolution (Ornstein, 1987).[2] Research evidence (e.g., the studies of REM deprivation producing a rebound effect) strongly indicates that REM sleep and REM-like waking activity are essential for maintaining neurophysiological and psychological equilibrium (Fosshage, 1997).

In dream mentation, as in waking mentation, we use (and reveal) our primary patterns of organizing experience (Piaget, 1954; Wachtel, 1980; Atwood and Stolorow, 1984; Stolorow and Lachmann, 1984–1985; Stern, 1985; Fosshage, 1994). Images of self, other, and self-with-other are intricately revealed. Dream mentation, like waking mentation, can reinforce, transform, or develop patterns of organizing experience.

While we may attempt in dreaming, as in waking mentation, to develop, maintain, and restore psychological organization, we vary as to the efficacy of our efforts. Affects are central in assessing the efficacy of a dream or dream scenario. The nightmare, for example, reveals a poignantly unsuccessful attempt to cope with a high-anxiety producing stimulus or conflict.

In addition, a dreamer's overall motivational aims may shift in priority. Developmental strivings may be thwarted as strivings to maintain familiar psychological organization and corresponding attachment patterns gain in priority. For example, a dreamer may first dream of empowering acts of self-assertion and, subsequently, in reaction to anxiety return to a disempowered, victimized position that is familiar and habitual, yet, at a considerable cost in terms of vitality (see Lichtenberg, Lachmann, and Fosshage, [1996], for motivational systems theory and dreams).

[2] Within the organization model, wish fulfillment is no longer viewed as a fantasied gratification of libidinal or aggressive impulses with a primary function of discharge, defensive process, or superego wish, but rather as an avenue of regulation and management of affective–cognitive experiences (Fosshage, 1987b).

DREAM CONTENT

Freud's (1900, 1923) postulation that dreams usually involve a defensive (disguising) transformation of the underlying latent content into the manifest content is unique to the classical model, differentiating it from all other dream models. Once drive and energy theory is eschewed, it is no longer theoretically necessary to posit the ubiquity of defensive or disguising operations in dream formation. While Erikson (1954) noted that the manifest content is also revelatory of the dream and dreamer, the utilization of the manifest–latent content distinction and the perceived need to uncover the latent content in dream interpretation remains dominant in classical psychoanalysis. In my view, the manifest–latent content distinction contributes to ubiquitous translations of dream imagery that potentiates the analyst's influence, at the expense of the dreamer and the dream experience, in understanding dreams.

In my view, dreams more directly reveal—through affects, metaphors, and themes—the dreamer's immediate concerns. Fromm (1951) spoke of symbolic (forgotten) language not as a language that disguises but as a "language in which we express inner experience as if it were a sensory experience" (p. 12). French and Fromm's (1964) problem-solving efforts, Fairbairn's (1944) object-relational processes, Kohut's (1977) self-regulation, Erikson's (1954) individualized ego modes of experiencing and relating, and what I posit to be developmental and regulatory processes, are all viewed as directly (manifestly) observable in dreams (Fosshage, 1983). Defense organizations, what we refer to as aversiveness (Lichtenberg, Lachmann, and Fosshage, 1992, 1996), are one route by which self-cohesion may be protected, and may appear directly in dreams or not, but they do not necessarily result in disguised stand-ins.

Rather than assuming a distinction between manifest and latent content and corresponding disguising processes, I use the term *dream content* (Fosshage, 1983, 1987a,b). This phenomenological concept easily incorporates the notion of various meanings that are associatively connected without assumptions about defensive transformations or levels of meaning. I believe that dream images are chosen primarily not for the purposes of disguise but for their evocative power and actual usefulness in thinking imagistically about the issue at hand, much as a waking person selects words to further the process of thinking meaningfully about internal concerns.

In eschewing the manifest–latent content distinction and positing that dream content is more directly revelatory, I am not suggesting that dream meanings are readily apparent. Dreams are often elusive and difficult to understand. Their elusiveness, in my view, is related to a variety of factors including: poor dream recall; lack of clarity in the dreaming process itself; metaphorical nature of the dream (Ullman, 1969); difficulty in understanding the meanings of images from a waking perspective; difficulty making sense when juxtaposing two different (i.e., waking and sleeping) mentational states; conflict between dreaming and waking mentation; and a less than optimally facilitative intersubjective context in which the dream is told and explored.

The idea that dream images are chosen as the best imagistic and linguistic language available to the dreamer at that moment to express and facilitate what the dreamer is thinking about, profoundly affects our work with and our understanding of dreams. Dream images, in my view, need to be assessed for what they reveal, metaphorically and thematically, not for what they conceal. While I may refer to these images as symbols, I do not understand symbols in terms of defensive transformations and stand-ins for "something else," but in terms of poignantly capturing meanings (more similar to memory nodal points). With this emphasis, each dream image as used within the context of the dream scenario can be appreciated better for what it conveys. For example, the "I" in the dream identifies the dreamer and the object images represent the dreamer's images of the other. Not assuming that these object images are projections of the dreamer's self gives us access to the dreamer's images of others, self-with-others, and important relational patterns. Exploration may reveal that aspects of the dreamer are projected onto the other; yet, eschewing the common assumption that object representations are self-representations, enables us to illuminate the patient's self-with-other relational patterns as well as the aspects of the self projected onto the other.

Dreaming mentation, like waking mentation, varies in significance to the dreamer. Dreams range from comparatively simple thoughts involving completion of daily tasks (e.g., mowing the lawn, completing a paper), to dreams that are richly significant, providing sweeping renditions of the dreamers' lives. Research has demonstrated that affect-loaded, imagistically dominated REM dreams are more important than non-REM dreams in consolidating memory and in dealing with emotional issues, and that the effect of dreams or waking thoughts and feelings varies (Kuiken and Sikora, 1993). Recognizing the variability in significance of dream mentation clinically frees the analyst and analysand from what can become a burdensome and daunting pursuit of a significant latent meaning in every dream.

GUIDELINES FOR WORKING WITH DREAMS

In these times of constructivism, we recognize that patient and analyst variably cocontribute to understanding the patient's dreams. In attempting to maximize the influence of the dreaming experience itself in arriving at a coconstructed understanding, I suggest five guidelines for working analytically with dreams.

Dreaming is an affective–cognitive organizing experience that is at times continuous with, yet often divergent from, preceding and subsequent waking states. We need, therefore, to illuminate, as fully as possible, the patient's dream experience. The first guideline is to listen as closely as possible to the patient's experience within the dream (an extension of Kohut's [1959] empathic mode of perception to working with dreams).

Analytic inquiry is initially aimed to fill out the dreamer's experience within the dream—the second guideline. I might ask, for example, "What were you feeling when that occurred in the dream?" "What were you experiencing?" Inquiry into the dreamer's experience facilitates the dreamer's involvement and affective reconnection with the dream experience itself and potentially counters the dreamer's waking construal of the dream—particularly important when it is divergent with the metaphorical and thematic structure of the dream. This focus on the dreamer's experiences implicitly validates its importance and increases the dreamer's conviction about the meaningfulness of the dream experience.

Dream imagery is not to be translated or seen as standing for something else but is to be understood in terms of the meanings captured metaphorically and thematically—the third guideline. When dreaming is viewed as an integrative and synthetic mentational process, the task is to illuminate more fully, through the dreamer's associations and elaborations, the particular meaning of an image as it is used within the context of the dream. Each image is like a word within a sentence, and sequences of images are like sentences and paragraphs that tell a story. Waking clarification as to the meaning of a dream image is facilitative of understanding, yet the image can be understood fully only as it is used within the dream context, for the context shapes the meaning.

Affect-laden images of self, other, self-with-other, and relational scenarios can all be identified. The overall drama from beginning to end can reveal starkly and powerfully the dreamer's innermost struggles and strivings. Once the dream's scenarios are identified, our analytic task shifts to identifying (when unclear) if, where, and when these themes have emerged in waking life or how they are connected to waking experience—the fourth guideline.

When defining transference in the broadest sense as referring to the patient's experience of the analyst (Gill, 1994), it follows by definition that all dreams reported to an analyst have transferential meaning.[3] We need to assess, however, whether the content of the dream is applicable or the process of communicating the dream carries the primary meaning for the analytic relationship (Fosshage, 1994). Most commonly, the content of the dream is understood as reflective of the transference. Facile translations of dream images to be stand-ins for the analyst aid in applying the content of the dream to the transference, but, in my judgment, potentially undermine the capturing of the meanings of dream images and their dream contexts as well as the meaning for the analytic relationship. As a fifth guideline, I never assume that the content of the dream directly relates to the transference unless the analyst appears in the dream or the dreamer immediately associates to the analyst. Otherwise, the process of communicating the dream to the analyst—rather than the content—most likely carries the transferential meaning. In analyzing a dream, relational patterns emergent in

[3] While I will use the term *transference* in this broadest sense to refer to the patient's experience of the analyst, I have spelled out elsewhere (Fosshage, 1994) the disadvantages of this definition. Essentially I think we are particularly interested in primary organizing patterns with which the patient assimilates the analytic relationship (Wachtel, 1980; Stolorow and Lachmann, 1984–1985; Lichtenberg, Lachmann, and Fosshage, 1996).

the dream need first to be identified and subsequently to be connected by the patient to waking life. If we sense that a relational pattern is occurring in the analytic relationship as well, even though the patient has not mentioned it, we can simply inquire, "I wonder if you are experiencing that here too?" The transference, in the sense of applying the content of the dream to the analytic relationship, can thus be addressed without translating dream imagery and without minimizing the patient's dream or associated experience involving relationships outside the analytic relationship.

This phenomenologically grounded approach to dreams validates the dreamer's experience within the dream and enhances conviction as to the meaning of the dream. Dream images are appreciated for their communicative value within the structure of the dream drama. Importantly, the dreamer can begin, or can continue to rely more on his or her own dream experience—rather than on the analyst's interpretive translations—to understand the dream. All of this facilitates an empowered and vital sense of self.

FIRST CLINICAL ILLUSTRATION

The first clinical example illustrates a profound shift in the patient's experience of the analyst that first emerges in a dream. The patient was a young physician. While competent in his work, he experienced a debilitating malaise or deadness and was having difficulty finding the right woman. To enliven himself he had tried a number of Eastern practices. A friend of his, and former student of mine, had strongly recommended that he see me. Although considerably skeptical about psychoanalysis and psychotherapy, on the strength of her recommendation he decided to give it a try—after all, what did he have to lose? He did not think that psychoanalysis worked and his primary perception of me was that I was a charlatan and not to be trusted. Only once during the first three months of treatment did he mention seeing me as solid, married, and having a home (I saw him in my home office), aspects of life which he wanted for himself.

The patient said the dream 'took place in your driveway. A young man was moving into your basement as a form of treatment. I told him that he's very lucky to have you—you were fair, reliable, trustworthy, had integrity and were not a charlatan. I was showing my old house where I grew up. I was selling it. Somehow I was going to move into here, your house, too.

We both recognized with surprise what a changed percept and experience of the analyst this dream was conveying. I asked if this corresponded with any waking thoughts he had had about our relationship and me. Without a pause he answered with conviction, "No." He said that in the dream he was moving in to live with me, but consciously he was only aware of his doubts. I highlighted that in his dream he was envisioning our relationship and me very differently as compared to his waking perspective.

I understood the dream and process material to illustrate the emergence of new images of the analyst and of the dreamer in relationship with the analyst that contrasted strikingly with his conscious waking percepts. To view dreaming and waking states as different self-states (literally, different states of mind) highlights their similarities and differences and avoids invalidating either. In this instance, these states were quite disparate. Interpretively we were able to note the difference without invalidating either. From a conscious waking perspective, distrust of the analyst was typically in the foreground. Previously the patient had only once hinted at an idealized selfobject transference (Kohut, 1971, 1984), in which the analyst was viewed as having qualities that matched some of the patient's sought-after ideals. Presumably these ideal qualities served as the basis for him to seek and remain in treatment, although his experience of them was at best far in the background in his waking states. While presumably the therapeutic interaction must have fostered the development of the relatively new percept, it was in his dream that the patient was able on this occasion to envision the analyst far more fully and definitively as trustworthy, a developmentally needed experience with an idealized other. The patient in his dream experience was envisioning and consolidating this new percept. Relating and affectively connecting to the dream in a waking state facilitated integration of the developmental movement emergent in the dream.

One analyst questioned if the patient is "struggling in the dream with the awareness of his envy, evident in the struggle in the dream and his devaluing associations still manifesting his distrust and suspicion"

(Melvin Lansky, personal communication). Rather than conflictual or "struggling with awareness" of envy that is conflictual, the content and mood of the dream is calming and self-enhancing, corresponding with an idealized selfobject connection. To the extent that there is conflict, it is, in this instance, between two states of mind, the dreaming and waking states. The patient's waking devaluation of the analyst was, I believe, an expression of a primary pessimistic view of the other leading to dejection, and was probably also a percept maintained to defensively ward off a hoped for, yet feared idealizing selfobject connection.

SECOND CLINICAL ILLUSTRATION

Dreams play a profoundly important role in developing and regarding our psychic life—an importance that in many ways even outdistances that accorded by Freud. On occasion, we witness dreams that provide a comprehensive and sweeping vision of our lives and ourselves. To conclude, I present a dream of this sort that portrays the shifting inner states of the dreamer.

The dreamer, a woman who was 39 at the time of the dream, was very bright and imagistically gifted. She was raised as a model child and had to freeze off from much of her affective life, in response to successful and extremely intrusive parents who had an agenda for her, and to incidents of sexual abuse from her brother and a neighbor. At the height of intense paranoid fears and suicidal ideation, at her request, she was hospitalized for one month to deal with her terrors in a more contained and, therefore, safer setting. The dream was presented in three parts:

> 1. A village: it extends up (and down) a slope. It is not a steep slope, but gradual and graceful; it is feminine. It is winter. I am looking down on the village as if on a model train set. There are clusters of houses nestled together in the snow. I see their roofs; they look like old leather books perched on each house. There are train tracks which wind through the village, unifying and connecting it, making it whole. There are green pine forests, main streets, central squares, country roads hidden under the snowfall. It is quiet, peaceful, lovely. I know that I am the village as well as hovering above it. It is the landscape of myself.

2. A feeling of fear. I am filled with the kind of terror which sent me to the hospital. It is huge, unmanageable, overwhelming. It is all over me, I feel it on my skin, and inside of me. I am paralyzed with fright. This fear is old, familiar. The village goes into a state of suspended animation. It is frozen and still; there is no movement. The me that is in the village ceases to feel. I have the familiar sensation of fear followed by an absence of feeling.

3. Time has passed like in the telling of the Rip Van Winkle story. There is the feeling of twenty years (but I know it has been more) going by. The village has remained in its state of suspended animation. I have lived without feelings all the time.

There is a thaw; the village comes back to life. The cottages are in the same place but feel as if they have been moved to new locations. The relation of the train tracks to the villages, and cottages looks the same when I view it from above, but the me that is *in* the landscape feels different. I am disoriented, but not afraid. I am thankful that the frozen sleep is over. There are icicles melting under the eaves of the cottages; the light falls with a different slant on the landscape. At the end of the dream I am only *in* the landscape, no longer above it. I am finding my way through unfamiliar terrain. The thaw has caused patches of earth to appear from under the snow. The landscape is no longer pristine as it was in the beginning of the dream (when it was a model—a model child) but I feel grounded in it; it is much more real and filled with vitality.

This dream speaks to us. It tells a dramatic story of an ongoing psychological transformation. The Rip Van Winkle sleep of twenty years had begun when the dreamer was 19, the beginning of adulthood, as she put it, and when she met her former husband. Brought up as a model child, she was graceful and feminine, and had achieved some peacefulness but at the cost of being "wintry" and distant from her own experience ("I know that I am the village as well as hovering above it"). In the analysis the patient began to reconnect with feeling, encountered terror, and froze to put a stop to it. Gradually, as she began to understand and work her way through the fear, she began to thaw, to be more fully "within" her experience, and to become more vitally alive. The dreamer is able to capture in poignant dream imagery feelings, self-states, and transformation, to ponder and to further consolidate these ongoing internal changes.

REFERENCES

Atwood, G., & Stolorow, R. (1984), *Structures of Subjectivity.* Hillsdale, NJ: Analytic Press.

Breger, L. (1977), Function of dreams. *J. Abnorm. Psychol.,* 72:1–28.

Bucci, W. (1985), Dual coding: A cognitive model in psychoanalytic research. *J. Amer. Psychoanal. Assn.,* 33:571–607.

——— (1994), The multiple code theory and the psychoanalytic process: A framework for research. *Annual of Psychoanalysis,* 22:239–259. Hillsdale, NJ: Analytic Press.

Epstein, S. (1994), Integration of the cognitive and the psychodynamic unconscious. *Amer. Psychologist,* 8:709–724.

Erikson, E. (1954), The dream specimen of psychoanalysis. *J. Amer. Psychoanal. Assn.,* 2:5–56.

Fairbairn, W. R. D. (1944), Endopsychic structure considered in terms of object-relationships. In: *Psychoanalytic Studies of the Personality.* London: Routledge & Kegan Paul, pp. 82–136.

Fosshage, J. (1983), The psychological function of dreams: A revised psychoanalytic perspective. *Psychoanal. & Contemp. Thought,* 6:641–669.

——— (1987a), New vistas on dream interpretation. In: *Dreams in New Perspective: The Royal Road Revisited,* ed. M. Glucksman. New York: Human Sciences Press.

——— (1987b), A revised psychoanalytic approach. In: *Dream Interpretation: A Comparative Study,* rev. ed., ed. J. Fosshage & C. Loew. Costa Mesa, CA: PMA, pp. 299–318.

——— (1988), Dream interpretation revisited. In: Frontiers in Self Psychology, *Progress in Self Psychology,* Vol. 3, ed. A. Goldberg. Hillsdale, NJ: Analytic Press, pp. 161–175.

——— (1989), The developmental function of dreaming mentation: Clinical implications. Reply. In: Dimension of Self Experience, *Progress in Self Psychology*, Vol. 5, ed. A. Goldberg, Hillsdale, NJ: Analytic Press, pp. 3–11; 45–50.

——— (1994), Toward reconceptualizing transference: Theoretical and clinical considerations. *Internat. J. Psycho-Anal.,* 75:265–280.

——— (1997), The organizing functions of dream mentation. *Contemp. Psychoanal.,* 33:429–458.

——— Loew, C., Eds. (1987), *Dream Interpretation: A Comparative Study,* rev. ed. Costa Mesa, CA: PMA.

French, T., & Fromm, E. (1964), *Dream Interpretation, A New Approach.* New York: Basic Books.

Freud, S. (1900), The Interpretation of Dreams. *Standard Edition,* 4&5. London: Hogarth Press, 1953.

——— (1923), Remarks on the theory and practice of dream-interpretation. *Standard Edition,* 19:107–101. London: Hogarth Press, 1961.

Fromm, E. (1951), *The Forgotten Language.* New York: Grove Press.

Gill, M. (1994), Transference: A change in conception or only in emphasis? *Psychoanal. Inq.,* 4:489–523.

Jung, C. G. (1916), General aspects of dream psychology. In: The Structure and Dynamics of the Psyche, *Collected Works*, Vol. 8. New York: Pantheon Books, 1960, pp. 237–280.

Kohut, H. (1959), Introspection, empathy and psychoanalysis. *J. Amer. Psychoanal. Assn.,* 7:459–483.

——— (1971), *The Analysis of the Self.* New York: International Universities Press.

——— (1977), *The Restoration of the Self.* New York: International Universities Press.

——— (1984), *How Does Analysis Cure?* Chicago: University of Chicago Press.

Kramer, M. (1993), The selective mood regulatory function of dreaming: An update and revision. In: *The Functions of Dreaming,* ed. A. Moffit, M. Kramer, & R. Hoffman. Albany, NY: State University of New York Press, pp. 139–195.

Kuiken, D., & Sikora, S. (1993), The impact of dreams on waking thoughts and feelings. In: *The Functions of Dreaming,* ed. A. Moffit, M. Kramer, & R. Hoffman. Albany, NY: State University of New York Press, pp. 419–476.

Lichtenberg, J. (1983), *Psychoanalysis and Infant Research.* Hillsdale, NJ: Analytic Press.

——— Lachmann, F., & Fosshage, J. (1992), *Self and Motivational Systems: Toward a Theory of Technique.* Hillsdale, NJ: Analytic Press.

——— ——— ——— (1996), *The Clinical Exchange: Technique Derived from Self and Motivational Systems.* Hillsdale, NJ: Analytic Press.

McKinnon, J. (1979), Two semantic forms: Neuropsychological and psychoanalytic descripting. *Psychoanal. & Contemp. Thought,* 2:25–76.

McLaughlin, J. (1978), Primary and secondary process in the context of cerebral hemispheric specialization. *Psychoanal. Quart.,* 47:237–266.

Meissner, W. W. (1968), Dreaming as process. *Internat. J. Psycho-Anal.,* 49:63–79.

Noy, P. (1969), A revision of the psychoanalytic theory of the primary process. *Internat. J. Psycho-Anal.,* 50:155–178.

——— (1979), The psychoanalytic theory of cognitive development. *The Psychoanalytic Study of the Child,* 34:169–216. New Haven, CT: Yale University Press.

Ornstein, P. (1987), On the self-state dreams in the psychoanalytic treatment process. In: *The Interpretation of Dreams in Clinical Work,* ed. A. Rothstein. Madison, CT: International Universities Press, pp. 87–104.

Piaget, J. (1954), *The Construction of Reality in the Child.* New York: Basic Books.

Reiser, M. (1990), *Memory in Mind and Brain.* New York: Basic Books.

Stern, D. N. (1985), *The Interpersonal World of the Infant.* New York: Basic Books.

Stolorow, R., & Lachmann, F. (1984–1985), Transference: The future of an illusion. *Annual of Psychoanalysis,* 12/13:19–37. New York: International Universities Press.

Ullman, M. (1969), Dreaming as metaphor in motion. *Arch. Gen. Psychiatry,* 21:696–703.

Wachtel, P. F. (1980), Transference, schema and assimilation: The relevance of Piaget to the psychoanalytic theory of transference. *Annual of Psychoanalysis,* 8:59–76. New York: International Universities Press.

4

Dreams in Clinical Works

Edward Nersessian

In lecture 29 of the *New Introductory Lectures on Psycho-Analysis* (1933, pp. 7–8), Freud lamented the disappearance from the *International Journal of Psycho-Analysis* of the section entitled "On Dream-Interpretation," and the fact that analysts behaved "as though there was nothing more to say about dreams, as though there was no more to be added to the theory of dreams." Now, one hundred years since *The Interpretation of Dreams* (1900), it may be useful to consider the fate of the study of dreams in psychoanalysis. I am a classical analyst, which in the United States refers to those who continue to adhere to Freud's theories and their subsequent development through the works of Anna Freud, Hartmann, Kris, Lowenstein, Arlow, Brenner, Beres, and Rangell. My education has been in what is commonly labeled the American ego psychology school and its modification by Brenner leading to modern conflict theory.

Prior to embarking on describing a personal view of the fate of dreams, I would like to say a word about another interest of mine, which is the newly emergent dialogue between psychoanalysts and neuroscientists. I hope that over time new insights will ensue from this important exchange, leading to a better understanding of the three aspects of dream theory elaborated in *The Interpretation of Dreams*, that is to say, the function of dreams, the meaning of dreams, and the dream as an entry point for research on the workings of the mind-brain. Many theories abound as to the function of dreams, yet we do not possess a fuller understanding beyond Freud's remark that the dream serves "to protect sleep" or to be more precise, to protect the "wish" to sleep. While most dream researchers dispute this role for dreams, to my knowledge nothing conclusive has been determined about why we dream, though it is quite likely that dreaming has a larger role in mental functioning than was anticipated by Freud. For example, research on affects and memory may, in the not too distant future, reveal the role dreaming plays in various aspects of these properties of the mind. Naturally, the function of sleep itself needs to be fully elaborated, and understanding sleep may contribute to the understanding of dreaming.

As to the meaning of dreams, our psychoanalytic view has come under serious attack over the past three decades, not just by work done on REM sleep by the Harvard researcher Hobson and others, but also by psychoanalysts relying on sleep research findings. It is encouraging that Hobson no longer considers dreams as meaningless, but instead thinks that salient memories and emotions serve as the primary shaper of dream plots. Disagreement remains, however, about the psychoanalytic idea that in a dream a wish is represented as fulfilled. My own training as a psychoanalyst combined with my readings in the neurosciences have led me to think that dreams probably play a role in managing affects, especially the so-called negative affects.

Whatever the eventual resolution as to the function and meaning of dreams, I firmly believe that we will all benefit from a sustained dialogue between psychoanalysts and neuroscientists, particularly in terms of elucidating the workings of the brain-mind. Recent brain imaging studies are showing great promise in this area, by demonstrating, for example, the areas of the brain that show more activity during dreaming (Braun, 1999). Naturally such a collaboration between psychoanalysts and neuroscientists will embrace many other areas of mutual interests and not just dreaming and dreams. Study of emotion, consciousness, memory, interrelationship between various brain disorders (traumatic, metabolic, endocrine) and mental functioning, motivation, desire and lust, are just a few of the areas where such a collaboration could yield significant benefit. This is the mission of the journal *Neuro-Psychoanalysis*.

Within psychoanalysis, and particularly within my own school, I could schematically describe two trends. First, up until the late 1950s, there was a move toward supplementing Freud's ideas, spearheaded by Otto Isakower (1954) and Bertram Lewin. In the years that followed, a second trend emerged, diminishing the importance of dreams both in clinical work and in psychoanalytic theory. Arlow (1963) and Brenner initially advanced this view, which was later enlarged upon by Brenner (1975). All four of these clinician-theorists have been important teachers at my institution, the New York Psychoanalytic Institute, and their writings form the backdrop on which my views on dreams in clinical practice have emerged.

Let me say right away that for my part, I continue to find dream analysis extremely useful. I am gratified with the help dreams sometimes provide and hope with the three brief examples that follow to demonstrate their usefulness. Naturally, not all dreams lend themselves to analysis, and not all patients work with dreams in the same way. Additionally, what constitutes a useful analysis of a dream also varies greatly. In my experience, dreams that lend themselves to the kind of analysis Freud demonstrated with his botanical monograph dream are rare, but do occur with some patients who seem particularly curious about their dreams. Lest anyone suspect these particular patients are students in psychoanalysis, let me dispel that notion. In my experience, people who are very knowledgeable about psychoanalysis report dreams regularly but rarely actually want to analyze them. Parenthetically, I would add that my own ability to contribute to a dream analysis also varies and seems to be not only a function of what I know about the patient, the context, the day residue, but also the particular state of mind I am in and the affective curiosity aroused in me by the dream. I do not know whether others share this feeling, but from experience I can see myself more or less interested in a dream, while remaining curious about the rest of the material. At times, such countertransference reactions can be profitably analyzed, but at other times they remain limited to one particular dream and are left unattended. It is also correct to say that one does not wish to analyze all dreams thoroughly, and especially in the early phases of an analysis it is sometimes prudent not to bring out all the latent themes that can be detected, in order not to arouse too much anxiety or excessive defensive intellectualization. Furthermore, it is important not to come across as a wizard of dream analysis early in a treatment, as this can have problematic consequences.

With these introductory comments, I will now present three vignettes. None of these examples demonstrates an exhaustive analysis of dreams, which as I have already indicated seldom happens, nor are particularly unusual; instead, I hope they show the usefulness of dreams in the everyday work of analysis.

Prior to reporting the first example, I would like to say a word about transference, which is often the focus in most dream reports in seminars and published papers. There is little or no doubt that in an ongoing analysis the transference will inevitably appear in the dream and that the person of the analyst, as a transference figure, distorted in the customary ways, will frequently be present. Since the analysis and analyst are often in the day residue, this is not surprising. I think, however, that we fail to take sufficient advantage of what dreams can offer if we do not attempt to go beyond and even beside the obvious manifestations of the transference. Too often, as soon as the evidence for the transference is detected in a given dream, it is interpreted, and all other potentially rich material is ignored.

I hope the example that follows illustrates this point. I should warn readers by saying that the elements of an erotic transference are so clear, that whoever has heard this dream has focused almost exclusively on it, but I would like to suggest that, though present, other affects were stronger.

EXAMPLE 1

The patient was a young married woman, with one young son, who had been in analysis for about three years at the time of this dream. She had a great need to be in control and put up a cheerful, intellectual, and friendly attitude to defend against intense inner emotions. One of her complaints was that since the birth of her son she did not enjoy sex with her husband very much, but on the day before the dream, she so enjoyed sex with him that they had intercourse twice. That night she dreamt that she was climbing up a cold white marble statue of a young male, and when she began sucking on the white and very smooth testicles of the statue, it slowly came to life.

The patient was then somewhat cheerful in the session and talked in the same upbeat way about her ongoing anger and jealousy of her husband who had surpassed her in professional success in the field in which they both practiced. From there, her thoughts went to my upcoming weeklong vacation, and since it was during spring break for the New York City schools, she assumed I was going away with my family and children. She especially focused on a daughter she imagined I have and toward whom she believed I was very loving and affectionate, not at all like the distant and cold professional I was toward her. She also reported talking to her mother the day of the dream. The mother, who had breast cancer, had complained about some aches and pains which had worried the patient in a passing way as to their possibly metastatic origin, but which she had later dismissed as just being the usual pains of old age or possibly a flu.

Naturally, I thought that perhaps the dream was expressing her feelings about my lack of affectionate availability to her, with the desire to transform me from a cold psychoanalyst to a warm, aroused, lively lover. I was struck, however, by her description of the texture and color of the testicles. Knowing her intense fear of the loss of her only surviving, very ambivalently loved parent and her inability to deal with the inevitability of this loss except through mild hypomanic defenses and an intense need to control all emotions, I chose not to interpret what seemed to me as the more obvious transference meaning of the dream. Instead, I asked her if she were very worried about mother, whom she knew had metastatic cancer in the bone and whom she wished she could keep alive. Somewhat to my surprise and for only the second or third time in the analysis, the patient began sobbing intensely and talked about the unfairness of it all. She revealed, while sadly crying, a series of fantasies about her mother's death, the funeral arrangements, whether her mother would be alive the next New Year, and so on. Prior to this point, none of these fantasies had been available to the analysis and concerns about the mother's health had either been minimized or dealt with in a very matter of fact manner.

I will interrupt this report here and once again stress that an excessive focus on the transference may obscure other useful avenues of exploration in the dream. I am not trying to oversimplify and to ignore how various issues are related, but instead to highlight the need to be parsimonious in interpreting a dream, and in doing so, hope to touch on what is affectively most charged at the moment. My next vignette has to do with the observation that there are times when a dream helps bring to light a childhood memory which has remained out of the patient's awareness up to that point.

EXAMPLE 2

A man in his early thirties, who had been in treatment for less than a year at the time the following dream was reported, initially presented with a depressed mood accompanied by obsessive fears about the well-being of his loved ones. Extremely intelligent and a good observer of the world around him, he had a rather severe inhibition about observing the world within; in other words, he had more voyeurism than curiosity and communicated with people with difficulty. He also had sex on his mind all the time.

"I am in this house, upstairs, and the room I am in is green. I am with a woman, and then there seems to be a danger, like the color green becomes dangerous, and we have to escape and I wake up."

Associations

I visited my parents over the weekend with my wife and went upstairs to the apartment my aunt and her husband used to rent in our house when I was a kid. I was trying to see if it was as I remembered it or not. We were there for Mother's Day, and my mom was happy that we went. That afternoon, I started thinking of J and wondering if I should call her and wish her a happy Mother's Day (J is a woman he is very attracted to and has been very flirtatious with). I decided not to because if my wife ever found out, she would kill me.

Analyst: In your dream you were with a woman, and there was danger.
Patient: I didn't think about it that way. It was the green color that was dangerous, and I can't imagine why I would be afraid of a color.
Analyst: Does the color bring anything to mind?
Patient: It is my mother's favorite color. In our house when I was growing up, everything was green—walls, curtains, bedspreads. Not upstairs though, only in our part of the house. My mother also loves plants, so we had plants everywhere, but my aunt didn't have any because she and her husband only lived upstairs a few months a year. I remember when they were away, I would go up there and play. In high school, I would go there with girls and fool around, but my mother never caught us. When I was much younger, eight or nine years old, I would play doctor with our next door neighbor's daughter who was my age, but I don't remember doing that upstairs. They had a big backyard, and we would go there and take our clothes off.

Following session:

Patient: "I had another dream. I was in my country house. There was a station wagon. I was in the station wagon, and there was someone else in it."

Associations

My car is not a station wagon, but my parents used to have one when I was a kid. I remember when I was 8 or 9 we took a long cross-country trip in that car. I loved that trip. It's funny, but what comes to mind is that one time my mother was very angry at me during the trip. My sister (two years younger) and I were in the back of the station wagon, and I think we had taken our clothes off under a blanket, and I asked her to touch my penis, and my mother heard it and was furious. Maybe the dangerous green is my mother. (Laughs)

Analysis: So did you also play doctor with your sister?
Patient: Oh, a lot. We were very sexual together when we were young, but I don't remember where we did that. I clearly remember the

backyard with the neighbor, but with my sister I don't seem to picture a place except that time in the car. But I just know we fooled around a lot.

Analyst: Could it have been upstairs?

Patient: Could have been, but I don't remember being upstairs with my sister.

In the next and last vignette, I think we can see the interrelationship between transference, memory, and dreams. Here, what was difficult for the patient to become aware of in the here and now brought into consciousness a memory about a repetitive occurrence in childhood which then facilitated getting in touch with her transference feelings.

EXAMPLE 3

The session was after the weekend, and Ms. C began by reporting on a fight she had with a good male friend G. A woman, L, who was a mutual friend was staying with her, and G had arranged to meet L on Saturday evening. My patient, upon hearing this, decided to accompany L to the meeting, and G was very upset. He felt that he was friendly with L independent of C and should be able to spend an evening with her alone. This story occupied a good part of the hour, but then the patient stopped, and after a brief silence said, "I had a dream last night. You will think it's significant. It is the kind of dream shrinks think is important."

After a few more similar qualifying comments, she reported the following dream: She was in a bathroom. It was very large and steamed up. I was there, and I told her to get undressed, that I wanted her naked. I was naked, but she did not really look, the way she always avoids looking at naked people. The situation was sexually very arousing. In real life, she would find such a situation—a man ordering her to take her clothes off—very exciting. She then went back to discussing the weekend events further, and then, changing the subject, she said, "I have been thinking about what you said in the last session. I agree that I want to be special here and feel my relationship with you is different from your relationships with your other patients. I realized that when I had complained to you about my breasts and that they are deformed and too small and not firm, that I was excited by it. I felt as if I were showing myself to you naked, I was drawing your attention to my body.''

In order to clarify the context of this material and the dream, it should be added that some two weeks earlier she had reported for the first time that when she was between the ages of 7 to 8 to 11 to 12, on a number of occasions she would be taking a bath in her parents' bathroom (the only bathroom in the house with a tub), and her father would walk in naked to take a shower in the shower room, which was behind the head of the tub. At the time she had reported this, she had not recalled any other feeling except that well, that is how it was in our house and a certain mild annoyance, yet in the transference with me whenever sexual matters came up, she would feel disgusted toward me and think of me as a disgusting, dirty old man. The dream not only helped bring together many of the issues we had been struggling with, but most importantly it brought forth an awareness of her own wishes and desires and made it possible for her to recognize the ongoing influence of her childhood experience in her current fantasies both within the analysis but also in the outside world.

We have celebrated the hundredth year anniversary of the publication of the *The Interpretation of Dreams*. I hope it is clear from the above that now, a century later, I continue to benefit in my work from the help offered to me by dreams. I predict that dreams have many more insights left to offer to psychoanalysts and to all interested in the study of mind-brain.

REFERENCES

Arlow, J. A. (1963), Conflict, regression and symptom formation. *Internat. J. Psycho-Anal.,* 44:12–23.

Braun, A. (1999), The neuropsychology of sleep, Commentary. *Neuro-Psychoanal.,* 1(2):196–201.

Brenner, C. (1975), Affects and psychic conflict. *Psychoanal. Quart.,* 44:5–28.

Freud, A. (1936), *The Ego and the Mechanisms of Defense.* New York: International Universities Press, 1966.

Freud, S. (1900), The Interpretation of Dreams. *Standard Edition,* 4&5. London: Hogarth Press, 1953.

——— (1917), A metapsychological supplement to the theory of dreams. *Standard Edition,* 14:217–235. London: Hogarth Press, 1957.

——— (1933), New Introductory Lectures on Psychoanalysis. *Standard Edition,* 22:1–182. London: Hogarth Press, 1964.

Gilmore, M., & Nersessian, E. (1999), Freud's model of the mind in sleep and dreaming. *Neuro-Psychoanal.,* 1(2):225–232.

Hartman, H., & Kris, E. (1945), The genetic approach in psychoanalysis. *The Psychoanalytic Study of the Child,* 1:11–30. New York: International Universities Press.

——— Lowenstein, R. M. (1962), Notes on the superego. *The Psychoanalytic Study of the Child,* 17:42–81. New York: International Universities Press.

Hobson, A. J. (1999), The new neuropsychology of sleep: Implications for psychoanalysis. *Neuro-Psychoanal.,* 1(2):157–195.

Isakower, O. (1954), Spoken words in dreams. A preliminary communication. *Psychoanal. Quart.,* 23:1–6.

Lewin, B. D. (1946), Sleep, the mouth and the dream screen. *Psychoanal. Quart.,* 15:419–434.

Rangell, L. (1981), From insight to change. *J. Amer. Psychoanal. Assn.,* 29:119–141.

5

Dreaming and Not Dreaming

Edna O'Shaughnessy

Freud's great work *The Interpretation of Dreams*, combined with the findings of a hundred years, constitutes what Sara Flanders (1993) calls *The Dream Discourse Today.* Today we know that dreams are of different kinds, and that not dreaming has diverse origins, and that during analysis the evolution of the transference and the course of dream life are connected. About the patient I shall present here, it would be hard to say which is more important—her dreaming, or her particular way of not dreaming.

Mrs. A, in her midforties, holds an administrative post and her husband is in finance. She admires him and she is also afraid of and for him. She speaks of his making nasty deals and his disturbing influence on family life, and how it is always she who must do what needs to be done (e.g., for their now grown-up son and daughter). Mrs. A sees her parents and her two brothers as disturbed, unlikeable people and herself as the one in her family her mother turned to.

At the time she dreamt the dream, Mrs. A had been in analysis for some while. At the beginning she was very anxious, did not like me, and withdrew, suspicious that after she disclosed that she wished she had gone to a different analyst that I had turned hostile. As these feelings and anxieties were analyzed over some months she became pleased to be my patient, which I think she genuinely was, at the same time as being unconsciously excited by a belief that she was my favorite who, unlike my other patients, was free of disturbance and had a special intimacy with me, just as she had felt she was, and is, the sanest in a disturbed family into which I think her disturbances were, and are, projected and hidden. Over a period, and with much difficulty, this phantasy seemed to give way and Mrs. A and I settled into an analysis with more real contact. Relations with her husband and colleagues improved markedly, and she gained a senior post, though she is currently disappointed at not being offered a promotion she expected, even though, and this is important, she had not contended for it.

However, I have been troubled that at a deeper level my patient has not changed. Though the analysis is ongoing it seems so only within certain limits; that is, it has become what I think of as an enclave (1992) in which the full potential of our work is never quite realized. Mrs. A remains something of an observer who is not fully participant, which leads to my prompting her or even saying things that are really hers to say. She apparently now dislikes nothing about me, has no strong feelings of envy or jealousy, or feelings of love or hatred toward me or anyone else. If I try to draw Mrs. A's attention to any of these features we get nowhere. In sum, though Mrs. A has improved it is within some "not get-able" structure—the psychic structure which came into view in her dream.

THE SESSION

The session with the dream was on a Monday. On the previous Friday, Mrs. A had been very agitated about a lump she had detected while examining her breasts the evening before. Mrs. A started the Monday session by talking in a lively way about her dreams. She said she had had two dreams. Now there was one. She had dreamt: She was in a beautiful place. The queen, Queen Elizabeth, was there. Mrs. A laughed and commented, "I'm laughing at myself for dreaming about the queen. I don't like her.'' She continued: But in the dream ''There the queen was, just like an ordinary person. The palace was beautiful, with many pictures and antiques, and there were lots of people there. The queen came over to me and spoke to me. She said she would show me round the palace herself. She was friendly and intimate. The queen took me about and pointed out things.''

Mrs. A then said, ''In the dream of my dream, I mean''—she corrected her slip of the tongue—''in the palace of my dream I did like her.''

''The queen took me and showed me where she lived in a little cottage outside. I told the queen I was amazed that she was living there, but the queen explained it. She said, 'What's the use of living in a palace? The Americans would come and bomb it.' '' After telling her dream Mrs. A fell silent. I waited for a moment, and then asked if she had associations. She answered ''No!'' as if I had asked a wrong and irritating question. A long silence followed. I found myself remembering the lump in her breast which had worried her on the Friday, and thinking that what had happened about the lump, or indeed anything else on the weekend, was absent, and by contrast, how bright and present Mrs. A's dream palace was. I also thought how meaningful her dream was and how it seemed to illuminate many troubling features of the analysis.

Mrs. A suddenly broke the silence to speak resentfully about her friend from Paris, Regine. She pointed out that ''Regine'' too means ''queen.'' She said how annoyed she is with the way Regine lives in London—Regine's always visiting them, just arriving, and her (Mrs. A's) husband doesn't like Regine's husband, yet if they both come he understand he has to be there. Mrs. A concluded, ''We feel really *put upon* by them. I can't just say, 'She's my friend, I'll see her whenever I like. I can't go there because my husband has nothing in common with Regine's husband.' '' I remarked that she also could not see me whenever she liked and I wondered whether with her worry about the breast lump on Friday this might have been especially hard for her on the weekend.

Mrs. A ignored the content of what I said and talked about Regine and how annoyed she was that Regine keeps visiting them. She fell silent again. After awhile, speaking as if remote from her session (i.e., with no glimmer that her thoughts might hold also some immediate meaning related to her or me), she said that yesterday she had heard her husband make a telephone call about a sum of money. She could hear him behaving very badly on the phone, though he didn't have as much money as people thought.

Mrs. A stopped and stayed silent. I felt all the work of thinking about what was happening was being lodged in me (e.g., that she'd felt put upon by my visiting her like an annoying Regine, first asking for associations and then making uninvited remarks about her breast lump, and having to wait for me on the weekend, and then feeling even more resentful, she had behaved badly and ignored me). Furthermore, it was I who had to worry that what with her resentment and our long silences, time was going by, and the potential of her insightful dream was at risk of being lost.

Suddenly, from the street outside voices and then a child crying could be heard. Mrs. A remained silent after these intrusions,, still passively waiting for me to speak. I remembered her slip of the tongue when she related her dream; how instead of saying, "in the palace of my dream" she had said "in the dream of my dream," and I thought she was dreaming her dream in the session, and wanted me, instead of being the psychoanalyst who annoys her, to act like the queen of her dream who points things out to her personally and intimately.

So I spoke about how it disturbed her when she did not like me and was annoyed when I asked for associations, or mentioned the breast lump, or that she couldn't come to me on the weekend. I said she was trying to lose her resentful feelings by dreaming her dream here with me. Suddenly, Mrs. A was attentive. She nodded her head. I continued saying that if I stop functioning like an analyst and become part of her dream, become a queen who shows her around like an ordinary friendly person (e.g., mention the voices and the crying child we'd just heard), then she feels we are both in her dream and she likes me.

I was sure Mrs. A was listening but she stayed silent, waiting for more from me. It was unclear now who was the queen, she or I. I commented that during the session she herself seemed to have become more and more like the image she has of me, a queen waiting to be served. And indeed Mrs. A went on waiting.

Eventually I spoke about how though she and I might seem to be here together in a beautiful dream palace, each of us is really being diminished. Her picture of me is that I, supposedly her analyst, admit to abandoning my real place (the queen doesn't stay in her palace but lives in a cottage to escape bombs). That is, I conceal my status to avoid rousing her hostility. She loses her active mind and what she really feels, and passively persuades herself she likes me as this queen, though enduring condescension and a false intimacy form me. I concluded by saying something about how with her dream she had been able to recognize a painful truth—that this bright dream palace is a false sort of place. Mrs. A responded with conviction: "Yes. I get your point," she said.

It was almost the end of the session. In its last moments, sarcastic and disparaging, Mrs. A almost shouted, "But are you not going to say anything at all about the *actual* events and people I mentioned?" This sudden eruption of antagonism and attack on the analytic enterprise was a bomb falling on the bit of analytic work we had done.

DISCUSSION

In the course of this session some marked, and I think interrelated, changes took place—in the mode of the dream, in the relations between Mrs. A and myself, and in the balance of Mrs. A's instincts.

The dream itself occurred in two forms in the session. There was the dream Mrs. A dreamt in her sleep, which she remembered and reported, and there was also what she called "the dream of my dream" which was not a dream but an enactment. When the session began, Mrs. A was awake and active. As she reported her dream she was able to comment on and laugh at herself. There was a glimpse of a lively self-reflective ego. She said, "I'm laughing at myself for dreaming about the queen. I don't like her," and a little later, "in the palace of my dream I did like her." At that moment she was herself very near to the insight that her dream palace was her defense against her dislike of her object. All seemed set for productive work between patient and analyst—until I asked for associations. As soon as I tried to work with her, her feelings changed. She was irritated. Her irritation and refusal to associate were important: They were part of not wanting us to stay patient and analyst, of wanting us instead to "dream her dream'' together: I should be like the queen who, although, as in the dream, there were many people present, singled her out especially to show things to, so that together we could look at her dream, which I think would then become in the session like a picture in her dream palace.

When I waited, instead of starting to enact her dream with her, Mrs. A was annoyed. She spoke of feeling ''put upon'' by an annoying little Regine who visited her whenever she chose and whom she can't visit when she wants to. When I took this annoying little Regine to represent myself, and spoke of my unavailability on a weekend when she may have been worried about the breast lump, she felt even more resentful and I think was alarmed by the rising violence of her feelings. She withdrew from contact with me and projected her guilt at ignoring what I said instantly into the husband (it is he she heard behaving badly on the telephone the day before).

An overall change then ensued. She no longer wanted to think about her dream or talk to me. She grew silent and passive. Her silence and passivity, soundlessly aggressive and intrusive, altered our relations. Mrs. A lost her initial lively contact within herself and with me through the projection of her active ego into me. She and I lost our distinctive identities and we began to fuse: We were queen and Regine (a name she pointed out also means *queen*) and she as much as I became a waiting queen. We were now in a setting where deeds were more important than words. I was in the dilemma of enacting her dream if I started interpreting its valuable content to Mrs. A, or neglecting its worth if I said nothing about it and then still enacted her dream, though less obviously, by being a queen with no real interest in her subjects.

I decided to do neither of these and to do something different. I addressed the overall change in our relations and the altered function of her dream, which was now not for analyzing but for enacting. I spoke to her about how she wished to make the session be the dream of her dream so she could lose the disturbing feelings of resentment she had toward me as her analyst and instead feel she liked me as the queen in her dream with whom she had especially intimate relations. In my view this was the key interpretation of the session. It reached her and she became attentive, and even though she was still half in her dream, she was also enough out of it to listen and to understand what I, still the active one, said. For her I too was half and half: half defined by her dream as the queen pointing things out to her, and also half her analyst interpreting to her.

And just as during the session her dream existed in two forms with a corresponding shift in our relationship, so there was a corresponding shift in the balance of Mrs. A's instincts. The striking discrepancy between my patient's capacity to dream a dream rich in meaning, with valuable antique pictures of childhood feelings and primary relations that had lasted to the present day, and her refusal to work with the analyst about it, reflected an unresolved conflict between her impulses to work with and her impulses to escape from psychic reality. When she dreamt her dream in the night and when she first spoke to me and told her dream, life instincts were in the ascendent. But as soon as I wanted to work with her, the balance tipped the other way, dislike of reality started to be in the ascendant and she wanted to cut off from and to depart from mental life.

The session went silent and the dream's potential for creative use between analyst and patient began to die. Mrs. A enacted her dream with me in the way she enacted it in her life, and there was the same loss of potential in analysis as in her life. I mentioned earlier that for some months she waited like a queen to be offered a promotion at work—without actively contending for it—and she was currently very resentful, though she took care not to show it, that another colleague whom she felt was less able and less hardworking than she (and I believe her) had obtained the higher post. In such ways she ended up identified with the unconscious image she had internalized of her analyst, undervalued and overworking. During the session, insofar as she enacted her dream, what took place was akin to what Ignes Sodre (1999), describing the fate of Emma Bovary in Flaubert's novel, called *death by daydreaming.* Sodre wrote in her paper, "in his exploration of the restrictive impoverishing quality of Emma's inner world, Flaubert offers a clear differentiation between the creative use of imagination which enriches life and its perversion into addictive daydreaming used to replace awareness of life, and so destroy real meaning" (p. 49). Emma Bovary was driven to suicide by the terrible enactments of her conscious daydreams. Mrs. A was not so extreme. When she enacted her night dream, she did not kill herself, but denuded herself and her objects, and contrived an inauthentic and somewhat deadened life in an attempt to escape the anxieties and pains of psychic reality.

However, there were some "nasty deals" inherent in this situation which was a declining one of increased persecution and guilt, all of which was split off and kept projected in the husband.

I will now leave my patient when awake and describe her when she sleeps. Mrs. A only rarely dreamt a dream like her queen's palace dream, the kind of dream Freud's classic theory is about. Mostly her dreams were static, images presented without associations, whose meaning and reference were left to me to determine. Until her dream of the queen's palace with its antiques and pictures revealed that these image dreams were pictures that were part of a wider underlying defensive phantasy, I had not even arrived at so clear a description of their nature as I have just given. Mrs. A reported also a third type of experience at night in addition to the few dreams like her palace dream and her many picture dreams. She was disturbed during sleep; she said it was not a nightmare, she was not dreaming, but she muttered and called out and was unable to wake, and her husband had to wake her.

Bertram Lewin (1946) conceived of a *dream screen* as the surface on which a dream appears to be projected. He linked the dream screen to the internalized maternal breast and connected the sleeper's relation to the dream screen with the waking transference relation to the analyst. In her valuable introduction to the *The Dream Discourse Today* (1993), Flanders[1] located the dream screen in the history of analytic inquiry into dreaming. Especially consonant with my Kleinian approach was Gammill (1980) who related Lewin's dream screen to Esther Bick's (1968) work on the skin and, most significantly, to Bion's (1962) work on the container, which converts a screen with its connotation of being projected into a space that can be projected into, a space which I understand to be the inner world of the object.

I would suppose that when Mrs. A kept in contact with her internalized object it gave her when asleep a space to dream in. Then she could dream dreams like her palace dream. When her dreams were merely pictures, she was beginning to intrude into her internal object with a consequent flattening of the dream space and a loss of her ego's dream function. This accords with Segal's (1980) account of the significant effects on dreaming of increasing degrees of projective

[1] See also the section Flanders calls 'The Dream-space'' in which she has assembled papers by Stewart (1973), Khan (1974), Pontalis (1974), Segal (1980), Gammill (1980), and Anzieu (1989).

identification with its concomitant loss of symbolization. On those disturbed nights when she muttered and had to be woken out of a distressed sleep, I think Mrs. A's projective identification into her internalized object had increased to the extent that she felt concretely inside her object and she had lost entirely both a dream space and the capacity to dream.

Analogous variations occur, we may recall, when Mrs. A was awake in the session. At first she had a lively ego, remembered her dream and related it to the analyst, then she cut contact with herself and her analyst, began to project her lively self into the analyst and half lost her dream as a dream by enacting it. Furthermore, Mrs. A grew increasingly passive, trapped in a state of projective identification in a phantasy world that for her was being concretely realized and she then needed the analyst to reach her to help her at least partially out of it. Harold Stewart (1973) noted about a patient not unlike Mrs. A how, "the intrapsychic and interpersonal changes that had occurred in the transference were mirrored by the changes in her experience of her dreams" (p. 124). Awake or asleep, Mrs. A's experience shifted uncertainly: She could have a dream about an unconscious phantasy and she could enact it and not dream it.

Gammill (1980) said about not dreaming, "This phenomenon can be found in a wide clinical range (characterological, rather than neurotic or psychotic), extending from the schizoid personality to the apparently normal individual . . . " (p. 127). Leaving aside the incapacity to dream of the psychotic patient who hallucinates rather than dreams (Bion, 1963), where should we place Mrs. A in the range of not dreaming? Mrs. A is unlike those patients whose world is static, a museum in which movement and psychic work are at a standstill, who never dream. I think Mrs. A is on the long continuum between enactment and dreaming, neither at the one end of enacting unconscious phantasies there is no dreaming of, nor at the other end of dreaming without enactment, but midway. Mrs. A could know her dream was a dream and she also enacted her dream as "a counter-belief"—as Britton (1998, p. 16) calls it—to psychic reality. She kept a precarious division between, on the one hand, emotional truth and object relations with contact, and on the other, deadening, falsifying forms of projective identification.

What kind of dream then is Mrs. A's queen's palace dream she told at the beginning of the session? I quote two authors: Hanna Segal (1991) writes in her book *Dream Phantasy and Art* "a dream is a way of expressing and elaborating an unconscious phantasy. . . . It provides a phantasy expression of unconscious conflict and seeks a phantasy solution—wish-fulfillment. . . . It provides also an intrapsychic communication between the unconscious and the conscious . . ." (p. 64). Jean-Michel Quinodoz (1999) described a special class of such dreams as "dreams that turn over a page." He wrote of their "clarity and coherence" and how "such dreams often reveal more clearly than others the structure of the unconscious intrapsychic conflicts" (p. 232). He called them "integration dreams." Mrs. A's dream is, in Segal's sense, an intrapsychic communication between her unconscious and her conscious. Its clarity and coherence make it potentially an "integration dream" in Quinodoz's sense. Yet as the session unfolded we saw that Mrs. A was not able to integrate her dream, that is, to work with the analyst and work through and keep the insight she was so near to at the beginning of the session, into her need to disavow those aspects of psychic reality that aroused her hostility. She said no to my request for associations, irritated and I think also alarmed that psychic work with her analyst would link the dream to the transference. Indeed the hatred she defended against finally erupted at my last interpretation about the painful truth that her queen's palace was a false and damaging place to both of us. Mrs. A was still unable to integrate either her violent envy, or, what is different, her dislike of me as an analyst who came and went, who waited to be served, plus as yet unspecified unlikeable qualities, or her guilt about the "nasty deals" in the queen's palace way of being, which I think is the most disturbing of all to her. At this stage, Mrs. A could not keep contact with day residues from session to session: Just as she never referred again to her breast lump, so she never referred again to her palace dream. Even as she had a dream about her queen's palace, she could not yet relinquish the actualization of it.

If Mrs. A's palace dream was not an integration dream that "turns over a page," what kind of dream was it? Money-Kyrle (1968) distinguished three stages of representation: concrete representation in Segal's sense of symbolic equation; true symbolism; and between these, a stage of what she termed ideographic representation. I think Mrs.

A's dream is best conceived of as an ideograph, an ideograph that can go either way, become more concrete or more truly symbolic, depending on what analyst and patient do with it. Not only the dreams of patients like Mrs. A, but also their other clinical communications, are often ideographs poised between concreteness and meaning, which pose for the analyst characteristic problems of technique (Joseph, 1989). The analyst has to try to interpret in such a way as to reduce unescapable enactments to a minimum. Moreover, since much of the patient's personality is often lost in the analyst, the analyst has to contain, and retain in herself, much that is obvious at times when it cannot be emotionally experienced by the patient. In Mrs. A's session, I struggled all the way with these problems, not entirely successfully, but not I think failing altogether either.

I end with the old question: Is the dream the royal road? At the beginning of the paper I described my concern that Mrs. A's analysis had become an enclave in which, though she was better, she had not changed at depth. Until her dream came I could specify what was wrong only obscurely. Mrs. A's dream of the queen and herself in the beautiful palace revealed her unconscious phantasy *in her own individual iconography.* What I had recognized only partially and in general terms, that Mrs. A was not fully participant, that strong feelings were absent, that many of her dreams were images she passively listened to me talking about, all this was given coherent meaning by her dream which revealed the whole of a deep defensive phantasy. I can now understand that her image dreams were part of a dream palace, in which when we discussed them we become a couple of queens. Her dream also confirmed my suspicion (though this is one of its several aspects that we did not get to in the session) that though she had overtly relinquished her sense of being mother's, and the analyst's favorite, that at depth she still existed in what was really a homosexual dyad that disavowed a dislikable and dysfunctional oedipal family of parents and contending siblings whose true state was still blurred by her projections.

To have a patient's dream in a session is like having a Rosetta stone in the session. When a dream is present along with the other languages of the analysis—the patient's actions, verbal and nonverbal communications, the analyst's interpretations, countertransferences, and actions—it is the dream that enables the deciphering of the patient's unconscious depths. I think the dream is the royal road though a slow one with those patients who are like Mrs. A.

REFERENCES

Anzieu, D. (1989), *The Skin Ego.* New Haven, CT: Yale University Press.

Bick, E. (1968), The experience of the skin in early object-relations. *Internat. J. Psycho-Anal.,* 49:484–486.

Bion, W. (1962), *Learning from Experience.* London: Heinemann.

——— (1963), *Elements of Psychoanalysis.* London: Heinemann.

Britton, R. (1998), *Belief and Imagination.* London: Routledge.

Flanders, S. (1993), *The Dream Discourse Today.* London: Routledge.

Freud, S. (1900), The Interpretation of Dreams. *Standard Edition,* 4&5. London: Hogarth Press, 1953.

Gammill, J. (1980), Some reflections on analytic listening and the dream screen. In: *The Dream Discourse Today,* ed. S. Flanders. London: Routledge, 1993, pp. 127–136.

Joseph, B. (1989), *Psychic Equilibrium and Psychic Change.* London: Routledge.

Khan, M. (1974), *The Privacy of the Self.* London: Hogarth Press.

Lewin, B. D. (1946), Sleep, the mouth, and the dream screen. *Psychoanal. Quart.,* 15:419–434.

——— (1955), Dream psychology and the analytic situation. *Psychoanal. Quart.,* 25:169–199.

Money-Kyrle, R. (1968), Cognitive development. In: *Collected Papers.* Strathclyde, Scotland: Clunie Press, pp. 416–433.

O'Shaughnessy, E. (1992), Enclaves and excursions. *Internat. J. Psycho-Anal.,* 72:603–611.

Pontalis, J.-B. (1974), Dream as object. *Internat. Rev. Psychoanal.,* 1:125–134.

Quinodoz, J.-M. (1999), Dreams that turn over a page. *Internat. J. Psycho-Anal.,* 80:225–238.

Segal, H. (1980), The function of dreams. In: *The Dream Discourse Today,* ed. S. Flanders. London: Routledge, 1993, pp. 100–107.

——— (1991), *Dream, Phantasy and Art.* London: Routledge.

Sodre, I. (1999), Death by daydreaming: Madame Bovary. In: *Psychoanalysis and Culture,* ed. D. Bell. London: Duckworth, pp. 213–234.

Stewart, H. (1973), The experiencing of the dream and the transference. In: *The Dream Discourse Today,* ed. S. Flanders. London: Routledge, 1993, pp. 122–126.

Discussion

Chair, Ellen Rees
Discussants, James L. Fosshage, Edward Nersessian, Edna O'Shaughnessy, and Audience Members

Ellen Rees stressed the importance of basing the discussion around a number of what we consider central questions and to keep it rooted in the clinical data of the dreams, to try to root it in things that can be used in analysts' consulting offices. First, how do we understand and use the manifest content of the dream? What is the role of defensive processes in the formation of dreams? What is the relationship of the dream to unconscious fantasy and to memory? How do we understand and use the references to the analyst in the dreams? Are dreams always about transference? How do we come to understand the meaning of a dream within a session? What is the role of the past in the formation of the dream—the past of the analysis and the genetic past? Can the dream promote psychological organization? How do we understand the relationship between the dream and the state of mind in the analytic situation?

Ellen Rees: First I will start with a question. How would each of the panelists deal with the productions of the other panelists' patients? Each of the panelists will then comment on how the other panelists understood and used the dreams they presented.

Edna O'Shaughnessy: I'd like to say a word or two about Edward Nersessian's patient's dream of the white marble statue. I think that was fascinating because it proceeded as if it were an erotic dream and I thought it was very significant that her analyst didn't take it as being an erotic dream and instead what he responded to was the emotional urgency of the patient in her denial of the mother's illness—possibly dying from cancer. I think we have come on something very important, namely, that you have to take on the dream in the emotional context between analyst and patient. I think, too—I don't know if Edward Nersessian would agree with this—that there is a transference reference. Had he not taken notice of where his patient was emotionally in regard to her mother, he would have been for his patient just such a smooth, stony, sculpture of an analyst—that she has to come and say, "Yes, yes, of course, I know you are going away on holiday and I'll do all that and I'll say all that." He responded to the point of emotional urgency, that he had meant for her such a stony statue. I'd begin with just that.

Edward Nersessian: In terms of my saying something about the other presenters' dreams, I don't think I could really add significantly to the work that the analyst has been doing with the patient for a period of time. The dream is a little moment in that work, and anything I would say would not take sufficiently into account the complexity of the relationship and the ongoing analysis. Edna O'Shaughnessy's patient's dream is fascinating and her way of dealing with it very interesting, because there were two currents. One had to do with the fact that the patient was dealing potentially or possibly with anxiety-provoking news—the examination of her breast. Edna O'Shaughnessy approaches it and tries to bring it into the analysis because, even though she doesn't explicitly say so, she thinks it's somewhere in the dream and in the dream to dream. But there is a whole other aspect which she brings in very skillfully, which has to do with the patient's unconscious fantasy and her way of doing work within the analysis and outside the analysis, and the repetition of that within the transference. It seems to me that the dream is similar to what Freud described as "a dream within a dream." This patient starts by saying she has two dreams, and then she only tells one. She goes back to the palace dream which takes her back to two dreams and makes it resemble the so-called dreams within a dream, which usually have to do with something so disturbing in a dream that it has to be doubly disguised or doubly defended or double avoided and has to do with a piece of reality. One could imagine that the piece of reality is the potential lump in the breast and that the patient is trying to move away from that disturbing fact in going to the palace. I think there is some further evidence for that because the patient also continues within the hour, which suggests that to get away from the dream completely would be too disturbing at that moment.

James Fosshage: It is always difficult, as we all know, to comment on each other's dreams and work but we want to use this really for illustrative purposes in terms of how we might have approached things differently. I just have a couple of comments about Ed Nersessian's examples. I thought it was very interesting and I think that Edna's point was very well taken that in fact he had *not* been the marble statue in the way that he had dealt with it. You can never do everything, but I would have wanted to come back at some point to have brought it more directly in the transference. I wouldn't just assume that, but I could consider it fairly safe to say, "I am wondering if you may experience me in this way?" In fact she did say it. I would want to get that discussed. The other issue that I experienced in terms of the green room dream, the green everywhere, is that Ed got to some memories around it. I would still want to know, why was the dreamer dreaming that right now? Why was it coming up? I wouldn't assume that it was just that those memories were emerging out of the inquiry. I would want to know the meaning of those memories right now—to make it more present day and to bring it in.

Now, I want to go into Edna O'Shaughnessy's dream in more detail because I would approach it, I think, quite differently. I want to just set this before you for consideration as another alternative. I want to go through the dream in detail. Let me preface this with a dream in which the dreamer came to the crypt of her dying father-in-law.

The patient immediately associated to me, that I was the dying old man. That theme of my being the dying old man was activated in the transference in the analytic relationship right through contributions by both patient and analyst. She thought I drove a Cadillac and saw me in an old cardigan sweater, both of which made me look like an old man. And she sensed my anxiety in an interaction. She got very scared; that was what seemed to activate the dying old man transference configuration.

In terms of Edna's patient's queen dream, she had dreamt she was in a beautiful palace. " 'The queen, Queen Elizabeth, was there.' Mrs. A laughed and commented, 'I'm laughing at myself in dreaming about the queen. I don't like her.' " Now, I would like to have gotten into the experience. There is some pattern here that is applicable to the transference. Here I would ask a question like: "I am wondering if you experience me somehow like the queen?" Now, interestingly, I think that as I listen to the whole session that it became clear to me in terms of understanding. She said, "I'm laughing at myself for dreaming about the queen. I don't like her." But in the dream, "There the queen was, just like an ordinary person. The palace was beautiful with many pictures and antiques, and there were lots of people there. The queen came over to me and spoke to me. She said she would show me around the palace herself. She was friendly and intimate."

I see that as a major change in terms of her relationship to the queen in the dreaming. She anticipated that the queen would be very elevated and would be very removed, and instead in the dream she was surprised by the fact that the queen was an ordinary person and was friendly and intimate. Now, I see that as a developmental change. For her, things were becoming friendlier with queenlike people and the analyst presumably is one of the queenlike people. I had this feeling that Edna O'Shaughnessy had felt very differently about that. She saw that as a defense against seeing her as the analyst, to bring her down to the level of being friendly and intimate, rather than the analyst who was not going to be that. In a peculiar way I sensed that she was acting, in terms of interpretation, somewhat like that queen. The analyst was not an ordinary person. I would have noted that the patient was moving ahead and saying, "Look, you are ordinary and also queenly. And I like that queen." And so there is a real change there.

"The queen took me and showed me where she lived in a little cottage outside. I told the queen I was amazed that she was living there, but the queen explained it. She said, 'What's the use of living in a palace? The Americans would come and bomb it.' "

What was very striking to me is that the queen was friendly, intimate, down-to-earth, ordinary—an ordinary person, and then all of a sudden it comes up that the queen anticipates that the Americans, the allies, are going to bomb the palace. So it conveys to me that the queen is very distrustful and there is tremendous distrust there, even of the Americans who presumably are the allies. I would want to get into that experience of what it was like for her to hear the queen say that the Americans might bomb and what that was about. I think I would have gone at it in a very different way.

Edna O'Shaughnessy: This is a central point and a central point of real difference. James Fosshage is quite right when he says that I took it in the way I did and you explain how you would take it, which is not the way I would take it. It is very important because the analytic setting is not an ordinary setting. It's a very special setting for both patient and analyst. Certain privileges and restrictions and a way of conducting oneself are imposed on the analyst that are quite different from how one conducts oneself with one's colleagues, family, and friends. We all know the horrible therapist who is therapeuticizing in his or her private life. It is a quite different role, the way I conceive it. It is a role in which the patient gives the analyst a very great privilege, the privilege of access to his or her own internal world. I start from this idea. For my patient, it isn't an ordinary friendly situation where I could say, "Hey, did you hear the child crying out in the street," as I would in an ordinary situation, it's an analytic situation. For my patient this has all the distressing meanings that are there in her life.

Always there have been situations in her life which are not symmetrical. Starting with the child, with the mother, with the parents, and now with the analyst. I am privileged to get this brought to me in the way that it is. Here is a woman struggling to like me and to like me on a false basis. That I would say, "No, no, really it is just ordinary" is all false and condescending. As I understood it, it is my patient's real insight to have dreamed a dream of what is one of her big defensive mechanisms in her life to deal with that I think she finds very difficult; that is, her own distress and nastiness, which she tends to project into the husband. So it is a very important and quite a different view of what is going on, and it is important to have it pinpointed in this way.

Edward Nersessian: To get back to Jim Fosshage's question about the green, the green is connected to the fact that I think the present is to some degree colored by the past. And in this situation, the patient was attracted to this woman and in trying to understand what particularly was attractive about this woman it seemed that there were similarities he was making between the woman and his sister. So that then the childhood memory was relevant in terms of that understanding. There are important differences between Edna O'Shaughnessy's way of looking at it and my way of looking at it, but there are similarities, whereas there are major differences in Jim Fosshage's way of looking at things and mine. It seems to me, for example, that in the first dream and in some of his descriptions, he doesn't feel that there is continuity between the dream life and the waking life; they are two separate states that don't even influence one another. When the patient is awake he thinks of Jim as a charlatan and when he is asleep he thinks of Jim as a wonderful guy. If that is in fact the way he sees it, we have a major difference in outlook. What is more, some of his questions about the issue of transference make me want to ask him about his definition of transference. To what degree does he feel unconscious elements come into the transference? To what degree is the transference only determined by the present relationship?

Edna O'Shaughnessy: Jim, I was very taken with what you say about the queen's distrust in this dream. I think that is a very good point because Mrs. A operates in a world in which she doesn't believe her objects can stand any flack, that they too will say, "Oh, I am not really a queen, I am just living in a humble little cottage. Nothing to envy." It works both ways with Mrs. A: She is very disturbed when she feels angry and I think she also believes, as Jim said, that the queen too would say, "Look, there is nothing here to be jealous of, envious of, nothing like that." And I think it is a very important point you've made about Mrs. A's objects which leads to this passivity. In her work she doesn't fight for promotion, but she waits for it to come, and when it doesn't come, she just goes on as before.

James Fosshage: You give additional meaning there: Her humility is what she uses to keep down her envy and also her expansiveness.

Edna O'Shaughnessy: Absolutely.

James Fosshage: So that really particularizes the meaning of it. I just wanted to say in agreement with Edna's earlier point that the analytic relationship is a unique, one of a kind relationship. There is nothing like it. I don't know if we would differ or not, but my experience is that when patients begin to move away from the elevation of me and the situation between us becomes more on a level playing field, I see it as a developmental movement, and I think that's what I was sensing in that dream.

Now, to Ed's comment, it is not true that I see that there is a discontinuity or that there is a lack of continuity between the dream and waking states. There may be a discontinuity or there may be a great deal of continuity between waking and dreaming state. It varies. I think that the traditional position has been that there is always continuity, so when the patient comes in from a waking perspective and is making associations from a waking perspective, those necessarily have to do with the dream. Sometimes it is absolutely true, they do. But I am opening up the possibility that sometimes there is a different mental state at that particular moment which may be quite different from what the dream was about and what the dreamer was dreaming about. We need to be open in order not to belie either state and not take one state—the waking state or the dreaming state—as a valid state. If anything, there has been a built-in bias that the waking state is the real state and dreaming is fictional. It's a Western bias, but both states are very real. What I mean by that is that they are both real experiences. Both need to be taken seriously; at times there is continuity and times there is discontinuity.

In terms of definition of transference, I am going to define transference briefly, although there are different definitions. One way to define transference is to define it as Merton Gill does, namely, that is the patient's experience of the analyst and the analytic relationship, a very broad definition. I sometimes lapse into that, but when I do I try to talk about the point that what the patient is concerned about is the analytic relationship. I tend to define transference more specifically as referring to primary organizing patterns with which the patient organizes and constructs the analytic relationship. Those organizing patterns are built up out of childhood, of course. Our primary organizing patterns are based upon lived experience. They are typically unconscious. We are unaware of their existence. Our principal ways of organizing seem like simple reality to us. As we know, those patterns have to be illuminated, particularly the problematic ones, in order for them to be suspended so that new experience can be assimilated and new organizing patterns be formed, like new percepts of self and self with other have to be formed. Those organizing patterns are utilized in dreams as in our waking mentation, in dreaming and waking mentation. When they are utilized, that is what is in the forefront at a particular moment. These organizing patterns could be activated in waking life or they could be activated within the dream. I will give you one brief example that I often use. A patient has a breakthrough session. For the first time he feels trusting of the analyst. He leaves the session. Two days later, he comes back and reports the following dream: "I came to your office, Jim, and it was eleven o'clock and it was the time for our next session and I found your door open and you had ten people in that office. And I said, Jim, you know, it is time for my session. And you essentially said, 'I'm busy now, come back another time.' And I felt crushed and dismissed." What activated that dream? There are all sorts of possibilities. I ask, "Did you have some feelings at the end of last session that didn't get talked about?" He replies, "No." "Did you have some thoughts between that session and this session?" The patient answers, "No, I felt very trusting of you, I felt for the first time I could trust. I felt very good about you for the first time in my life until I had this dream this morning." What happened? One view is that the dream was serving the function of restoring previous psychological organization, the older state of being, probably in reaction to anxiety. The same thing could have happened in fantasy. You know, the patient started to say, "Uh oh, watch out, I am trusting him, but I may be in for trouble here." So the dream was different from the waking state, but the function of it was not developmental, it was restoring the prior older psychological configuration.

Edna O'Shaughnessy: I want to come back to one of the dreams in Jim Fosshage's paper, the dream of the female patient who had been a model child and who brings this long beautiful dream in which there is a thaw of the previously very frozen village and landscape. I would like to raise a few questions because there is this most striking manifest content which I absolutely understand and I thought it spoke to all of us. Jim stressed the story of her ongoing psychological transformation. Another possibility is that just as she's always been a model child, she has become a model patient. She knows the analyst has an agenda, like her parents always have had an agenda, and the dream might be seen as saying, "Look I'm your model patient. You've done beautifully." Or is it, as the analyst took it, that it really was a tribute, a gift so to say, that said, "Look, it was like this and I have thawed, I am no longer split up between there and down below, I've come together." We have to consider both of these possibilities. Jim, how would you work in the session to differentiate these two?

James Fosshage: I really appreciate the question, Edna, and I think you are quite right that the patient would be in danger of becoming a model patient because she had been such a model child. The question is, why didn't I see it that way? That's a huge question, but the change that was going on was very palpable in terms of this person, and her vitality had increased immeasurably. The affects are what are really so crucially important in terms of assessing. In terms of: Do you believe this dream is a straightforward presentation of the transformation, or is it some defensive attempt or an older characterological attempt, which is an old way of adapting, that is coming forth in the dream? It's interesting because I think we always have to ask that question: Is a patient accommodating to us or can we believe in the authenticity of their affective experience? We are constantly having to do that. I believed in the authenticity of her affective experience at this moment.

I went through this line of thinking before since Hanna Segal and Priscilla Ross were discussants of the case previously mentioned. I think that there is a tendency that some of us have not to believe the patient when what the patient says doesn't correspond with our particular model. We believe the patient most easily when whatever is going on corresponds to our particular model. We are all subject to that possibility, because we are all using models to understand our patients.

It is something that we have to guard against and one of the statements I have made is that we all, as analysts, have to believe our patients sometimes. It is absolutely essential that we have to believe evidence of their progress, we have to believe the authenticity of their affective experience, sometimes. Not everything is defensive. Every analyst has to do that. And this particular time I believed this patient.

Edna O'Shaughnessy: I'm not going to be put in the position of having a theoretical model that I don't believe my patient. I think that what emerges from our interchange is that you have to inquire with the patient at the given time, "What does this mean, really? How is it brought? How is it functioning in between patient and analyst?" And I certainly don't think that I have any more of a preconception that I don't believe my patient than anybody else does.

Edward Nersessian: Jim, you also place a certain evaluative quality on the dream, as if the dream is able to evaluate and review some kind of progress that the patient is making or has made.

James Fosshage: I'm saying that it's up to the dreamer to evaluate that for himself or herself.

Edward Nersessian: You see the changes in the dream as indicating some changes in the patient, so there is an evaluative quality which I don't see, normally. If it is there then it is in every other aspect of the patient's life. In my experience, when people have a dream and then they have terrible anxiety or terror, they usually wake up from it. This patient did not wake up from it but continued to sleep. So that it seems to me that the latter part of the dream, which was highly intellectualized and logical and calming, was a way that the patient dealt with the anxiety. But what was the anxiety about? What is the traumatic nature, what is the trauma that could cause such an intense anxiety in the dream?

In other words you are saying it seems like you noticed a change in the object relations, in the relationship with the analyst, as in the first dream also, happening in sleep. The patient thinks of you when awake as a charlatan, but when asleep as not a charlatan, and you see that as a progression. The patient is progressing in the quality of his relationship with you, so in that, you give a function and a role to dreams that are quite different from the way I look at dreams. I am not saying you are right or wrong, I am just trying to underscore the difference. There is an evaluative quality.

The general idea, that we are still to some degree holding onto, is that dreams are there to protect sleep. That is one function of dreams in the classic model. The function of dreams to my mind is that they protect sleep. I believe dreams do other things, as I said in the paper, probably dealing with affect and the ways of dealing with the more difficult negative affects. But I don't see the dream as having a degree of intellectual sophistication to present an evaluation or to present an assessment or the kind of self-reflection that would go along with knowing that something is changing in oneself.

James Fosshage: This is where, of course, we part company. Initially, you talked about the function of dreaming being to protect sleep, but you also mentioned affect regulation and I would agree on the affect regulation part of it. When you say that dreams are not that "intellectual," I would object to the term *intellectual* and say *cognitively sophisticated.* I think that what we are talking about is cognitive sophistication and that's where there is a major difference because the classical model has never included the complexity of cognition that I think dreams are about. There is a converging of new models that move in the direction of seeing dreams as a very complex cognitive activity. You know, when there is some movement within the classical theory from the topographical to the structural model of the mind (of course the ego participated in the formation of the dream), it opened the door to the possibility that sophisticated cognitive activity could be included and participate in dream formation. A major thrust in the classical model is that dreaming doesn't involve sophisticated cognitive activity and my model does.

Cognition can be very elementary, and it can be very sophisticated. Now when you talk about evaluation, I think that the dreamer can see things in a new way that may occur in the dream. They may be able to image something, to envision something new, to see it in a different way that they have not been able to see within their waking mentation before. It can happen both ways. Breakthroughs can come in waking mentation and the dreaming can hold on more, as I just gave an example, to the older organizations. Or vice versa, the dreamer has a breakthrough, says something for the first time, sees that it is possible to do something for the first time. I don't see that as evaluative, but that there is an overall developmental thrust. Now, our motivational models may differ. I think that there is an overall developmental thrust, in keeping with Kohut's theory, to develop, to grow. It is the self-realization or self-actualization motivational model, and certainly that is very different from the classical model.

Now, when you said that the last dream was potentially highly intellectualized, I think this is where you say that we have to listen to the affect. We have to go back to the affective experience of the dreamer. It is the only way. The classical model positions you not to accept this sophisticated cognitive activity as part of dreaming. It therefore positions you to say it is defensive or intellectualized. My model says, this sophisticated intellectual activity is a part of dreaming; it can occur in dreaming; therefore this activity may be intellectualized or it may be authentic and affectively grounded. I would assess it by going to the affects of the dreamer.

Ellen Rees: I want to raise the question, to what degree is the model of each panelist influencing the way he or she works with dreams? I think it is beginning to emerge why it is that the model which each panelist brings to the interpretation matters whether we are talking about how to understand the relationship between states of mind in sleep and in dreaming, the nature of the imagery in either state, or the role of defense. This question regarding models is starting to emerge. Other questions are coming to the fore around the role of countertransference, and how the panelists would understand the role of countertransference in working with a dream.

Edna O'Shaughnessy: Not one of you mentioned that word *unconscious.* I mean surely, regarding Freud's great discovery, even a hundred years on, is it not the case that everybody in this room still thinks that in one way the dream expresses our repressed or our unconscious state of mind? We need this as an assumption so that we can understand how psychic work can take place. It develops a language and does some putting together. Do we not all still hold to these fundamental tenets?

Edward Nersessian: Well, I do. I'm not sure to what degree Jim Fosshage does. Are we influenced by the theories that we use to work? I don't think that there is any question about that. When I read the paper I tried to qualify myself and say that I am a classical analyst influenced by this or that, because there is no question that when I work, anybody looking at my work would know where I come from. So yes, my model does influence me totally. I don't see it working any other way. There is still something I am not able to properly put into words in asking Jim Fosshage: There is almost a quality of Janet's ideas about different levels of mental state that comes across in his presentation of the dreams. I wonder if that is something you would like to comment about.

James Fosshage: First of all, there is no question about models. We all have our models. Whether or not they are articulated, we have models. We have ways of organizing the data. Of course they are going to influence how we see the dreams. There is a perfect example we have here on this panel. How do we try to assess the models? Ultimately we try to assess them in terms of what models or what pieces of models are helpful to us in terms of facilitating our understanding of the patient and the facilitation of the analytic process of the patient's growth and development. Now, in terms of the unconscious, Edna, I am sorry I didn't hear all of the attributes you gave the unconscious. Would you repeat that for me?

Edna O'Shaughnessy: Let's put aside the very disturbed patient—because when the mental structure has become fragmented and is not functioning in an ordinary way, it may be a bit different—but from the borderline to the ordinary, it seems to me that dreams ordinarily do express what is unconscious. Freud used to think of the totality of the dream as the repressed unconscious. I certainly still think of what is unconscious. However clear the manifest content might be, I still have the feeling that there is something that has to be found out, and that is unconscious for the patient. In a dream, psychic work, perhaps of various kinds, is done; a language and symbolism is found and some putting together is done. Now, isn't this just what we all think, or is it not?

James Fosshage: Certainly I would agree with you that there is a lot that is going on at an unconscious level every moment of the day, waking and sleeping, by definition. Dreaming to me provides the most direct—and Freud was right in a certain way—direct road—and I would change it a little bit, not the unconscious because the concept of the unconscious was seen as a sort of repository of repressed ideation. I think that the unconscious is much larger than that, and I don't think it is a repository, but I would say that the dream is sort of the royal expression of unconscious mentation, the most direct expression of unconscious mentation we have. So I would see conscious and unconscious as levels of awareness, and I believe that is always going on and always varies. But I think the unconscious is not just a repository of repressed ideation, wishes, and so on, but that active mentational processing is going on at an unconscious level all the time.

So far as the role of the countertransference is concerned, I think a great deal depends upon your definition of countertransference. We have enlarged the usefulness of countertransference, it no longer represents just the pathological aspects of the analyst, but rather the countertransference can inform us about our patients. I think *countertransference* is a problematic term. I prefer just to talk about the analyst's experience. I define countertransference from a *totalist perspective*—as the analyst's experience of the patient. Every analyst uses countertransference, if you define it in that way, as the totalist perspective. How we use it, how our models shape it, will vary from analyst to analyst. Our experience of a patient is always filtered through our subjectivity. But we will all filter it through our subjective experience of the patient, because there is nothing else that we have to go on. That is my understanding. We utilize our experience to understand, and that's what we have been talking about.

Mark Solms: The point is being made that we all start from our own models and that influences how we interpret the dream and we see here the consequences in action. We start from different levels, that makes us see the dream differently, and we come to completely different conclusions. This affects our actual everyday work with ordinary patients. This was the problem that I have raised before. I contended that this is an untenable situation for a discipline. Everybody is allowed to have his or her own model, the models contradict each other in important respects, and that has actual practical implications for our clinical work. We can't carry on with everybody being allowed to have his or her own model. There has to be some way to predict. There is something we can do about it. Because of recent developments in the neurosciences, it is possible for us to put some of these general theoretical model type of questions to the neurosciences, which have other methods available to address these questions in ways that analysts on their own patently can't address using our ''I'm going to see what is important in this session'' kind of approach. We have a good case in point: Jim Fosshage says that his model, unlike the classical model, assumes that all sorts of sophisticated cognitions are possible during dreams. The classical model holds that primitive things are going on. Now, does neuroscience have something to say about that? Indeed it does. In neuroscience, we have people doing brain image studies, clinical neuropsychological studies, lesion studies, and so on. We have all come to the same conclusion that a part of the brain known as the dorsolateral prefrontal convexity, the highest evolutionary development in primates and in all mammals, the thing that makes us most complexly self-reflective, the thing that is most specifically human about us, all this evaluative, categorical, self-reflective type of thinking, plays absolutely no part in dreaming. It can't. That part of the brain is inactive. When you damage that part of the brain it has enormous implications for your ordinary cognitive activities. You are really disabled, but your dreams remain identical. They are unchanged. Imaging studies show that part of the brain is simply switched off during dreaming. The primitive parts of the brain, the limbic system, the emotional and drive and reward seeking centers, are highly active. That says something—it imposes constraints on our theorizing, on what sort of models seem to be more likely to be correct.

Steven Ellman: I want to go back to the inner-REM period. If you look at that part of the REM period that is really defined as a REM period, where there are bursts of eye movements, at that point there is no self-reflective aspect to the mentation. The mentation at this time is confused, sensory, vivid. It is the most emotive and affect-laden at that point, so that complex mentation—I would absolutely agree with Mark Solms that we have very good data—that self-reflective function is virtually gone during active components of REM sleep.

James Fosshage: You talked about the reflective function; what about complex cognitive functioning?

Steven Ellman: I guess it depends on what you mean by complex functioning. What I would say is that it is the least complex functioning, the most toward the emotional, affective life, and it is also the most confused. On our self–object differentiation scale, you have the greatest possibility of self and object images being confused in terms of that, and so how do you want to rate that in terms of complexity? I would tend to say that it is less complex. But there I think before one gets into that you really need to have some independent idea of complexity and what one means by that.

James Fosshage: What about the possibility from a neuroscientific perspective that sophisticated mentational processing is going on so that to the extent that a new perceptual angle could be achieved within a dream or the envisioning of a new resolution to a conflictual state?

Steven Ellman: I certainly think that is possible. It does occur under some conditions. There is the possibility that if you travel you actually have more REM sleep, and so when you are in new situations, REM starts to increase. But if you are in a situation and you know there is no way of solving it, REM sleep starts to diminish.

Morton Reiser: We have come across a very interesting disagreement here, not an impasse, that illustrates something about what goes on between analyst and patient in the therapeutic process. What seems clear to me is that different analysts use different models of that dream process. I believe it is reasonably clear from what Mark Solms said that these different models correspond differently to the studies of what is happening in the brain during dreaming. Now what is striking here is what is happening between patient and analyst. Mainly it seems to me, as Otto Isakower used to say, that you teach patients how to free associate and you teach them how to dream and work with dreams, essentially through *instrumental conditioning*, although I don't think he used that term. But, in a sense, I was struck by Jim Fosshage's patient's dream and that she had learned how to dream dreams that turn you on. In a sense you expand on the dream appropriately and that must have some effect on her. There is some change in her that is related. We are not all doing the same thing and describing it in different ways. These different models do have an impact on the transaction between the analyst and the patient, and have an effect on the patient that we can measure as therapeutic or antitherapeutic.

Arnold Rothstein: The state of knowledge in the field is such that we have competing models that people choose because of their own subjective biases, and we don't have a methodology for resolving those differences yet. With all deference to Mark Solms, I don't think that the neurosciences yet can give us sufficient data to adequately demonstrate the efficacy of one model versus another. I think your rendering of neuroscience reflects your subjective bias and affiliation toward your models. That's my view of it. In terms of the dreams specifically, the dream that is dreamt in REM sleep is not the dream that is reported in analysis. There is a very interesting paper by Noy (1969), who introduced the concept of tertiary revision which hasn't really been picked up that much. Freud introduced the idea of secondary revision where he indicated that a patient makes sense of the dream, so that it is logical. That's when he or she wakes up and remembers. But by the time the patient gets to the analytic session and all the things that influence them to report the dream, not the least of which is the transference, he or she has revised the dream. These revision processes leave room for the kinds of things which Jim Fosshage is interested in. Now I have radical differences with Jim, but I can't prove to him that my biases are better than his biases. So, that's the state of ignorance that the field is in. That's why we have these meetings. I think it is very important to just accept that level of subjectivity and try to hope that the neurosciences give us enough data ultimately to be able to be more certain. In order to be a panelist you have to have a kind of certainty.

James Fosshage: In regard to what Mark Solms was talking about with regard to multiple models, and that this is a sorry state of affairs from his vantage point: You know it took a long, long time for psychoanalysts to accept and appreciate that there indeed were multiple models and that there were different models. Today, part of the ferment in the field is created by the fact that there is a pluralism of models and there is a more open consideration of different models. So I think that is to our benefit and will result in a far greater creativity and development of useful models as we go. I don't think that we can or should foreclose prematurely. On the one hand, I am with you that we need to move toward developing those models which are going to be more in keeping with what we know about the brain. That will be most facilitative, as I have said before, in terms of our understanding of the patient and also in fostering the patient's development within treatment. We will always have multiple models because models are expressions of our individual subjectivities and we are never going to get molded into one subjectivity where we are all going to agree. So I think that we are slated for multiple models.

I really appreciate what Arnold Rothstein said, because I think that does seem to be the state of affairs. I wanted to clarify because what Mark Solms and Steve Ellman were talking about is that there seems to be a neurocapacity for self-reflection; that's a very complicated concept, self-reflection within dreams, but as Steve indicated that does not eliminate the possibility for more complex processing, cognitive processing, going on. As a matter a fact I have a quote here from Mark Solms, who says, "I think that both my and Braun's findings suggest that dreaming is a higher mental function generated by forebrain mechanisms." And there is another quote by Braun that says, "I think there are points of departure for Freudian theory, rather than metaphor or symbol, dreams may constitute more direct, albeit distorted, access to unconscious processes, and really dreams may be less disguised and more apparent than commonly believed." Again, these are neuroscientists who are trying to find their way around as well.

Edna O'Shaughnessy: Granted all the potential power of neuroscience and the fascination of it, which in a bit of an amateur way I feel myself, I wonder if we are not forgetting something. One of the great things that Freud did was to discover a method for exploring interiority, what was going on internally, and psychoanalysis has this ability, and

I think we should remember this. At present we have many models of the mind, not of the brain, but of the mind. One of the important things at the moment is to try to see how different approaches really use their thinking, and once we can do that we might be able to understand how concepts are used and whether they may or may not be congruent. Are we actually in different words describing something similar? Let us hope in the future that our multimodel plural state will gradually converge into a more unified science, I would say. From the point of view of the mind, using what I think is one of Freud's greatest discoveries, the discovery of the particularly strange thinking in the analytic session, which enables what is inside to be externalized out there for analyst and patient to see.

Edward Nersessian: That's very true. In fact, some neuroscientists are interested in the particular way that we observe the mind as a tool for their own studies.

Audience Member: I have, for years, been having an ongoing argument with a colleague who is a professor of research psychology. He's not interested really in clinical matters but he has proposed the question: Is the unconscious smart or stupid? He has a lot of research data to indicate that the unconscious is stupid, but my own view from working with a lot of dreams is that there is a lot of smartness in the unconscious too. I think what Mark Solms raised as one avenue of research is important, that you look at what is happening in the brain, and which parts of the brain are active during the dream, or not. I think that methodology though has to also be balanced by looking at the dreams themselves. I think we have seen in history a number of important intellectual discoveries that have been attributed to work done in dreams. Probably many of you know that Elias Howard, who invented the sewing machine, said that he got the idea for where to put the eye in the needle of the sewing machine from a dream in which he saw a primitive ritual going on, where these people had spears that had a hole at the end of the spear instead of at the top. And then he woke up and put that into operation and it worked for the sewing machine. Now, there is an example of an inspiration that came from the image of the dream but it was worked out in waking life. I think that raises a very important question about which part of the complex intellectual activity is involved? And there may be a number of parts; an inspiration that may come from the dream then has to be worked out in waking life.

In terms of testing things scientifically, many of us balked at that question because we are clinicians, we don't have research projects, and don't have graduate students, and don't have a whole system for doing this kind of research, and so we are not going to do this kind of research.

A formulation of a number of testable clinical hypotheses would be very useful. There are people here who do clinical empirical research and we could talk about what kind of studies could be done to actually test these out. I know I have clinical observations that I have made—I think very often if the dream refers to the countertransference and the analyst doesn't pay attention to the countertransference implications, each successive dream will become more and more direct until finally the analyst appears in the dream and it's spelled out and practically hits you on the head, but still sometimes the analyst doesn't notice it. I think that's something that I observed anecdotally, but it could be tested and be tested I think with relative ease.

James Fosshage: I want to address Mort Reiser's comment on my patient's frozen village dream which has been nagging at me. He suggested that the dreamer dreamt it because it turned me on—essentially. That I was able to influence her dreaming process to that degree. I wouldn't agree with that. I would say that I picked the dream because it turned me on. I think that's true. I think there is also certainly a subtle influencing process that goes on. But to say that I influenced her dreaming process to the degree that she gave me exactly what I wanted, I think that sort of influence I don't have.

REFERENCE

Noy, P. (1969), A revision of the psychoanalytic theory of the primary processes. *Internat. J. Psycho-Anal.,* 50:155–178.

Clinical Panel 2

Chair, Ernest Kafka

6

Overcome by Strange Emotions: Dreams and Affects

Elsa First

In Freud's *non vixit* dream of October 1898, the dream narrator remarked that he was "overcome by strange emotions." This is the dream in which old friends from Brucke's lab, Fleishl and Paneth, both dead at a young age, reappear. In real life there had just been a memorial for Fleishl, whom Freud admired, envied, and loved, and in whose death Freud felt implicated because he had introduced him to cocaine for pain control to wean him from morphine. Paneth fades, under a "piercing look," from the dreamer who is "highly delighted," and who says he "now realized that Ernst Fleischl, too, had been no more than an apparition, a '*revenant*'; (1) and it seemed to me quite possible that people of that kind only existed as long as one liked and could be got rid of if some one else wished it" ([1900, p. 421] cited by Anzieu [1986 p. 379]). I am evoking the *non vixit* dream because I want to discuss affect in dreams. Also we are meant to show how we each work with dreams and how we came to that understanding.

I have learned much from studying Anzieu's approach to dreams in his work on Freud's dreams.

Anzieu (1986) considered the *non vixit* dream to have been a landmark in Freud's self-analysis, which Anzieu viewed as a working through of depressive position anxieties as part of a midlife crisis (Jaques, 1965). In the *non vixit* dream Freud rehearsed affects relating to grief, loss, concern, survivor guilt, wishes to triumph over others. Through associating to the dream, so Anzieu has deduced, early childhood memories Freud had already recovered (including the death in infancy of his brother Julius) became linked up with childhood affects. Freud did not lay his ghosts entirely to rest with this dream, but he engaged with them meaningfully.

DEPRESSIVE AFFECTS IN DREAMS AND PSYCHIC REALITY

My theme here is to consider dreams as a containing place for trying out affects; especially depressive position affects around wishes to harm loved ones. In containment, affects can be experienced and subsequently communicated. Part of the current interest in affects and affect containment is the recognition that increased capacity for affect tolerance is in itself therapeutic, and a vehicle for increased integration. I am suggesting we look at this aspect of work with dreams. I am also more broadly interested in the usefulness of dreams in treatment in building up the dreamer's capacity to hold and appreciate psychic reality.

How has my work with dreams changed, since my original Anna Freudian training at the Hampstead Clinic in the 1960s? Changes in and debates over the use of dreams in analysis have been thoughtfully reviewed (Blum, 1976; Pulver, 1987). My understanding of play in child analysis began changing first. I had learned to consider play as the expression of an underlying fantasy to be understood and interpreted as a compromise between wish and defense. But if I let myself take a more experience-near stance, I was struck by how often children seemed to represent states of the self or states of mind as well as the state (we might say phantasied state) of their object relations. Play in treatment seemed more reflective than I had supposed, more concerned with representing what a child knew about himself and his dilemmas. A tilt toward looking at play as potential communication (First, 1994) rather than disguised gratification helped. One brief example: A 6-year-old boy had been adopted at birth. His parents reported that when the adoption came through unexpectedly they were heavily committed to career projects, and didn't take personal notice of him until "too late." Early in treatment, the boy drew a house with a stick figure in front. He cut a doorway around the figure and folded it open revealing a layer of paper behind. Another door was cut and so on, through perhaps six layers to a final blank background, which he indicated as "Mr. Nobody." I understood Mr. Nobody as representing an internal state of emptiness, linked with his experience of not being recognized. It also evoked anticipation followed by disappointment. (I was disappointed to find no one after the suspense of doors opening on other doors.) The empty house with Mr. Nobody in it had further meanings in terms of his self and object representations, and his apprehension of the parents' unacknowledged feelings about themselves and the adoption. I grew more respectful of play as an effort to register nonverbal but complex understandings of internal object relations. This carried over into finding in dreams the mind's efforts to formulate and reflect on the current state of internal experience. Today, in brief, I would find affinity with a recent statement by Peter Fonagy (1997) of how dream theory and practice have changed.

1. "Many no longer consider dreams to be invariably wish fulfilments . . . they are as likely to be attempts at resolving conflict as expressions of it" (p. 76).

2. "The act of dreaming is a significant act of representation or symbolization" (Fonagy, 1997, p. 76). I would combine these two points, seeing the dreamwork as an effort to create new symbols rather than disguise desire and circumvent censorship. Fonagy's "mentalization" parallels Bion's idea of alpha function: Raw experience needs to be rendered dreamable and then needs to be dreamed about before it can be thought about as part of what Winnicott might have called a personally lived life. In some way the dreaming itself is a first processing, or mentalizing, and the dreamwork is a further shaping, a "meta-representation" in Fonagy's language. In this view, dreams

make experience into psychic reality and dreams *are* a royal road—to psychic reality.

In Donald Meltzer's (1983) account of "dream life," he speaks of dreams as "internal drama to whose debates we wish access" (p. 89). He uses the term *debates* rather than *conflicts* because dreamwork may be trying to symbolize and lay out a dilemma so it can be explored. In my view some of the struggle and conflict Freud apprehended in dreams was an effort to elaborate states of ambivalence. Affect is meaningful. Meltzer explains that Freud could not see affect as containing meaning because to do so he would have had to see affects as being genetically prior to ideas; he could not do so because he thought that behind the dream were prior dream thoughts that had been conscious.

TRANSFERENCE, DREAM, AND INTERPRETATION

I assume transference contextualizes dreams. Dreams also can contribute significantly to making transference a psychic reality that can be acknowledged. Any dream told in treatment is as likely to have a transference dimension as it is likely to have an infantile one. We may not arrive at it with the patient, and we may prefer not to interpret transference if we can't get there collaboratively. Nonetheless, appreciation of the transference meaning of a dream can be mutative in a privileged way. A dream that recognizably works over something from a prior session can establish a new sense of continuity between sessions and intimacy between two minds. Sometimes interpretation ahead of the patient can seem right: For a self-hating patient who needs to deny relatedness interpreting a dream as an expression of transference may suggest the analyst can bear holding the patient and himself in mind together.

Of course the telling of a dream and work on it are part of the momentary transference–countertransference matrix and interpretation can be part of a transference enactment. In what follows, however, I am focusing on how dreams and the work on them may contribute to building psychic reality. It is of course hard for patients to work on dreams collaboratively if neither dreams nor transference have much psychic reality yet, or just then. In the first brief example, no interpretation is made, but the communication of dream affect helps resolve a temporary impasse. In the second vignette, the transference meanings of a dream and its precursor dream are lurking but not explicit. In the third vignette, transference is obscured but later gets recognized.

CASE EXAMPLE 1

Patient A was a 30-year-old woman with an eating disorder who when more ill had endangered a fetus by not eating enough and underfed a toddler in compliance with obsessional anxieties and compulsive routines. For several weeks before this dream she avoided treatment, insisting she couldn't find childcare competent to keep her girls from fighting with each other, and she refused to come in with the children because she wanted her sessions for herself.

In the dream, A sees her 2-year-old daughter dead and laid out naked. She watches as her 4-year-old daughter and a bigger companion who in the dream has the same name as the 4-year-old start to "play rough" with the body. The body arches "unnaturally." The thought in the dream is that they may be torturing her. Increasingly upset, the watching mother intervenes, angry at the older girls. She turns the body over, smooths it out, and rests her cheek on the buttock of the dead child. In the dream she is crying, and she cries in the session as she tells it.

In my view this is not simply a dream in which the patient gratifies disowned wishes to harm the children or to be beaten, though there does seem to be a beating fantasy in it, and perhaps identification with the father who beat her on her buttocks, and the arching back could represent orgasm/death by shock. I think this dream shows a patient touching on grief over her destructiveness toward her children and herself. She represents herself as becoming able to notice mistreatment and wanting to stop it, though a death has already taken place, perhaps of her child self. The doubling of the older daughter I think expresses understanding that she identifies with this daughter, and a dawning realization that she is using this daughter as her agent. Her own sadomasochism is becoming more of a psychic reality, less split off, as is grief over deadness. This dream was presented in supervision. I asked if any feelings from the dream communicated themselves to the supervisee. Yes, and they were "strangely intense": Listening to the dream, the male supervisee felt the patient's cruel wishes to hurt her children. Previously, he had felt this mother was entirely dissociated from the ways she teases and psychologically torments her children, and was himself too horrified to bear it in mind. I presume the supervisee began to feel the cruelty as part of the patient's psychic reality because in and through the dream the patient was also integrating it. A significant outcome was that the supervisee felt readier to confront and less afraid the patient would quit if he did so.

In the following weeks they both became able to focus on how A was allowing her children to get into states of distress, and to pay attention to events A was leaving out of her story and out of mind about what made the children distressed.

CASE EXAMPLE 2

A woman in her early forties, Ms. B, dreams that she and the man, Fergus, with whom she has been in a relationship for several years, are staying in a country cottage and planning to go on a long bike ride together. An uninvited visitor arrives just as they are about to wheel their bikes out. This is Winnie, a former girl friend of Fergus's. Ms. B explains: Winnie was flamboyant and retro; she looked like a 1940s movie star, and bossed Fergus around. The dreamer tries to get Fergus to tell Winnie to leave, but Fergus is too easygoing. Winnie is making herself at home as if she had a right to the place, and is moving in. The dreamer then tries to get Winnie to leave, but Winnie says: "I don't listen. I don't listen to anyone and I only do what I please." The dreamer backs off. Affect: I was angry at Fergus for not trying harder and angry at myself for not getting him to try harder, and frustrated because we weren't getting to go on our trip.

This dream was thrown carelessly into my lap near the end of a session and I evidently wanted to rescue it because I let my belief in its meaningfulness show. In this dream, I commented, you seem to be trying to work something out: What is getting in the way of you and

Fergus getting together. Don't you think so? You pick Winnie to stand for what is getting in the way, interfering.

Ms. B acknowledged that the anger she feels in the dream is how she is feeling about waiting for Fergus and herself to figure out their next step. But Winnie was years ago. I also commented that Winnie's movie star style and her showing up unannounced evoked Ms. B's mother (who would show up unannounced at foster homes where the patient had been placed, take her out for treats, and disappear again). Ms. B said she didn't want to think about that. I had hoped it would lead to some awareness of her conflicts over not wanting to be like the entitled mother.

I thought that the patient was trying to represent and think about an encapsulated omnipotent part of herself. It has been hard for the patient to reflect on the obstacles in her relationship with Fergus as an internal reality rather than in terms of the external logistics of their finding a place to live together, or her efforts to be patient while waiting for Fergus's separation agreement to be negotiated. Being able to have a dream in which she considers the problem, and represents omnipotence as part of the problem, marked a step in internality and reflectiveness.

A previous dream had shown Ms. B and Fergus waiting on a park bench for "brain surgery." She linked this with their difficulties in talking to each other about their feelings, although they feel intimate and loving sexually. The brain surgery was going to help them with this problem. The tops of their skulls would be cut off. She also thought this odd surgery was to help them with the state of being "cut off" from their feelings. An intelligent woman friend shared the waiting bench. There was an implication that brain surgery might involve a brain transplant from the friend who knew how to think and verbalize feelings. The unacknowledged violence of the brain surgery scenario in this dream was replaced, I thought, by the capacity to be angry as a psychic reality in the following dream, the "Winnie" dream. In working on the brain surgery dream the patient had discovered evocative and idiosyncratic associations linked with specific personal history in relation to one element (the bench). This capacity to develop associations had seemed a step in enlivening individuation for this patient who was often trying to conform with some idealized version of others' expectations, as she had in foster homes. (The bench associations incidentally pointed to themes of weddings and feeling like a usurper.)

Considering dreams as argument I now wondered if the argument of the Winnie dream may center on whether she wants to kick out or keep the encapsulated entitled part which also may be the only part of her that can feel entitled to a home of her own. We returned to the Winnie dream in a following session. I wondered whether Winnie could also be a part of the patient she was afraid of. She strongly disagreed, then reconsidered: Winnie in the dream or Winnie in real life? Winnie in the dream was ho-hum, acted as if she had all the time in the world, sat around leafing through fashion magazines, sure she'd get what she wanted eventually: That could be her taking her time with Fergus, not pushing.

But Winnie in real life was so "aggressive." Tales of Winnie's outrageous self-centeredness and ruthlessness followed. If Winnie wanted to meet someone important she practically stalked him. The patient had a "horrible vision," of what she feared the therapist might mean: that maybe she is deluded in how she sees her relationship with Fergus, mad to think he wants her and she could have him. Suddenly she is in touch with a terrible doubt about the relationship and the accuracy of her perceptions, a doubt that evidently had been warded off by a covert entitlement. She also, however, seems in this moment to see Fergus as a separate person at whom she can be angry as in the dream where, she now recalls, he just goes on tinkering with his bike while she gets upset over Winnie. I bear in mind that Winnie could also represent an impervious aspect of the therapist who may be felt as more intrusive as the transference deepens. We are just beginning to be able to work collaboratively on dreams.

CASE EXAMPLE 3

A dream from an analysis: The patient, D, a married woman in her fifties, had the previous day completed a challenging project with much less internal interference than before.

> The patient, D, watches a woman who in the dream is an acquaintance she hardly knows, spoon feed a toddler who is severely handicapped. The dreamer thinks the handicap is probably incurable. The acquaintance is calm and patient with the handicapped child. This caregiver seems not

> to realize or not to mind that the child is incurable or will never have a future. The dreamer can hardly bear to watch this scene. She goes into an adjoining room and reads a book to another child.
>
> Later in the dream she walks down a cobbled street with little shops like a mall in a college town. She is accosted by a "weird, dirty old man." He is soliciting her to come into a club or join a cult or donate some bodily organs or fluids. The dreamer tells him she is not interested and walks away.
>
> Still later, she is solicited a second time. This time the dreamer learns that the old man is not soliciting for a perverse club or a mad cult but is collecting donations of some bodily substances in a supposedly good cause—they will go to congenitally handicapped children. Again she refuses to donate, and walks away resolutely. D felt intense troubling feelings in this part of the dream and shame on awakening.
>
> D was dismissive of the first scene, and blocked in associating to it. The feeling that she could "hardly bear to look at the scene" of the handicapped child seemed a representation of her resistance, or dissociation.

D's immediate spontaneous associations were to the names of the bodily substances wanted for donation and these led directly to the medical conditions of a chronically ill father, and a seriously handicapped sister, both dead for some years. "Dirty old man" D connected with an older man, a celebrity in the arts, who had had an affair with her while she worked for him after college. She also associated to a character in an opera, a shabby old man who keeps reappearing, asking for money, perhaps as blackmail, representing the shameful secret past of the opera's heroine. (In the opera, D explained, it is ambiguous whether he was the heroine's real father or maybe was her pimp.) The affects in the dirty old man scene linked to sadomasochistic fantasies of the past of surrender to a hated and hateful object. They also linked with the strain trauma of witnessing abuse in the family around the management of sister's and father's conditions, scenes in which the family members' cruelty was disavowed and the patient felt complicitous or humiliated.

The patient connected finishing her project with walking away from the solicitation to sacrifice her substance. But what about the persistent shame? As we wondered about this the patient recalled that when she said no in the dream there were briefly braver feelings of anger and guilt about walking away. Somehow she fell back into "being a part of them."

The scene of the nice, indifferent caretaker was only returned to weeks later when the patient was complaining of the analyst being a Pollyanna: "So maybe there was something about me being a Pollyanna in that dream with the handicapped child?" D then could try to look at the dream scene and acknowledge she felt she was incurable in ways the analyst didn't want to notice—or D didn't want to bring up because she couldn't bear more rage. D remembered a further fragment: The dreamer is afraid the other woman will feel criticized or mocked if she overhears D reading to the more healthy child. We could then enquire into the Pollyanna transference as well as some concealed competitiveness. The patient got scrappier, more irritable, and frankly critical. The affect state she had in the dream when she couldn't bear to look, and her experience in the analysis when trying to look: numbness, head filled with cotton wool, became associative links in their own right: first to experiences of the mother's impermeability and denial of others' pain, then to infantile experiences of D with psychosomatic sequelae.

The uncaring caregiver I thought could be also the projection of an omnipotent part of the patient, which would be content to leave her unable to live, in order to remain in omnipotent denial. This dream set an agenda for the treatment, pointing to work not done. I hope I have suggested how focusing on affects helped keep the work alive.

REFERENCES

Anzieu, D. (1986), *Freud's Self Analysis.* Madison, CT: International Universities Press.

Blum, H. (1976), Changing use of dreams in psychoanalytic practice. *Internat. J. Psycho-Anal.,* 57:315–324.

First, E. (1994), The leaving game or: I'll play you and you play me: The emergence of the capacity for dramatic role play in two-year-olds. In: *Children at Play: Clinical and Developmental Approaches to Symbolic Play,* ed. A. Slade & D. Wolfe. New York: Oxford University Press, pp. 111–132.

Fonagy, P. (1997), Dreams of borderline patients. In: *Dreaming and Thinking,* ed. R. J. Perelberg. London: Institute of Psychoanalysis, 2002, pp. 76–89.

Freud, S. (1900), The Interpretation of Dreams. *Standard Edition,* 4&5. London: Hogarth Press, 1953.

Jaques, E. (1965), Death and the mid-life crisis. *Internat. J. Psycho-Anal.,* 46:502–514.

Meltzer, D. (1983), *Dream Life: A Re-Examination of the Psycho-Analytical Theory and Technique.* Perthshire: Clunie Press.

Pulver, S. (1987), The manifest dream in psychoanalytic practice. *J. Amer. Psychoanal. Assn.,* 35:99–118.

7

A Traumatic Dream: A Dream in Which the Analyst Appears as Himself

Robert D. Gillman

You would think that the analyst would appear in recognizable form in a high percentage of patients' reported dreams since the analyst is part of the day's residue for four or five days of the week, but such is not the case. These dreams are infrequent, although not rare (Rosenbaum, 1965). In most dreams the analyst is represented in displaced form, rather than as himself, so that only associations tell us in what fashion the dream figures portray the patient's thoughts and fantasies about the analyst. We have known since Gitelson's (1952) paper that these undisguised dreams can appear in response to countertransference.

My thesis is that the analyst appears in dreams in response to an event that takes place in the patient–analyst relationship that the patient experiences as traumatic: In the context of the transference, the event is sudden and unexpected, momentarily disrupting established compromises. The dream represents a new compromise in which the focus on the analyst as himself or herself serves as a defense against deepening transference and the recovery of early conflicts.

The undisguised transference dreams have the *form* of traumatic dreams in which the patient is attempting to relive and master an overwhelming external event (Renik, 1981). An exposure to the person of the analyst outside of the customary analytic framework, or the impact of his countertransference interventions in an intense transference situation, can constitute a minitrauma. These analytic surprises and disruptions activate too suddenly, and too strongly, unresolved conflicts from childhood. As in other traumatic dreams, a piece of a troubling experience—here a representation of the analyst as himself—is in the dream content, but the story of what took place is distorted and reenacted in disguised form.

Many of these dreams occur where there has been a break in an abstinent analysis in the analytic barrier, a break in the transference picture of the analyst. Common events are telephone conversations, meetings outside the office, talks about insurance forms, the patient hearing outside information about the analyst, a discussion of termination or other arrangements. For example, when I arranged with two patients to meet in my home rather than in my office, one immediately had an undisguised dream. For him, entering someone else's home, a stranger's home, had forbidden conflictual meanings from early childhood. The undisguised dream of a 28-year-old man followed our agreement to change from twice-a-week analytic therapy to analysis. In his dream, a 4-year-old boy and several adults intruded into the analytic room. In associations, analysis represented for him breaking through defenses against intimacy. He had avoided intimacy in his life because of narcissistic vulnerability to having to share someone's attention. The dream represented the arrival of a brother when the patient was 4 years old. At this time he was denying any possibility of early rivalry or jealousy toward the brother.

But an undisguised dream can occur through actions of the patient outside of the analytic frame without any contribution from the analyst: One patient had a dream in which I appeared the night after he drove down my street and saw my house.

More complex events that evoke these dreams, less easily specified, take place within the analysis itself. While the patient soon learns a great deal about the analyst's personality with its quirks and idiosyncrasies, there are countertransference actions of the analyst that surprise the patient. They are unexpected, beyond what the patient has come to anticipate in the analyst's character. These two groups of events, the break in the analytic frame and countertransference, are the day's residue that seem to account for the appearance of a large number of undisguised transference dreams. In a third model, several authors reported cases of early sexual overstimulation, both in male and female patients, where their experience of the analytic situation itself was enough like the childhood events to evoke these dreams. For these patients, erotized or erotic transference evoked signals of the traumatic helplessness of childhood seductions (Gitelson, 1952; Rappaport, 1959; Yazmajian, 1964; Rosenbaum, 1965).

The patient thrusts the analyst forward as an actor in the dream as a defense: The patient's dream momentarily serves to repress those conflictual memories that are reappearing as transference feelings. The patient is saying, in disavowal, "Freud was wrong, the analyst represents no one but himself, with no symbols to be deciphered" (Yazmajian, 1964; Pazzagli and Hartmann, 1980). By putting the analyst in the manifest content, the patient insists that the dream is only from above, from the day's residue and not from below, the contribution of the unconscious conflicts (Rothstein, 1978).

CASE 1: THE TRAUMATIC IMPACT OF THE ANALYST'S INTERVENTION (GILLMAN, 1989)

The patient was a married woman in her thirties, with one son. She was a graduate student in history. Her Viennese refugee background contributed to her choice of studying the history of psychoanalysis. Her episodes of depression and difficulty completing her dissertation led her to begin analytic treatment. As a thorough historian, she had managed to search out and read just about everything I had written. Now in the fourth year of analysis, she had developed a strong positive father transference. She had recently spoken of her love for me, sometimes in a sexual context, sometimes in terms of warm friendship. She spoke with much hesitancy and conscious withholding of thoughts having to do with early childhood activities. I addressed her shame and embarrassment and her fear that I would not like her if I knew those thoughts. Her interest in my writings had sharpened and she hoped I would give her reprints of my papers she had not otherwise located.

Hour 1

''I'm anxious. There was that plane crash and now my husband is flying to Denver. I'm afraid I'll lose someone I love.'' I said, ''You had so many losses even before your mother died.'' She said, ''Yes, my grandparents died before I was 10. Not such a loss for me but my mother was so upset. And there were so many aunts and uncles who died. My father's partner died''—she hesitated—''He was short. I hesitated to say that about him because it would hurt your feelings.'' I said, ''Then you would lose my love?'' This was the first time I had spoken of ''my love.'' On other occasions I said, ''I wouldn't like her any more.'' Even though it was appropriate to her associations it took me by surprise and I wondered about countertransference feelings I hadn't recognized. She said: ''I'm upset you said that but I can see why you did and it's reassuring.'' She then went on to talk more about her husband's trip.

Hour 2

''I had a dream about you. You gave me your paper. I thought it was the one about depression but it turned out to be your oedipal paper. I saw the date, it was 1920. Then I realized that that was a reference and the paper was one you had just written. I thought, now that he has given me that, he will give me a reprint of the depression paper.

''Yesterday I thought I got a gift from you. You said [she hesitates] 'You're afraid I won't love you.' I was going to paraphrase it as if I didn't remember. It made me feel like a person. You did write a paper on the superego, oedipal. 1920 is the year my father was born. You have been driving the Oldsmobile, your wife's car.'' (This was her conclusion, since I usually drove an older car, a small Fiat sedan, and she liked me for letting my wife drive the better car.) ''I was thinking that you were ill.'' I said, ''And now my wife is ill?'' (This was an earlier fantasy of hers when I drove the newer car.) She said, ''Or away visiting your children early for Christmas. Here I am fantasying from nothing. What if she really were in bad health. Can't we drop this? It's ridiculous.'' She recalled a dream in which a woman appeared in a ''ridiculous'' dress. ''I don't even know your wife.'' She then told how she had recently been warm and compassionate with an older woman. She then described some of her husband's recent awards. ''How does this all hang together? You won't answer, I can tell. Sometimes you surprise me—Freud's advice to physicians, something about even-hovering attention.''

Hour 3

''Are you sick? You looked bad at the end of yesterday's hour'' (I was not sick at the time. Her father was seriously ill.) ''I had a dream. You came over to the couch, but I said, 'You don't look well.' And you said, 'Yes, let's end the session.' ''

She then shifted to talking about her anger at some of the things her husband had done recently. She then gave details about members of her father's extended family. ''So many deaths,'' she said.

Comment

There were two experiences that were traumatic for this patient, followed by dreams in which the analyst appeared, recognizable as himself, with the manifest focus on the analyst taking some action in relation to the patient. The first was when I said, ''Then you would lose my love.'' It was the first time I had said ''my love,'' and for her it was a gift, a declaration of love. But it conflicted with her need, in the father transference, to see me as a devoted husband in a marriage she could not threaten. The trauma is represented only in part, and in disguise. I am not declaring my love in the dream, but I am giving her a reprint of my paper—the extent of entitlement her guilt will permit. The second trauma, seeing that I have driven the newer car, brings a fantasy that my wife is safely out of the way. In the dream, the analyst comes over to the couch but defensively he is made sick like the older father and the dream ends the hour prematurely. Then a critical attack displaced to her husband dispels the erotic fantasy of the transference.

There are two defenses characteristic of undisguised dreams: First, the conflicts from the past are represented as exclusively current and less conflictual; second, putting the analyst forward as himself defends against the impact of the transference: The patient is saying, "you represent only yourself." The replication of the actual event in disguised form can be reassuring insofar as the vivid dream story, like a screen memory, is different from the dreaded fantasy. It is paradoxical that the appearance of the undisguised analyst is a disguise to hide the traumatic event (Pazzagli and Hautmann, 1980; Renik, 1981; Sirois, 1994).

UNDISGUISED DREAMS STIMULATED BY THE ANALYTIC SITUATION ITSELF (Gillman, 1980)

Case 2

My patient was a woman in her forties whose early childhood was marked by sexual and exhibitionistic overstimulation. She had probably managed to gain the parental bed during intercourse. Her mother never affirmed that patient's self-worth. The mother was no protection against men's frequent exploitative attention to her beauty and precocity. Her beloved father was away for a year when she was 5. She vowed at that age to avoid future disappointment by never wishing for anything. Her disappointment coincided with the internalization of a strict superego resulting in great anxiety with guilt, shame, and feelings of humiliation over the prematurely stimulated libidinal and murderous wishes. The resulting conflicts led to a fateful and far-reaching compromise we call the oedipal resolution, resulting in renunciation of wishes, and a character of inhibition, masochism, sexual unresponsiveness, innocence, and phobia.

At every stage of development she resolved threats to her equilibrium by adding new solutions. She handled murderous fantasies to younger siblings by inventing rescue games, and by a remarkable altruistic surrender to a deformed sister. At puberty she began a series of shameless acts, exposing herself to danger to prove how innocent she was, and futilely hoping her mother would set some limits. In adolescence she avoided boys and stopped writing for the school paper because her name was published. She married an ardent suitor in college but kept it secret for three years lest anyone accuse her of sexual or caring wishes. She could not show caring feelings for husband or child.

Buying a house was a traumatic event causing a rift in her compromise solution. She panicked when she had to expose her wishes by signing her name to the documents. She became phobic of signing her name in public except when it was a gift for her mother, or in the presence of someone "too old to have sexual feelings." The second traumatic shattering of her equilibrium, which led her to seek analysis, was when she became aware of sexual feelings for a man at work. She developed a driving phobia which required her to change her job.

Before analysis began she said: "I've heard about the transference but I won't be caught in that trap. I simply won't think about you when I'm not here." Early in analysis she said: "The greatest humiliation is to have one's wishes known." Her undisguised dreams were 20 percent of the total, double the average. Her dream associations were rich in the beginning. But, as the analysis progressed, the inertness, passivity, feelings of innocence, and renunciation of wishes that characterized her past and present life were now entrenched in the transference. In the third year her undisguised dreams took on a frank sexual content, but she avoided associations. The dreams seemed to express the helpless protest and humiliation potential of early experiences.

For example: "I had a crude dream. You started having intercourse with me and I protested that it was not part of psychoanalysis, and you said, 'What do you know.' Then it was at home in my bedroom and I heard footsteps, and I said, 'For God's sakes, stop, my mother is coming.' Then you went to hide in the closet and changed into my husband getting into his clothes."

In the course of the session I reminded her that I was in the dream: Did she have any thoughts about me? She replied: "I never have any thoughts about you that I'm aware of." At this time the patient took no responsibility for her dreams; they were simply sleep phenomena like meaningless pontine discharges.

As the analysis progressed and as she could allow herself to be interested in the psychological meaning of her dreams, the undisguised dreams began to reflect her analytic gains: The sexual content disappeared, there was an end to her helplessness, there were dreams in which she was the active one and critical of me.

Comment

This patient belonged to the group of overstimulated patients for whom the analysis itself threatened, like a potential traumatic force, to disrupt further her fragile compromises. I was like the seductive father who was saying, "Surely you have some wishes," at the same time like the humiliating mother who offered no protection against them. It is possible that the construction of exploitative sexual undisguised dreams helped the patient maintain her isolation of the transference fantasies from her waking life. In her analysis I found it hard to find extra-analytic events or countertransference events that might have motivated the formation of her many undisguised dreams.

SUMMARY

The dream in which the analyst appears recognizable as himself immediately catches the attention of the analyst—like seeing your name in print. There is a danger that the dream itself mobilizes countertransference reactions, that it will be the focus of the analyst's attention. This dream occurs in less than 10 percent of all dreams, frequently enough to be studied as a phenomenon in its own right, but not so frequently as to be unremarkable. The dreamer is insisting: "The dream is about you, not about me." These dreams have been studied sporadically over the past 50 years. For many of them a preceding precipitating analytic event can be specified, but for many it cannot.

These dreams alert the analyst to the possibility of a countertransference enactment that he was not previously aware of. They also alert the analyst to the possibility of the patient's private or subliminal fantasies and impressions about the analyst. Such events can be experienced as traumatic in that they threaten to disrupt the equilibrium of important compromises. The undisguised dream functions to defend against such threat. There is one group of patients, those overstimulated or abused sexually in childhood, where the analytic situation itself is experienced enough like the childhood events to elicit these undisguised transference dreams.

As in other traumatic dreams, the patient attempts to master the anxiety by depicting something of the actual event—in this case a dream picture of the analyst. But the actual event is distorted in the dream. It has the vivid characteristics of a screen memory. There are two defensive structures that appear to be common to all of these dreams. First, by putting the analyst forward undisguised in the center of the dream, the patient is denying the transference meanings of the analyst. Second, the patient sets the scene in the immediate present, most often in the analytic room itself, to deny any representation from the past.

I think of dreams as new compromise formations, attempts to make a disguised coherent story to master the affects and conflicts that have been mobilized in the analysis. Analytic dreams occur in the context of the transference–countertransference of the analysis. I place special emphasis on the defensive aspects of the dream in relation to the transference. It would be impossible to think of undisguised transference dreams without considering their meaning in the here and now of the analysis.

It follows that I pay attention to the manifest content, the coherent story the patient presents. The story displays defenses, affects, and conflicts, but we can also see how dreams change in the course of an analysis to reflect new self and object relations, new adaptations, analytic progress. For example, in my phobic patient's dreams (case 2) there was eventually an end to helplessness, a new autonomy, and in one late dream she was my teacher showing me how to do things right—all corresponding to changes in her inner and outside life.

Yet I don't think of the undisguised transference dream as a "typical" dream in Freud's sense of a unifactorial dynamic. It requires associations to discover the spectrum of latent meanings. It alerts us that something may have taken place between analyst and patient that challenged a transference fantasy, or resonated so strongly with conflicts from the past that the patient found this particular adaptive solution to the current impact of the analyst, in an attempt to integrate a disruption into the existing equilibrium.

REFERENCES

Gillman, R. D. (1980), Dreams in which the analyst appears as himself. In: *The Dream in Clinical Practice,* ed. J. M. Natterson. New York: Jason Aronson, pp. 29–44.

——— (1989), The undisguised transference dream as a traumatic dream. Paper presented to the Atlanta Psychoanalytic Society, April, and the Cleveland Psychoanalytic Society, May.

Gitelson, M. (1952), The emotional position of the analyst in the psychoanalytic situation. *Internat. J. Psycho-Anal.,* 33:1–10.

Pazzagli, A., & Hautmann, G. (1980), The psychoanalyst as a character in dreams and the analytic relationship. *Revista di Psicoanalisi,* 26(3):368–379.

Renik, O. (1981), Typical examination dreams, "superego dreams," and traumatic dreams. *Psychoanal. Quart.,* 50:159–189.

Rappaport, E. A. (1959), The first dream in an eroticized transference. *Internat. J. Psycho-Anal.,* 40:240–245.

Rosenbaum, M. (1965), Dreams in which the analyst appears undisguised: A clinical and statistical study. *Internat. J. Psycho-Anal.,* 46:429–437.

Rothstein, A. (1978), Towards a place for "the analyst undisguised" in the psychoanalytic theory of dream analysis. Paper presented at the midwinter meeting of the American Psychoanalytic Association, New York, December 14.

Sirois, F. (1994), Dreaming about the session. *Psychoanal. Quart.,* 63:332–345.

Yazmajian, R. V. (1964), First dreams directly representing the analyst. *Psychoanal. Quart.,* 33:536–551.

8

On Analytic Dream Conversation in an Interpersonal Mode

Paul Lippmann

Clinical and theoretical work with dreams has declined and changed dramatically since the early days in which dreams and psychoanalysis were intimate partners. For analysts to meet together to talk about dreams is a rare event within psychoanalysis these days.

There are many ways by which one comes to an interest in dreams. My own childhood nightmares led to extended periods of blocking out dreams. This antagonism to dreams was relieved decades later through intellectual and artistic interest stimulated largely in the clinical situation. That is, patients told their dreams because they often thought an analytic therapist would or should be interested. In this way, we dream listeners share in the ancient archetype of dream knower, dream healer, dream shaman. Over time, I began to relax and to allow dreams their playtime, and then, I could begin to relax with my own (Lippmann, 2000).

In addition, I come to the study of dreams through the rich clinical interpersonal tradition in New York City. But also as a postdoctoral clinical psychology fellow, in the early 1960s, at the Austen Riggs Center in Stockbridge, the spirit of David Rapaport's chapter 7 seminars still echoed. If you can imagine putting these seemingly divergent influences together, you have an approximation of two of the analytic roots of my thinking about dreams. In the interpersonal approach (i.e., at the William Alanson White Institute), there never was a particular theory of dreams, never a singular clinical approach to dream interpretation, and certainly much divided opinion on the nature of the unconscious. This led to an atmosphere of relative freedom in thinking about dreams. To this diversity was joined the quality of Erich Fromm's dream seminars and later Edward Tauber's, in which playfulness, intuition, and an openmindedness were seen as virtues. I learned to find my own way with dreams within a general clinical approach that was not doctrinaire, that was as attuned to the real world as to the inner world, that allowed the therapist considerable individual latitude, including the possibilities of direct engagement with the patient, that was closer to patients' experience than to theory, and that anticipated many of the recent changes in modern psychoanalysis.

On the other hand, there was Rapaport's Freud. For me, this included an appreciation for mental architecture, for layered, complexly interwoven psychological themes, in which drives, defenses, day residues, and infantile experience, join together in carefully constructed, yet remarkably fluid ways. It gave me a sense of the universe within each dream image—including the distinct possibility that it could all make sense, if one had the desire and the patience to apply Rapaportian learning to Freudian creation (our secular version of the relationship of Talmud to Torah, from which much of the spirit of psychoanalysis arose).

There is also an oppositional quality that stimulates an interpersonalist to move to Freud. I am sure if I came home from a Freudian atmosphere, I would be Jungian, and vice versa. This oppositionalism is helpful in working with dreams, because one is so constructed as to look at the other side of things, and with dreams there is nothing but other sides. I have been asked to consider how my thinking about work with dreams has evolved since first reading Freud's opus. Because of the aforementioned oppositionalism, I had been working with dreams for some time, and often in interesting ways, before I undertook a serious reading and rereading of *The Interpretation of Dreams* (Freud, 1900). I find it the most passionate and instructive reading on all matters psychoanalytic—together with the letters to Fliess (Masson, 1985) and with related writings that engage with the dream book (e.g., Erikson, 1954) and brings to the surface the book's own unconscious (e.g., the ongoing commentary on the Irma dream and its extraordinary and hidden story). Also, I believe it important not to assume we are better at our work than were the originators. The vanity of modern psychoanalysis, particularly in the increasingly dominant relational form, is seen in the belief that we have achieved significant progress and have come a long way in our theory and in our technique over the last one hundred years. I think this assumption can be argued.

I would like to offer some orienting remarks before turning to specific discussion of analytic work with dreams. In thinking about dreams, the following distinctions are necessary between (1) dreams along with their primary experience and direct effects; (2) dream interpretation, including ideas, associations, and amplifications about the dream (i.e., what we think of the dream's meanings); and (3) the usefulness, for the purposes of treatment, in work with dreams in psychotherapy. These three are *not* synonymous. Unfortunately, they are often intermingled and confused. I believe each needs to be thought about separately and then in interaction with one another.

Also, I prefer to engage, in my work, in what is best termed *dream conversation*, which can include, but is not the same as *dream interpretation*. The former as a term is less lofty, more collaborative, and closer in spirit to an attitude that I find more useful in clinical work with dreams than suggested by the term *dream interpretation,* which, while often useful, is not the only way or even the best way to engage with dreams. Interpretations have a way of following the dominant ideology. In the early days, all dreams were seen as sexual in latent meaning. More recently, all dreams are seen in their transferential meanings—involving a singleminded search for the analyst (like Elmo) in the patient's dream. One could say, in a brief history of our field, that we have moved in one hundred years from prurience to narcissism.

After receiving an invitation to participate in this symposium, I decided to select, for discussion, the very next dream that came along.

While this may be a slightly risky procedure, it guards against the tendency to select only ''meaningful'' dreams, since it is possible that all dreams are potentially meaningful. And so, I will present the dream of a patient, a simple dream on the surface, along with commentary that will include some sense of how I proceeded with him. But also, it should be mentioned, that in interesting work with dreams, it is never the same from one dream to the next or one patient to the next. There is, obviously, no one way or best way that fits all. Dreams, as a most creative phenomenon, deserve a fresh approach each time.

He ambled into the office, a tall, strong, blond, handsome, but country-shy, kind of guy—in his forties, but from afar looking, with longish hair and attire, much younger, a schoolteacher. I have known him for about five years, in once a week, more recently in every other week analytic psychotherapy. By this I mean that often through dreams and a careful study of fantasies, our work has the depth, the passion, and the elucidation of unconscious fantasy that often characterizes psychoanalysis. Such a view is of course in contrast to a widespread and mistaken defining of psychoanalysis by number of sessions or use of furniture.

In any event, when we two meet, we have come to look together at the inner workings of the patient's long-standing compulsion that includes masturbating while smoking, or smoking while masturbating—they go together. While this behavior has many sources and meanings, along with interesting and complex advantages and disadvantages, it also adds to his tendency to ''go away'' during intimate sexual relations and, further, removes him more completely from sexual desire for his fiancée, a woman for whom he left his wife and four children. I had a hard time with him at first and he with me, as I disapproved of him, to put it bluntly—while he worked hard for me to show some premature and, hence, artificial affection for him. A narcissistic standoff. We both understand things a lot better now. In the process, we came to know about his innermost life and we are lately both feeling close and enjoying learning together. He is a deeply changed man, in part because of his son's recent suicide gesture and the accompanying outpouring of hatred expressed to him by this son; in part because of the love from and for his future second wife; in part because of our work together. His occasional ''disappearance,'' "absence," and "going away," which turned out to be profound emotional and cognitive disconnectedness both from intimate others and from his own feelings—two layers of removal into some inner awayness—has become much less frequent and is less necessary.

As he begins his dream, I reach for my pad on the floor to my right. (In an example of reverse conditioning, I once absentmindedly reached toward the pad and a patient said: "Oh, that reminds me, I had this dream last night.") So, I reach for the pad as he begins his dream, and I say, "Hold on, I'm coming." We both begin to laugh at the many meanings we understand in my remark. When possible, I enjoy a lightheartedness in my work and we both like to laugh. We enjoy joking and humor—both dark and light—about sex, baseball, labrador and golden retrievers (he once referred to himself in a slip as "a golden retreater"), women, fatherhood, money, work—all the important things for two guys to talk about.

So here is his dream. He says:

> I'm walking with Janet (his fiancée). Her mom was coming this next weekend for a visit. It was 3 A.M. I woke up with this dream. So, I'm walking with Janet, in the dream, and we look in at the kitchen and Janet's parents are doing the dishes. Bill, her dad, and Alice, her mom. Everybody has a cold—raw around their nostrils. He's rinsing the dishes and Alice is putting them in the dishwasher. They are there to be with us for the wedding.

This is the dream. Kindly take a moment to collect your own images and ideas of the dream. It has immediate context within the therapy since we have, for some time, been talking about the upcoming wedding and have shared the slow and difficult process of the patient's coming to readiness for this event, given his need and capacity for emotional and physical disappearance.

Also, there is the context of his other dreams and our way of talking about them. He is a deeply inner man, who, in therapy has awakened to awareness about his implicit fantasy life and its complex implications. He has for a long time kept company only with himself, in his own mind, in his own way, and has limited capacity for too much contact with others. I recognize some of this quality in myself, and so we both value the need for "getting away" into oneself, from time to time—including getting away from each other. We have learned a great deal from his dreams, including hints about gender mix-ups, feminine identification, the need for power and adoration, the murderousness hidden with love, and so on. And these have helped in working with his symptom and with his life in general. His own ways of thinking about dreams were slow to show themselves, but of course, as with everyone, he has a longstanding style of regarding his own dream life that is important for the analyst to learn about and to respect.

Also, I like short dreams. They give one the opportunity, or the illusion, that one can hold the whole thing in one's hand or mind, at once, and then the associations, elaborations, amplifications, asides, memories, and all connective ideation spill out the sides until they collect again into new forms. With long dreams, one carves and trims, stretches and pushes, until one finds, like a sculptor, various inner shapes and essences. But there is always more. Like painting, one works on it for a while and then turns to other things, and perhaps later chooses to return.

"When Janet woke up, I told her: 'I just saw your dad in a dream and he looked great.' But that he had a cold, I didn't tell her that."

I find myself most interested in the communication of dreams both to the analyst and to others. When someone tells you they saw you in a dream, or your daughter, or your dead father, your ears perk up. There is something about being in someone's dream and being told about it that most always brings a rush of interest and suspension of realism. A boyfriend speaks with hurt tone: "In the dream, you were with another guy and you were kissing him." Even though she is virtuous and loyal, the girl friend finds herself feeling guilty and disloyal. Within *his* dream, she is somehow real. Or the patient says, "We were lying on the couch together," or "I came to the office for my appointment and there were so many people at a party, I couldn't get in. And you were having a good time and didn't notice me." And the therapist feels, in both instances, implicated, responsible, guilty. In ancient times and in various cultures, dreams were thought to represent the soul's actual nighttime travels and encounters, and so the report of the night's adventures were taken as actual events. Perhaps with all our modern, enlightened convictions, we still sometimes believe that dreams depict reality.

"He looked great?" I asked. He continued: "Really good, thinner; his tone and colors were warm; the emotional tone, warm. Janet's been sick for a couple of weeks. Getting better. I've been healthy except my back.'' Janet's been sick? Your back is out again? I need to remember to return to these.

I was puzzled about who was coming for the weekend visit. Was it future mother and father-in-law? I asked some orienting question that made it clear I had forgotten Janet's father, her beloved dad had died six years ago, shortly before she and my patient began their romance. So this was a dead man washing dishes, in the dream, with his live wife who was, in reality, on her own coming for the weekend to help with the wedding plans.

''What about their washing the dishes?'' I asked. ''I knew him only briefly when he was alive,'' he replied. ''I liked him very much. A good man. It was good to see him.'' These words: ''a good man,'' in the way said by my patient, carried significant weight and feeling. ''The dishes, it was just like they were getting along well. You know, something quiet, domestic, warm, useful. There was an awful lot of tension, usually, between her parents. Here, they were really doing O.K. I guess I dreamed Janet's oldest wish—that her parents get along. Anyhow, when I told her, she was very happy.'' I guessed there was more about washing dishes. It is such an interesting couple thing to do in many families. There was lots to inquire about in regard to the ''life of dish washing'' for the various couples in this patient's life (his mother and father, he and his first wife, he and his fiancée, perhaps even he and I, when alone and when with the other, when good feelings and when bad enter the activity, etc.).

When some sort of activity is highlighted in a dream, I often go for amplification of the activity (bike riding, ladder climbing, apple eating, sex). I could wish to know more about the experience within the dream and forget all else, if the spirit moved me (subsequently, we often conjure up various justifications for the direction our interests take us). I usually think along with the dream. I enjoy the internal commentary. I keep in motion, rarely empty-headed until the dream is finished. While, at times, I can be entirely still internally, I usually like to get into it, in my own mind, and sometimes aloud. Even without trying, the images mentioned provoke images in my mind. Their cat becomes my version; their old room becomes my version. There is always much to ask about, later on, or as we go along, as I try to turn my mind's images more and more to their version—the differences provide enough to occupy me for some time in dream conversation. I especially enjoy coming back to the specificity of the images dreamed, particularly when subsequent memories, day residues, associations, amplifications, and interpretations move into territory some distance from the original dream images. It is often enriching when original images and their subsequent elaborations reinforce or contradict one another.

In the dream, my patient was seeing his fiancée's dead beloved father in domestic and friendly interaction with her mom. The patient tells Janet about it, in his half sleep, leaving out the sickness part, and leaving her happy and sleepy in his arms—a lovely gift, a message from the other side, a blessing from the father. I wasn't sure what there was about all this, but at this point in our conversation I got it. The emotional meanings suddenly entered my feelings. While interested and engaged, I had felt somewhat outside the situation. But at this moment, I was suddenly inside the experience; my heart filled and I became briefly tearful. "You're bringing her dead father along for the wedding plans." His tender gesture, when recognized, opened feelings in us both. At this moment, my mind took me to my son's wedding some years ago, prior to which my Hasidic nephew insisted I visit my father's grave to personally invite him to his only grandson's wedding—which of course I did. One doesn't casually reject such a dream of an idea from such a dreamy Hasid. We all felt my father's proud presence at the *chupah.*

At this point in the session, my own experience joined with the dreamer's image as he moved forward and poured out his feelings about a number of dead people he hoped could attend, including his beloved younger sister who had died a suicide years earlier. I thought once again about my own dearest friend who had died a suicide almost twenty years ago, and how he and I loved to analyze dreams together. His spirit was in the room as well. Some party. The relations between the living and the dead are very rich especially when thought about in dreams.

Sometimes when one's ideas join the dreamer's, it can lead to an opening for both, or sometimes to doors closing. For example, a patient reported a dream to his analyst of playing a marvelously curved clarinet—curved something like a saxophone, but clearly a clarinet. The jazz it created was deep and excellent—all the more wonderful since this patient never played clarinet, although his brother, wife, and children all did. The clarinet and its keys were vivid and detailed. The analyst early showed a slight and sly smile (like the man in the TV ad who takes the opera stage to announce Lotto-time, before the audience rushes out and he mumbles: "cool" with this smile). The analyst was joining his association of clarinet as phallus to the patient's image. The latter quickly felt annoyed by the analyst's slight smile along with its knowing presumption and the patient clammed up about the rest of the dream.

The evening before the night of the dream, my patient recalled playing a recording of his grandfather's lovely singing voice. He and Janet and his future mother-in-law were doing the dishes and dancing around to his father's father's singing. More tears as the day residue and its story told itself. This grandfather was also being invited to the wedding plans, in the expanding fantasy. Through tears, the patient thought of all the people he had loved and who had loved him and whom he wished could join him at the wedding. At this point, I mentioned my Hasidic nephew and the invitation to my own dead father. As we shared ourselves around the growing thematic elaboration, it became clear to both of us that my emotionally "disappearing" patient had always been, if anything, a too deeply feelingful man who was capable of crying, laughing, dancing, hating too much, loving and hurting too much, if he hadn't developed a way of turning away and inward. He could easily disintegrate into too much feelingfulness if he hadn't learned, early and repeatedly, to "disappear" his feelings. We spoke of the way smoking-masturbating had helped him calm down and close down some of the too-much feeling of everyday life. We found ourselves at this point in an advanced stage of discussion about the symptom, in which one sees, even tenderly, some of the virtues and strengths in a hated and shameful behavior that had been the subject of exhaustive analysis of conflict and compromise.

He also spoke with feeling about how he had felt earlier in the week when some of his work was positively recognized. This theme brought us to the way many men feel, and hide their feelings, and show their feelings to each other in subtle ways at work and in sports. He is a big guy and shares the psychology of big guys, including the fearful attitude of others that big guys can be dangerous and violent. He remarked that really big guys never get hugged right unless they bend way down or are sitting or lying down. I don't remember exactly at what point, but I made a slip about "four square meals a day." And he burst out laughing saying, "it makes perfect sense, three and square don't go together as well as four and square." He was cooking.

But then, the darker side of the dream and of the wedding plans began to show, evolving out of the image of the "colds" and the "redness around the nose." We were near the end of the session, and I mentioned that I wished we had more time to talk about the redness around the noses. I wasn't sure why, but that detail wouldn't go away. He launched right into a series of ideas that were lined up and waiting within near-awareness. His fiancée's lingering upper respiratory illness, which wouldn't go away, had led to scary fantasies of lung cancer—both he and she smoke, another aspect of his guiltiness about the masturbation-smoking. The redness around the nose was a small sign—in the midst of lovingness—of disease, death, suicide, murder, hatefulness. He had recently read a report on the power of viruses and was alluding, he later thought, to how little control we have over life and death. He mentioned some science fiction he had been reading on the inevitable and frightening victory of the virus. But at the same time, the red noses led him to remember a relative who used portable oxygen through a nose tube that made his nostril area red, like in the dream. This relative was a smoker and died of lung cancer as did Janet's father. "I guess that's why I didn't mention his cold. I didn't want to remind her of how he died. I didn't want to remind her of the lung cancer, of the smoking, of our smoking, of my smoking." With this elaboration, he added another level to his understanding of his smoking-masturbation in relation to Janet's father's death; that is, to the terrible understanding that he was contributing to his sweetheart's "suicide," in the manner of her father. The combination of darkness and light, love and hate, in the feelings of this dream and in our discussion brought us to a strong sense of the extraordinary mixture, complexity, and contradiction in this man's makeup and in his life within himself and with others. This simple dream opened to "the whole story," as it so often does, if one can take the time.

Not every clinical conversation about dreams can move the therapy forward. But in this instance, it did—including the opening thought about his symptom, increasing his sense of connection through the generations (an awareness sometimes lacking in his alienation), strengthening his bond with his fiancée, acknowledging ambivalence, deepening his knowledge of his own contradictions, and adding to his ability to carry on his self-analysis, largely through dreams.

I have found that it is not difficult to join a patient's dream, through one's feelings, visualizations, and interpretations, but it requires a willingness to "stay with a dream's images" for as long as possible before linking such information with what one knows about a patient. The images, themselves, contain material that often opens new ground, unexpected vistas, hidden themes, overlooked experience. This potential makes it all the more important to let the dream show itself gradually rather than interpret prematurely.

There is, obviously, much more that took place in this session and in work with this dream that I can present in this brief example, but I hope some idea of the spirit with which I approach a dream has been communicated.

REFERENCES

Erikson, E. (1954), The dream specimen of psychoanalysis. *J. Amer. Psychoanal. Assn.,* 2:5–56.

Freud, S. (1900), The Interpretation of Dreams. *Standard Edition,* 4&5. London: Hogarth Press, 1953.

Lippmann, P. (2000), *Nocturnes: On Listening to Dreams.* Hillsdale, NJ: Analytic Press.

Masson, J. M., Ed. (1985), *The Complete Letters of Sigmund Freud to Wilhelm Fliess: 1987–1904.* Cambridge, MA: Belknap/Harvard University Press.

Discussion

Chair, Ernest Kafka
Discussants, Elsa First, Robert D. Gillman, Paul Lippmann, and Audience Members

Elsa First: I was very struck when I got Paul Lippmann's paper that this was a revenant dream and I was reminded of how in various tribal traditions dreams were considered to be sent by the ancestors or by the recently dead who were not reconciled with you, to remind you of issues that weren't reconciled and things you should look out for or things that you still had to work through in relation to them, or, as we would say, in relation to the internal parental objects. It is very striking that so many of the dreams in the papers presented were about death and loss and the return of ghosts. It goes with my sense of dreams as a place where depressive affects are rehearsed and where people learn to tolerate grief and loss, not just in the sense of overcoming trauma but in the sense of being able to have that as an internal experience.

Ernest Kafka: Well, maybe I can quote a couple things you said Elsa. You said something about ''an attempt to resolve conflicts by creating new symbols.'' That was one thing. ''Trying to symbolize and lay out a dilemma so that it can be explored,'' to which my reaction was, à la Paul Lippmann, but, how would this work in dreams that aren't remembered or dreams that are remembered but not communicated or dreams that occur without being in analysis and having anybody to talk to?

Elsa First: I think dreams, without being in analysis, can still be serving a function, or they would have died out by now, they would have dried up. I could address Paul Lippmann's patient's dream as an example of that and my patient's dream, but I am tempted to say what my grandfather, may he rest in peace, used to say, ''It's a good thing you asked me. You might have asked somebody who knew.'' But I think in Paul's patient's dream there is a dilemma. He is aware that he is stepping into his wife's father's shoes, this guy; that is, they met and they got together at the point where the woman had just lost her father, right? And now comes the dream where he brings back the dead father-in-law with his lung cancer to wash the dishes and get ready for the party. And in Paul Lippmann's way of hanging out with the patient, first they go through the affects of the grief and wanting to invite the dead, and then they get into what I would think had to do with guilt, and destructiveness and the worry that what he is bringing into the marriage may be more lung cancer rather than more life or more happy dishwashing. I think that is the laying out of a dilemma in the patient's mind. Other people might look at it as more of a denial, that was only undercut when the analysis and the patient hung out together around it and with their own reverie and so on. I think that there is a dilemma there. Can I be her father and bring back that attachment without bringing back the lung cancer? And what am I bringing into this family? Is that an answer?

Ernest Kafka: I don't know how a dream can be therapeutic without somebody else to be involved with it and put some input into it or react to a person's dreams. If there is nobody to say, ''Oh, washing dishes, it's a clean-up operation. What's dirty? Is it just dishes?'' Because otherwise how is this person going to get the point? Maybe the way Freud did. Because Freud didn't get the point of the relevance of this to his ambivalent attitude about his father. What Freud did was he discovered that the seduction theory, which accused essentially the fathers of being responsible for the ailments of their children, was his fantasy. He realized this because he realized that he had been very eager to put down his father. But all of these issues about curing people, saving people, the disappointment about the cocaine, the tremendous drive to discover and to do something new, I don't know if he ever gave too much sign of understanding that it had to do with atonement and guilt and whatever. He said, "I'm not guilty, I don't have to do it" in the dreams—that was one of the major interpretations. Did he really help himself beyond a certain degree even with his analytic work with his dreams, by himself?

Elsa First: Anzieu thinks he did. I don't think that he went as far as he could have. If you look at the patient I presented, who first has the dream of the brain surgery, and I think she is waiting for a violent transplant from the analyst with all the other meanings it has, to a dream in which she has a fully rounded character that she wants to get rid of who says things like "I don't listen to anyone," and where she experiences anger, I think that is a move forward that is partly accomplished by the dreaming. Now, it is always a question, as with child's play, Is something worked out in the playing? Is it worked out in the playing with someone else? Is it being used to get rid of certain psychic contents? Or is it being used to own and experience the psychic contents? But I still think there is something that we are trying to process in a constructive way, so far as the theory of dreams goes, not just in a self-deluding way, through having dreams, at least sometimes.

Paul Lippmann: First of all, we are not only dealing with the meaning of a dream. I think we are meaning addicted and meaning addled. There's a lot of things to do with the dream that have little to do with the dream's meaning. First of all there is the dream's effect, just the effect of having a dream. A person who has stopped smoking but feels like smoking again has a dream that they are smoking and it is greatly enjoyable but they wake up in a state of enormous guilt and upset because they think they have broken their word and when they realize it was just a dream they are so relieved and they renew their determination not to smoke. A lot of dreams have an effect, affect people, without any inquiry into meaning. But meaning is important, and it often takes two people to make four meanings. But it is tricky when you invite someone to look into your dream. Because people, like Narcissus looking into the pool, when people look into a dream they see their own face. Freudians see their theory, Jungians see their theory, and yet it depends how nervous you are about people putting themselves into you. You might not feel so good about this dream having somebody put their prints into it. At the same time, it certainly always opens more meanings to have someone else look into the dream with you. So, it's a mixed deal. It depends on how schizoid the person is, how schizoid the analyst is, how much respect there is for the privacy of dreams, how much need there is to work on a dream. It's a very lighter than air experience and it takes delicacy and the ability to experience, to appreciate music, sometimes to know whether to enter a dream, how much to enter a dream, how to play with a dream, and so on. I think it's a mixed deal, and you get the good and the bad. Not only with dreams, but in any experience with another person. It's a mixed deal.

Robert Gillman: I think what Elsa brought up about child's play is very relevant. Because children play—there are a number of child analysts who feel that the play itself is therapeutic done in front of the analyst even if the analyst doesn't interpret it. I think that child's play done alone is also therapeutic because he or she is mastering something, working out some fantasies or overcoming some hurt with repetitive play and I suspect that dreams have that function too. Although I can't give you any evidence, I suspect that dreams of that kind are therapeutic, kind of a play function of repeating ideas.

Paul Lippmann: I was whistling in the dark in that it was about sex. It was clearly about death. I mean the statistics are amazing. I had no idea that thirteen out of sixteen dreams involve death in one form or another. Clearly there has already been a very intimate relation between both sleep and death, and dreams and death, and dreams and life after death. It has been considered by some that dreaming about someone who is dead was the earliest evidence for life after death. That people have the real experience, "He's still there. I spoke with him," with the meaning that clearly there is life after death in some form. So the relationship between death and dreams is very important. In the manifest content of dreams are there more dreams about death in, let's say, Mexico than there are in the United States? In Mexico, which takes a very open-hearted view of death and celebrates death in ways that we cannot dream of, are there more manifest dreams about death in that culture than there are in this culture where we seem to be absolutely tyrannized out of thinking together about death and about aging? And especially where we have the technology to keep ourselves looking young and all of that stuff. So, with Jung, I think dreams are a place where things can take place that may not be able to take place in waking thought; that is, there's a compensatory function of dreams, perhaps. We dream about death in a culture in which honest discussion about death is a little bit difficult, that may be a hypothesis. Another hypothesis is that in the dreams of patients of more orthodox analysts the analyst will appear undisguised more than in the dreams of patients of interpersonal analysts. We make ourselves somewhat more available in the session on the outside. I think my patients dream much less about me undisguised.

Robert Gillman: About twenty-five years ago when I was first aware of them, I asked three senior analysts about the frequency of undisguised dreams—I had already read Rosenbaum's paper which said over 9 percent, another paper said less than 1 percent, one said 2 percent, and one said 2 or 3 percent. I don't know whether that is because of Gittleson's paper in 1952 that said you are bad if your patient has those dreams; it shows countertransference, or it is because analysts are uneasy. They think, "What did I do wrong? Or why am I in this dream?" But everybody underestimated. This question is one I have wondered about: Does it make a difference with an interpersonal analyst?

Elsa First: While we are on the subject of the undisguised analyst, in this respect Mark Blechner seems to have a contrary view of the undisguised analyst, that such dreams represent comments on the patient's perception of the analyst's countertransference. In a way it is a response to a breaking of the frame thing, but in a way it's that the transference is primary. It's not that an analyst being undisguised is a disguise for an earlier trauma, but that the current situation is where the action is.

Audience Member: We should understand that we are talking about remembered dreams, which may be 5 percent of all dreams, 5 to 10 percent? There is a vast number of dreams that nobody ever knows about and that's where most dreaming takes place. We are talking about an infinitesimal number of dreams that reach awareness and then memory and are told and then are analyzed, and all of psychoanalytic thinking about dreams is based on that. There's a huge life of dreams that never reaches awareness that is part of our mind's capacity.

Mark Blechner: Well, I personally don't believe that only dreams that have the analyst in the manifest content are about the countertransference, I think any dream told to the analyst can be about the countertransference. I think actually Gitelson's paper was very valuable because at least any time an analyst heard a dream where he or she appeared in the manifest content they would think, "Oh, what's my countertransference involved in with this patient?" But in point of fact, it is not only restricted to those situations, and as I wrote in a paper in 1995, I think we should always be considering that possibility.

This isn't really what this conference is about, about countertransference, and I would go back to the dead. But I do think there are probably differences in the different schools as to how we use the word *countertransference* even now. I think that all those characteristics you are describing are a part of the countertransference and when I say that the patient's dream refers to the countertransference, it is referring to the way the analyst is in everything that the analyst brings to the situation, including his character, his intelligence or lack of intelligence, all those things you were talking about. At least in the interpersonal school, all of the aspects of the analyst as perceived by the patient are a part of the countertransference. But I think that there are big differences, as we all know, in the history of analysis as to what is included in countertransference. But I wouldn't want to exclude any aspect of the analyst as perceived by the patient.

Robert Gillman: Paul Lippmann talked about his imagery in listening to the patient's dream. He sees his own dream in listening, and I had always assumed that everybody did that but I am not sure. I don't know what it means that I have an image that comes from my experience, and what I am familiar with, and I don't know exactly how to compare it to the patient's image except that we both sit down and draw it or something like that. I had an interesting experience with a patient who told me a dream about a flat tire. His bike had a flat tire. I realized after he finished telling the dream—maybe my mind was wandering or something—that I had no picture of it. And I said, "You know, I don't have any picture of this dream, could you tell me again?" And in the second telling he said, "The tire had a bulge in it so I knew it was flat." Well, it turned out that his wife was pregnant and it turned out that he had great ambivalence about this pregnancy and the whole dream depended on the image of it, as he experienced it. And I realized how important that image could be. But I don't know what other experiences there are. Is there anybody who doesn't have their own image of the dream?

Elsa First: I would just add that I think that along with trying to visualize the dream I more primarily try to follow the affects and get some affective attunement to what the patient was experiencing in the dream.

Audience Member: Paul Lippmann mentioned that 90 percent of dreams never get told to anybody, and after all, dreams occur—REM sleep occurs—way down in the philogenetic scale. So Stephen Jay Gould would say that humans don't dream so that Freud could discover the interpretation of dreams. That is, dreaming has a biological function, and it is an adaptive function in the minds of many evolutionary biologists, namely that one of dreaming's functions is to compare strange new situations with situations that are encoded in memory, that the individual or the animal has encountered before. A good part of what is happening during the REM period is this matching of new strange experience to old experience, which is a way of problem solving. So that dreams can have a function even if they are never told to an analyst or anybody else.

Elsa First: This part was on the clinical use of dreams, not on what dreams are for when no one is around but what use can we make of dreams when they are brought into treatment. It would be nice to focus more on the difficulty with a patient's dream as Paul does, and what is it we do when we are doing that, and how is it in fact useful for the treatment or not.

Robert Gillman: Well, I quite disagree with you. If it is true that we dream during waking periods also and true that dreaming involves the times when otherwise contradictory or paradoxical experiences can be brought together and similarities discovered and relationships created, then if we can understand how that works and what interferes with that function, then it would be very useful. More people could dream while awake and they could come to more conclusions and have more creative understanding of insights than they otherwise might. A question came up in the other panel about what is unconscious thinking. As a former piano player, I know that there is a tremendous amount of thinking that goes on unconsciously. When I was very involved with the music, in my sleep I would dream that I was practicing and that I was memorizing a piece and when I woke up I could play much more of it than I could before. Doesn't the mind compute all the time what probabilities are? Probabilities are the estimate of what will happen in response to a certain activity, or what will be the result if one acts on a certain impulse.

Audience Member: I am interested in the uniquely human aspect of dream storytelling. A dream seems to me to be a kind of performance or a dance or a piece of art work or a story that we tell somebody—those dreams that we do tell. I am wondering if analysts from different schools have to restrain or react differently to their reactions to the dream? Would Robert Gillman be more restrained if he thought, "Oh, what a beautiful dream!"? Would Paul Lippmann say that? Is there a difference in the way we allow ourselves to react to our patients' dreams in terms of our theoretical models? Or is it really much more a function of the patient, the working alliance, where the patient is at developmentally, the moment, the hour? Is there any kind of theoretical underpinning to the frequency with which we might share with the patient either being delighted by a dream or kind of befuddled?

Robert Gillman: I don't know if I am ever delighted by a dream. I think the most delighted I was by a dream was when a 9-year-old girl spent five consecutive days analyzing a dream. And she'd come and say: "Let's solve that dream. Let's work on it." I think that was the most delighted I ever was by a dream but not by the dream itself.

Audience Member: Isn't the dream a kind of creation?

Robert Gillman: It is a creation, sure, but so are a lot of associations creations, and I thought my 9-year-old patient was so creative in the way she spoke that I thought everything was something of a creation, but the dream itself was not special.

Paul Lippmann: Obviously there are wide individual differences and it's not a function of creativity or investment in the arts. I've just learned that Robert Gillman is a pianist and is involved deeply in music and appreciation and love of everything that is involved in music. But we are very opposite on that. I'm glad when somebody wants to work on a dream. I feel strengthened by it, interested in it, there are places to go with it. I have experienced delight. I recommend Bert States's, *Dreaming and Storytelling* (1993). It is like somebody comes back from their Odyssean travels with a story about wonders and they tell you what they have seen, and it is very hard not to be delighted, sometimes dismayed, because they will also tell you about all your shortcomings. They tell you about your stupidities and your uglinesses and they will tell you what they came back with. There's a patient I remember who dreamed over many years—she's a daughter of Holocaust survivors and her parents between them had lost three babies (both had been married before). They married after the Holocaust and she was born. Every time they looked at her their eyes filled with tears. So, they never saw her she felt, they saw the dead children, whenever they looked at her, from the very beginning, and this is an adult speaking. She said she never felt that she existed in their eyes. So she was invisible, she felt, in certain deep ways from the time she was born. She devised a plan and we never spoke of it, it was entirely unconscious, the plan took place in dreams over years, which she realized in one of the last of a series of dreams. In one of these last dreams, her parents are standing at the bedroom door, watching—her parents are both dead now—watching her and her husband having intercourse. And she looks over to them as if to give them instruction, "This is how you do it." What she has been dreaming of for years is the parents coming over from disparate parts of the planet, one in Japan and one in Poland. Then a year later one was in England and one was in San Francisco, coming closer and closer together, until this dream, when they are standing outside the door watching her and her husband have intercourse and her interpretation was that at the moment she was trying to show them how to make love. And at the moment that they were able to make love she would be able to enter their love making and be born as a visible being. I was delighted, moved, not only by the work that went into it, but by the dream process itself, which she had developed in her mind to solve the problem. I couldn't have imagined it but she did. And that kind of experience we have time and time again.The things people come up with to solve their dilemmas unconsciously and consciously, but certainly unconsciously as in dreams.

Elsa First: I think that her solution is also a way of changing her internal experience, as if she is saying, ''If I could experience my parents as together and loving each other after the Holocaust then I could imagine them as looking at me and really seeing me, not only seeing their grief.'' So she's done some internal work, and that's what is shown in the dream.

Audience Member: An experience that some of us have had was to leave a session, maybe where a patient has dreamed and maybe not, and then dream that night about the patient. So one of the things that we have not quite touched on is the analyst's dream: Its appearance or nonappearance the next day, and also the experience of dreaming together and experience in non-dream-like things in free association, finding out that there's a convergence of material, that the patient also has a similar image.

Paul Lippmann: The narrowest view is that it's a bad idea, a sign that the patient has gotten into you too much. A little broader than that is a recent dissertation at the University of Massachusetts Psychology Department which reports that dreams in which the patient appears come about at difficult crisis times, at impasses, at countertransferential problematic times, and that this is a form of self-supervision. Something about the patient is knocking on your brain and trying to say "pay attention to his." This broadest view is that we are always dreaming about each other all the time, and what you do with it is a matter of what you think you should do with it. There is a wide latitude in the whole area of talking with people about one's dreams. Edward Tauber (1954) was the first person whom I'm aware of, I think, who wrote about this. Ferenczi lived it, in a way, but Tauber wrote about it and was roundly condemned within the psychoanalytic world for daring to write about sharing his dreams with patients. Whether he was right or not right he was willing to inquire into the possibilities of such an approach and today that is written about a lot more easily. I think people are now talking about sharing a dream with a patient, it's become much more commonplace now. So there's this whole range of response from bad news to good news.

Robert Gillman: Those of us who have treated colleagues who are treating patients find they occasionally bring in dreams in which their patients are involved. If the analyst is ill, or if the analyst has some worry or concern, that may get transferred in the dream into some concern about that analyst's performance with the patient which is then reworked in the dream. The patient is substituted for the analyst who has been having some problem, and in the dream this is somehow represented. Otherwise, patients represent children of analysts, siblings of analysts, in the same way that other people do, and sometimes the dream has to do with the day residue of what went on in the analysis.

Robert Gillman: I woke up and realized that I had dreamt an examination dream, and I was very puzzled because life was going on and nothing was coming up that was like an examination. I went to work and my second patient walked in and I realized the dream was about the examination the patient was facing. So there was a countertransference overidentification that I recognized the moment he walked in; it could just as well have had the patient in it.

Paul Lippmann: Dreams could be used to point the way to neuroscience, but dreams can also point the way to social experience. We dream about each other, we think about each other, we are in each other's dreams. We communicate in dreams with each other under the surface. I think that's a very important side of dreaming and I think in our rush to neuroscience we need not to overlook the history of the social binding that took place in dream experience. In almost every ancient society, dreaming had to do with cohesiveness in the society. Two weeks ago I took part in the social dreaming program at the William Alanson White Institute. It is still rich in my mind—the clarity with which a group of people talked with each other about their dreams and associated freely to them, the clarity with which it became clear how deeply connected we were under the surface. Analysts rarely talk about dreams with each other. We may talk about our patients' dreams, but the old days when analysts talked about dreams all the time with each other over dinner and over drinks and on shipboard and on a walk in the Alps and in letters—dreams, dreams, we would tell each other dreams and this extraordinary new discovery of the royal road, for the most part, has stopped, except between very intimate friends. I hope there are those intimate friends who are therapists who still talk to each other about their dreams because there is a lot to learn from each other, but as a group we've gotten nervous about our dreams as though they are dirty little secrets, that talking about them will reveal too much. That's an enormous change in climate from the early days of a hundred years ago when dreams were the very stuff that people spoke about with each other. Now Freud was maybe afraid to say a little bit too much to Jung because he might lose his authority, and I'm sure Jung was afraid to say a little bit too much to Freud, which might show how much he wanted to kill him. But still one exercises tact and good manners in all things and yet the overall possibility of talking together with each other about our nightly excursions is severely limited and I think that's a sign of the times, the ways in which dreams have almost disappeared from psychoanalytic discourse, brought back by neuroscience, perhaps.

Audience Member: Apart from psychoanalytic discourse, all you have to do is to turn on afternoon TV so see complete primary process on display. MTV is replete with it.

Paul Lippmann: From the dream group to social dreaming experiments to new age interest in dreams to Jungian preoccupation with dreams, dreams are still very much alive, just not as much in our world. It is possible though that we are still working with dreams as much as we ever did and enjoying them but not talking too much about it. This might not be such a bad thing, because we so heavily excused our concentration with our models that I think dreams sank under the weight of our models.

Audience Member: What allows a dream to be remembered? Which dreams do we remember?

Robert Gillman: The last dream of the night, that's the main one that I know of from experimental work. The recent memory is an important factor in what is remembered.

Elsa First: I think internality has something to do with it as well. We find when patients are more in touch with themselves they can remember dreams; when they are less in touch with their internal life it is harder for them to remember their dreams, so I sort of thought that was a rule of thumb. There is a fluctuation in how much we are in touch with our dreams just as dreams themselves vary in how much integration of psychic experience shows in them from severely borderline dreams up through neurotic dreams. If a treatment is tapping into some ongoing level of psychic development, if the patient wants to share it on some level, then the dreams are remembered more clearly. Ernest Kafka said he thought dream mentation was a continuation of creative thinking, trying out alternatives, putting things together in new ways and so on. What is different between that and my sense of dreams as working out issues with internal objects?

Ernest Kafka: Just the terminology. It's just in the words. Internal objects don't mean much to me but they mean a lot to other people. Isakower insisted you could not understand somebody's dream if you didn't see it. You had to see it with the patient. And I never concurred. I really had a tremendous amount of difficulty. I don't see things; I don't have a visual memory. Other people do, so that's different for me. So it's a matter of people's brains working differently and some of them get visual things and others don't.

Audience Member: How about work with what comes to mind? Some people when you ask them what comes to mind, nothing comes to mind. But you ask that same person, ''What do you see?'' and something opens up. On forgetting, one of the important advances of REM research is that we found out that all forgetting dreams and dream references were not resistances. I think that was an important error that has allowed analysts to be angry, frustrated, disappointed. We should be more broadminded about the appearance and disappearance of dreams.

Ernest Kafka: I want to say something to Bob Gillman. Freud's idea that there are no useful associations to typical dreams is wrong. There are associations, and there are changes in examination dreams. The examiner changes; as a matter of fact in the course of analyzing people, very often the examiner is gradually seen as a more benevolent person, more like the parent who is wished for, rather than the parent to whom is ascribed the patient's hostility and the patient's projected resentment. People get better, their dreams get more comfortable very often. Margaret Mahler, after her friend Ravi Bach died, used to say, ''Every once in a while I have a bad day, but at night I dream, and Ravi comes to me and he says, 'It will be all right, it will be all right.' ''

Howard Shevrin: So far there has been no direct reference to the fact that dreams are hallucinated, that they are experienced as real experiences. So that when Mahler was looking forward to dreaming about her lost friend it was because it would be, as long as the dream lasted, in a sense a real gratification. And even those people whom we hold very ambivalently, when they come back in a hallucinated form, we experience these ambivalent feelings in a real sense, which may be one of the reasons why, as Elsa First has been saying, that affects are more available in the work with dreams, because they have an effect and experience as real in the dream. Now, why it is that dreams are hallucinated, why it is they appear to us as real experiences, we know has never received an adequate explanation. One explanation that I think we have heard during the course of the symposium thus far is that it is one of those things that happens at night when we sleep. We go into a different state and that different state happens to be a hallucinated state. Well, that is one way of trying to explain it. We know that Freud tried at least two related explanations. One is that it was a regressive phenomenon that was activated through the energetics of his energy model, the perceptual apparatus, and furthermore that it had a developmental implication, that it returned the individual to an earlier state of hallucinated gratification, and I know there is a lot of criticism of that from many different people. But I don't know of any other explanation as to why it is that in the middle of the night at certain times we experience something as real. Furthermore, that we benefit clinically from the fact that they are experienced as real in various ways, but we don't seem to address the issue as to why it is that certain things have to be experienced as real, others go into a fantasy, and still others go into a symptom.

Steven Ellman: I am sorry that Howard Shevrin thought that all that was said was that sleep was necessary. I tried to say in my presentation that the reason I thought dreams were real was because a motivational system was activated that had an affect attached to it, and that in addition, when that happened sensory events come into play, and so the whole thing feels quite real and in fact, if you make a lesion of the centers that are inhibiting muscles, the animal or, in some neurological conditions, humans will actually act out the dream as real and will perform a variety of behaviors. Juvey did this in cats and it looks like the cats are having sexual experiences or aggressive experiences and I thought I had tried to say that the motivational system that is activated makes the experience real.

Audience Member: I think this is a excellent question about the realness of the dream not only in the way Steven Ellman responded but also, if we take it again from neurophysiology out into the social world, we might notice that our technology, not only in movies, which seem very real to some people, but in the explosion of the development of the possibilities of virtual reality, our contemporary technology is working with the dream experience. Not calling it the dream experience, calling it all kinds of things, but we are developing the technology that will make it possible for people to believe that something that isn't there is there and actually going on. I think that is a very important question in parallel with the neurophysiologic question.

Another Audience Member: Why we dream is a viable question. The question of why, of course, is a function question—what is the function of dreaming? And certain dreams have a paradoxical nature, which we call REM, and it involves the autonomic nervous system, the activation of the autonomic nervous system, preparing the individual for fight and flight. Whereas other dreams may involve fantasy and may be more cold in nature rather than hot, as in opposition to a REM sleep. So if we look at the functions of these two types of dreams, how would you then categorize these two types of dreams bringing about two types of physiological reactions, one being sympathetic reaction, the other one being parasympathetic in nature, REM versus non-REM dreaming? How would you try to understand the meaning of these two in relation to, say, the analyst or in relation to the everyday life situations? I would like your comments about that.

Robert Gillman: In the Lumier films of approaching locomotives people got terrified and ran out of the theater. I think we have actually gotten acculturated. There is something about the visual that makes us have such difficulty in differentiating but also in movies that we get so absorbed in, rather than the other sense.

Elsa First: I would like to say that when you come out of a movie you can still remember it as real but also as only a movie and the same is true with a dream, which is the difference between a dream and a hallucination. I was once teaching something about Bion and his view that hallucinations are one end of a spectrum and dreams are another, because the person who is hallucinating does not know that it's inside him, but thinks it's outside him. One of my students discussed a patient, at I think it was Bronx State, who didn't want to be moved when patients were being moved because the walls were being painted in the room, because his dreams were in the walls. That's a hallucination. I guess part of the reason I'm drawing on the Bion tradition to talk about internality, is that when you have the dream, yes it is gratifying and real to you while you are in it, and then afterwards it is also something you can see as a part of your psychic reality and begin to appreciate how much internal psychic reality colors your everyday experience which is part of what treatment is about, isn't it?

Ernest Kafka: The child learns to distinguish what was a dream and what was reality. I remember my daughter at about the age of 2½ or so greeting me in the morning with the question, ‘‘When are we going to get the dog?’’ I said, ‘‘What are you talking about?’’ She said, ‘‘Well, you showed me the dog and you told me that we were going to pick it up today.’’

REFERENCE

Blechner, M. J. (1995), The patient’s dreams and the countertransference. *Psychoanal. Dial.,* 5:1–25.

Gitelson, M. (1952), The emotional position of the analyst in the psychoanalytic situation. *Internat. J. Psycho-Anal.,* 33;1–10.

Rosenbaum, M. (1965), Dreams in which the analyst appears undisguised: A clinical and statistical study. *Internat. J. Psycho-Anal.,* 46:429–437.

States, B. (1993), *Dreaming and Storytelling.* Ithaca, NY: Cornell University Press.

Tauber, E. (1954), Exploring the use of countertransference data. In: *Prelogical Experience,* ed. E. Tauber & M. Green. New York: Basic Books, pp. 127–148.

Clinical Panel 3

Chair, Ruth Imber

9

Bringing in the Dreamer: Some Reflections on Surprise, Dissociation, and Analytic Process

Philip M. Bromberg

In a paper titled "Potholes on the Royal Road: Or Is It an Abyss?" (Bromberg, 2000), I noted that sixty-five years ago Theodor Reik (1936) made the startling suggestion—startling because it was so far ahead of its time—that there is no royal road to the unconscious, and if there is a road at all, it is to be discovered most vividly, not in dreams as Freud (1900, p. 608) suggested, but rather through the experience of surprise, in that surprise allows an analyst to find something new which will then create its own technique. In other words, the road to the patient's unconscious is most discoverable at these moments when the

This chapter revises and expands the original version of this essay published in *Contemporary Psychoanalysis*, 2000, 36:685–705.

analyst becomes aware of his own unconscious participation in its construction while being consciously engaged in looking for it. Put in contemporary terms, some aspect of what is unconscious in the patient and unconscious in the analyst is always present in what we call ''enactment.'' It is the enacted piece of each partner's impact upon the other that makes the royal road a bumpy road and makes it all too evident that the raw material from which the road is constructed is drawn from the unconscious not only of the patient but also of the analyst. It is the bumps in the royal road—what Reik called ''surprises''—that provide the greatest leverage for therapeutic action because they are the most powerful ongoing source of novelty, unpredictability, and spontaneity—the true wellspring of the unconscious. Paving the potholes in the royal road, that is, bringing the bumps from the level of enactment to the level of conscious perception and conscious thought is the biggest, and I feel, the most interesting part of the analytic work.

I believe that working with dreams is, exactly as Freud said, an indispensible aspect of the process I've just described, even if it isn't literally a ''road'' in the way he perceived it. I think that Freud was correct in his view that dreams provide something unique, and I want to share a few of my thoughts about what this ''something'' is, and how I use it in my own work.

Sometimes a patient starts a session saying ''I don't have anything to talk about today; I wish I had a dream.'' We're all more or less familiar with this, and most of us would agree that the meaning of it can be fully grasped only as an event that is unique to the analysis in which it occurred. Nevertheless, I think that there are certain meanings that tend to emerge more than others, and I've found these to be typically organized around the concept of resistance. It is as if the patient were saying: ''If I had a dream I would be spared having to think about why I have nothing to say today.''

But there is another version of that opening remark, one that occurs much less frequently, and when it does, captures my attention more than the first. It was in fact said very recently by a patient who I'm going to talk about in more detail shortly. The remark was, ''I *fell* like I want to tell you a dream, but I don't *have* a dream.'' As the session progressed, the patient's ''felt need to tell a dream'' was more and more clearly understood as expressing the same thing that the dream itself would have expressed had he indeed arrived with one—a voice from a dissociated part of the patient's self that was ready to be heard, but that the patient was not quite ready to acknowledge as "me." There are many variations of this opening remark, and I've come to discover that more often than not, if such a comment is not seen routinely as "resistance," it will be found to convey the message I've just described, as if the patient were saying, "I don't have anything to talk about today, but maybe somebody else in there does."

My approach to working with dreams is simply a reflection of my overarching self-state perspective on the human mind and my belief that, no matter what one's theoretical persuasion or loyalty, a clinical stance derived from this perspective optimally facilitates enduring personality growth within a psychoanalytic relationship. Edward Tauber and Maurice Green (1959), two of the White Institute's most creative researchers and interpersonal analysts, published a book called *Prelogical Experience*. It remains today a landmark in psychoanalytic thinking about the mind, self-states, dissociative processes, and dreaming, and points the way, predictively, toward much of the work currently being done in brain research. They write:

> [S]ubthreshold perception is an ongoing process covering a broad spectrum of different states of consciousness. The subthreshold processes are, so to speak, busily engaged in picking up huge packets of sensory input and in sorting, filing, and organizing this input in ways that defy understanding. Scientific discovery and verification of this important aspect of man's inherent equipment open up new and promising possibilities for extending our understanding of essentially, nonverbal, dissociative aspects of human functioning" [p. 83].
>
> [S]ome of the subthreshold perceptions of the self [emerge in] dream content. And, possibly, such amorphous forms may be the stuff out of which presentational experience of the self can be created in awareness [p. 91].

I believe they were more on target than they could ever have known, especially in regard to how this understanding translates itself clinically in working with dreams, and here I can summarize my own clinical position in once sentence: I believe that when a patient brings in a dream, the analytic task is to enable him or her to "bring in the dreamer."

If one holds the view, as do I, that a dream is the most familiar special case of the more general phenomenon of dissociation, the normal self-hypnotic capacity of the human mind, then dreaming might be considered among the most routine day-to-day dissociative activities of the mind—its nocturnal function being an adaptational effort to cope with minimal levels of not-me experience without interfering with the waking illusion of central consciousness. One of its manifestations in psychoanalysis is to contain and hold, as a separate reality, unprocessed experience that is not safely containable at that moment within the ''I'' that defines the analytic relationship for the patient. In other words, the use of a dream in analysis might, at one level, be thought of as a transitional experience that allows the potential linking of self-states that are hypnoidally disconnected, permitting the voices of other self-states to be heard and to find access to the dynamic structure that the patient defines as ''I.'' The process through which this takes place is one that I feel is not adequately described by the term *dream interpretation.*

I would depict the process as a gradual development of dialogue between the waking self-state of the ''patient-as-patient'' and the sleeping self-state of the ''patient-as-dreamer''—dialogue that is shaped by the creative use of the projective and introjective process that takes place between patient and therapist as part of every analytic relationship. The analyst, by engaging in an affectively personal relationship with each self-state of the patient, finds out in detail its own story, thus allowing the patient to experience ''who he is'' with a sense of clarity and personal authenticity. And for the therapist, it is not necessary to work as hard to ''figure out'' what things ''mean,'' and how they are connected to the past. A similar sentiment has been expressed by Cecily de Mouchaux (1978) in a clinically illuminating paper on the nature of dreams (which she calls ''night thinking''). In describing her work with a patient who ''began to feel like . . . someone who had swallowed their twin . . .'' (p. 449), she writes that ''dissociation with no access to consciousness, as in the numbing or freezing stages of the primary stress response, gives way to dissociation with partial access to consciousness via night thinking, and this provides a trial ground, a way station on the road to integration'' (p. 448; cited in Bromberg [1998, pp. 297–298]).

With regard to how this shapes my own clinical approach (Bromberg, 1999, pp. 60–61), I start from the fact that a dream, in its essence, is a nonlinear reality and must be related to as such—not as a kind of story or a kind of movie, but as a real space in which the patient has been. By accepting that the dreamer is inside his dream (inside a separate psychic reality) then not only our way of approaching dreams in psychoanalysis is changed, but everything that takes place between ourselves and our patients is experienced differently, including how we perceive and use the transference and countertransference field.

In chapter 1 of *The Interpretation of Dreams*, Freud (1900) suggested that waking and sleeping realities may not be as experientially unbridgeable as one believes them to be when awakening from a dream, but the implications of his insight were not subsequently pursued by Freud with respect to the analytic process. He wrote: "The unsophisticated waking judgement of someone who has just woken from sleep assumes that his dreams, even if they themselves did not come from another world, had at all events, carried him off into another world" (p. 7). "Thus the dream experience appears as something alien inserted between two sections of life which are perfectly continuous and consistent with each other" (p. 10). Historically, most analysts have tended not to see a patient as potentially able to "reenter" in a session what Freud called "another world," and thereby access the self-state of "dreamer" without losing the one of "patient." For the most part, they have tended to collude with their patients' waking experience of a dream as something alien.

I have found that most individuals, particularly in the presence of an appropriately involved other, hold the capacity to reenter their own dream space while simultaneously retaining their waking reality, and that, in treatment, some people do it more easily and more naturally than others. I am persuaded from my own work and that of others (especially that of Robert Bosnak [1996], a Jungian analyst), that this is accurate, and what we call the therapeutic use of potential space in psychoanalysis (Winnicott, 1967, 1971) is effective because patient and analyst are simultaneously utilizing this capacity in the interest of a shared goal—each of them embraces the other's waking reality as if it were his own "dream."

If one views the normal process of human personality functioning (including patient and analyst), as a shifting conjuration of multiple self-states (what Freud in 1908 called *part-egos),* it is then not too difficult to conceive of the analytic process as a relationship involving an interconnection between the multiple realities of both people. The next step is to accept that our "dreaming" reality is simply a different state of consciousness, and that just because it takes place during ''sleep'' does not make it any more inherently unbridgeable to waking reality than are any two dissociated self-states. A familiar example of this is the phenomenon that we refer to as *pavor nocturnus* or ''night terrors,'' those cataclysmic eruptions of somatized anxiety into terrifying dreams which continue to be felt as real even after one is fully awake and which the mind and body cannot shake off for a long while. The main point is that looked at in this way, the two people are not just relating to one another through a unitary, ''waking state of consciousness,'' even though we might want to believe so, but through many different self-states, one of which, at least potentially, is that of the ''dreamer.'' In other words, the other's subjectivity, although it cannot be directly known except by its ''author,'' it is in fact experientially accessible as if it were one's own ''dream,'' opening a space in which the waking reality of each person makes room for a potential ''dreamer.''

In this same vein, I feel quite drawn to Marianne Goldberger's way of using *daydreams* (see chapter 10), and can easily translate how she works into a version of my own approach. She repudiates the idea, as do I, that just because night dreams occur in a ''different state of consciousness,'' they provide a more ''royal'' access to the unconscious, and she makes a strong argument for the sometimes superior access provided by daydreams because they ''at times have more immediacy'' and allow patients, as she puts it, to ''make playful use of their imaginations.'' In my own way of working, one could argue that I attempt to turn night dreams into daydreams.

I hearken back to Count Alfred Korzybski's (1954) frequently cited admonition that one should not mistake the map for the territory. In this same sense one should not mistake the reported dream (the map) for the dream reality (the territory). If, as Reik (1936) implies, the royal road to the unconscious is created (by the experience of surprise), rather than discovered (by the ''interpretation'' of dreams), then what links dreams and surprise? My answer is *affect.* Take nightmares, for example; they are unique among dreams (as are ''night terrors,'' technically not really dreams but a stage IV sleep phenomenon), because they are so affectively powerful and affectively vivid that the affect sometimes even spills over into ''waking reality.'' What I am calling the territory of the dream (the dream reality) as opposed to the map (the dream text), is organized by the affective experience while dreaming. This is true even if there is no affect, because the "presence of an absence"—to use Bion's language—is still the most personal substrate of the dream reality as experienced by the dreamer. So, the analytic work, as I see it, is to make every dream a "nightmare," not by the fact that it is frightening but rather by the fact that it is affectively vivid and immediate.

The general principle is to see a dream as part of a session rather than as a "thing" brought into a session from the outside. It is not a narrative to be "understood" but a reality to be experienced in as much detail as if it were taking place "now." That is, to return to Count Korzybski, I try to help a patient return to the dream experience, and feel into it as the "territory" rather than *tell* it as if it were "only" a story—a map of the territory for which associations will then decode its meaning. So, I try to ask for details in a way that most helps a patient enter the dream as a here-and-now experience. In a way it is a version of what Edgar Levenson (1988), expanding on Sullivan's (1954) concept of the "detailed inquiry," called "the pursuit of the particular," but using a dream as if it were no different from a reported event that took place in what we call the "waking world." For example, "What is it like as you are seeing that man in the corner? Not "what *was* it like?" "Where are you standing in the room? Look around you and describe what you see." Look up. How high is the ceiling? Where is the light coming from? You say you are feeling somehow close to this man. Does he seem to be aware of your presence? In what way do you feel close? And so on. The idea is to enable the patient to get further and further into the dream *space* and not simply remain in the dream *text*.[1]

What happens varies between patients. Some can go there freely while others can't, but for those who can lend themselves to it even minimally, the affective experience of being in the dream becomes increasingly vivid and real, and there is where the real point of all this begins to become clear. For one thing, the patient's associations to the dream, as they arise, will tend to arise more spontaneously because they are "affect-derived" more than "narrative-derived." But equally

[1] I am particularly indebted to Robert Bosnak, whose 1996 book, *Tracks in the Wilderness of Dreaming*, provides many of the illustrative questions selected here as examples.

important, the patient–analyst relationship is itself now drawn into the construction of the royal road. As I said earlier, the road to the patient's unconscious is always created nonlinearly by the analyst's own unconscious participation in its construction while he is consciously engaged in one way or another with a different part of the patient's self. So, while the analyst is leading the patient deeper and deeper into the affect of the dream experience, the self-state of "the dreamer" enters the session through enactment.

In one way it is no different from what takes place when you are helping patients talk about real-life traumatic events from their past. What begins as a story being "told" becomes an event that is relived, at first subjectively and then drawn into a relational enactment. Similarly, when a *dream* is being "told" and gradually relived subjectively, those aspects that represent unprocessed real-life experience (frequently, unsymbolized experiences of the analysis itself) will, like all unprocessed experience with high affective significance, be enacted in the patient–analyst relationship. In other words, the analyst is not simply a "guide" accompanying his patient on his journey down the royal road, he is a participant in the road's construction, and, we hope, in the repaving of its potholes.

I want to present a clinical vignette about dreams and "surprise." But it isn't about surprise in any dramatic sense, and that's why I chose it. There was no burst of something that emerged in a wondrously transformational moment. What happened was a surprise in a different way. My patient surprised me by being in a place, developmentally, I had no idea he had reached, and the fact that he knew and I didn't, was what was most important to him. At the same time, I also surprised him, by responding to his unanticipated confrontation of me in a way he didn't expect. Each of us had to deal with something unconscious in ourselves and in the other that was being enacted in our relationship—something dissociated of which we were each a part, and which neither of us was able to fully grasp and process alone, even though each of us was experiencing some part of it personally. We either escaped the dissociative cocoon together, or we both remained trapped in it. It's an example of the kind of moment a patient tends to remember as meaningful years after his or her analysis has ended, but can't really say why—a "surprise" moment when the "personal" and "professional" are unexpectedly bridged, and the bridge becomes an affective marker in personality growth that is enduring and far-reaching.

Daniel was a man in his early thirties whom I had been seeing in three times a week analysis, on the couch, for six years. He had been sent to me for analysis by his internist who had thrown up his hands trying to diagnose Daniel's mysterious leg pains, a condition Daniel had apparently suffered from since adolescence. I say apparently, because for Daniel, there were no such things as facts, and this included historical data. He was concrete to a fault. Mental representation of his past, as something upon which he could reflect, did not seem to be possible. Everything was like a snapshot on film that had important parts slightly blurry. If he couldn't see it as if it were a sensory image in front of him, happening now, maybe he was just imagining it. I can still remember our initial interview, when I sat trying to record the usual developmental stuff I ask about when I first meet someone, and each time I wrote down something he said I had to cross it out. I ended up with three pages of scribbles that looked like I was a dyslexic second grader. It's hard to describe the sensation of being told that such and such happened at such and such a time during someone's life, and having it disappear like the Cheshire Cat in *Alice in Wonderland,* fading a piece at a time, until all that is left is the grin. You are probably thinking at this point, ''Yeah, poor guy, I know what it's like treating a world-class obsessional,'' but he wasn't really *that*. It wasn't that he ''undid'' what he had said; it was more as though he put me into a state that made me not sure he had even said what I thought he said in the way I thought he had said it. Nothing was connected to anything else. ''Snapshots of his life!'' But they were snapshots that had never even been put into an album. He had more than a few issues that had to do with trauma, dissociation, and hypnoid states. We had worked together for six years in what I believed to be a pretty good analysis, and even his leg pains had disappeared, or so I thought. In any case, his internist was happy with me.

However, it was not an easy analysis. Working with transference–countertransference enactment to access dissociated self-states played a big part in it, but despite our seeming success it always felt as if there was ''someone else'' in there who was more angry at me than was ever expressed to me, and that this part of him had never been allowed to have a voice. The session I want to talk about took place after we decided to start talking about termination.

Without fanfare, he had canceled the previous session because of pains in his legs. In the past, he had cancelled other sessions for this reason, but it had not happened for a long, long time, and I thought we had come to grips with that symptom and that we were finished with it. So I found myself a bit grouchy when he came in for his next session. I was determined to ''get to the bottom'' of the transferential meaning of his leg pains ''once and for all,'' even in spite of the fact that I knew full well that the return of symptoms during a termination is more or less expectable. He arrived the following session, in an upbeat mood, with a dream.

> I'm running a race on a *concrete* and asphalt surface with someone else who is running behind me. In the dream I'm a novice; he's a pro, and I'm always thinking he'll catch up but he never does. I just keep running my race but with an eye on him. There's a bend in the road and he thinks I'm going to make a wide turn because I'm a novice, but I don't. I effectively cut him off from passing me. I even get stronger toward the finish line and I end up winning. But it's my first race and I'm not sure which line is the finish line, so I keep running just to make sure.

I, with my own agenda, went immediately to the fact that many of his earlier dreams had been about running races, and said, ''Running seems to play a prominent part in your dream life.''

He growled, ''Hmm. I don't think so! I don't see that. It feels like you are switching the subject.'' Then:

> I just remembered another dream I had last night. I was in a room talking to you. I was sitting up and you were facing me. You were telling me things that weren't fitting. You were sounding very intelligent but you were wrong. Then, somehow, we were near each other. I'm not sure if we were on the same couch. But Carol was sitting at the other point on the triangle. Carol was talking and I was thinking that she would be a perfect match for you. I was pissed at you. The reason I was dreaming of Carol is that she's always weaving irrelevant theories. She has to be right. She can't admit she's wrong. When she talks to someone, she talks with an exclamation point.

I said, ''It does sound like me. I do often talk to you with an exclamation point. In fact, I think I fit very well with that guy who keeps trying to get ahead of you. Actually, I was all ready to do it again today. I wanted to figure out why your leg pains had come back, like it was a personal defeat if I couldn't.''

He replied:

> ''You don't give me enough credit. I'm very bright. I know when things are right or wrong. In fact, I even have a quote from Harry Stack Sullivan, who said that ''In the present state of our society, the patient is right and you are wrong.'' [Actually, I never knew about that quote, and wasn't at that moment delighted to have it brought to my attention; but in an unexpected way I found myself more interested in where he was going with it than whether it was leading me to where *I* wanted to go.]
>
> ''You compare me with an 'average' patient,'' he said angrily. ''So you make 'average' interpretations. I'm not average. I'm me. Behind my vagueness is a sharp brain—and you don't give me enough credit.'' [There was a long pause and I was feeling kind of stunned at his directness.]

He now had a pained look on his face that came and went, and came and went. I could sense his vacillation between a wish to dissociate ''just in case'' the presence of shame began to feel too great, and his simultaneous struggle to stay alive with me in the moment. I said, ''I can feel how terribly hard it is for you right now to hang in with me, after having just said what you did, and I'm thinking that maybe it's because a part of you might be scared that it's too much for our relationship to bear. Does that feel right, or am I off base?''

He replied:

> Yeah, It's hard to believe you are willing to hear this. It's hard to believe I haven't hurt you badly and that you're secretly hating me. I never said anything like this to you before. Actually, I don't think I felt it this clearly before. But I'm not finished with you yet. There's more. It's strange, though. Now that I said that, I also feel like I want to tell you that I appreciate your saying what you just said about how hard it was to hang in. You didn't have to say it, but you somehow knew I needed it. It wasn't just empty words, and it wasn't false sympathy. I *was* starting to get fuzzy. I was trying not to. I was fighting to keep myself from disappearing, and maybe I would have stayed here anyway, but your knowing about my shame—even though you didn't use the word—made me feel like it was worth staying here. You could have just let me be ''grown-up'' all by myself, and I might have done it, but another part of me would have continued to hate you. I can still feel that other part now—the part that hates you—but it really doesn't feel like a different

> part of me. I feel like I know something about you that I wasn't clear about before, and it's OK to know it.

I then asked him if he would like to go back to the running scene and try to let himself feel into it physically. We had done this before, so he was already familiar with what I meant. When he indicated that he was there, I then asked him to look around, and focus on visual images, sounds, physical sensations, and even smells. After a few moments he said, "It's funny. I can feel what a hot day it is. There's steam coming off the concrete." I asked what it is like to be running a race on such a hot day. He paused, and said that he felt great. "The heat's not getting to me, but I can see the face of the guy behind me, and *he's* feeling the heat. He looks like he's pushing too hard—wanting to pass me—and I'm seeing everything he's doing, and I'm getting stronger as we get to the finish line."

I ask what it's like to see him so clearly and he replies that it feels great; "Especially when I cut him off." I then asked him to move closer to the guy, so he can see his face very clearly as the guy is trying to pass him. When he indicated he had done that, I asked what the guy's face looked like. He began to fidgit, and said that right now he feels like I'm pushing too hard. "I don't want to look at his face any more. I think you want to lead me somewhere." I said, "Like I want to be ahead of you?" He replied, "Yeah, exactly." And then he got the point, and grinned. "Yeah . . . I see it now. It's weird. Suddenly I don't feel threatened by your leading me someplace. All right; I want to get back into the dream now, and look at his face." There was a long pause. "I can't figure it out, but he looks happy. He doesn't look angry that I'm going to cross the finish line and leave him behind. I feel a little sad now, and I don't know why."

I asked him to feel into this guy from the inside, and let himself experience what it is like to be him so that he can see himself through this guy's eyes. (This, also, is something he had done with me before in working with other dreams.) After a minute or so, tears began to run down his cheeks. "He likes me. He's feeling good for me, even though he lost the race. He's surprised at how strong I am at the finish line. He didn't know I had it in me because he saw me as a novice—but he's really happy for me that I ran my own race." I then asked, pushing it a little more, "What's it like to know he's feeling that way toward you?'' He replied, ''I want to come out of the dream now. I can feel what the dream is about and I want to talk about that.''

> I know why you keep trying to get ahead of me. Carol has a friend who looks like she is made up of feathers. She floats around, but underneath she's summa cum laude. I told Carol about being angry at you and she didn't say anything. First I felt hurt and then I felt better because she didn't jump in right away with something that was supposed to make me feel better. I began to feel like I could do something else besides feel helpless. It was weird! I could actually feel the pains in my legs start to go away in a way that they hadn't really gone away before. I liked it but I didn't like it. It didn't feel like ''me.'' I guess I don't know who I really am without my leg pains. As a kid, with pains in my legs I was powerless to run my own life and that felt like ''me.'' I couldn't have been athletic if I had wanted to. If I stop analysis, part of me feels like I'll be letting you win—maybe like you will win the race. You won't have to keep on following me, trying to keep up. You will get to your goal. But where will *I* be? All alone?
>
> So I guess I keep a race going—but you keep it going too, in your own way. You keep trying to ''one-up'' me; to get me to buy your ideas. And I always feel like it's my fault that you're needing to be right. But I'm not feeling that now. And it doesn't feel as alone as I thought it would. I sort of feel like I can give myself some of what you were giving me.

During the next six months his associations led to his recognition that as he was getting ready to leave analysis and go off on ''his own,'' he was more and more aware that he was being shadowed, as if by another part of him. ''Running,'' at this point, had become his metaphor for his newly found love of living life for its own sake—being in the immediate experience, but trying to get somewhere also. The guy behind him was, in this sense, the self-image he had always been burdened with—filling the emptiness of his being by compulsively ''pushing'' to get to some future goal—proving he was not a failure, proving he was good for something. The ''shadow'' runner in this dream was a version of the self-image that he used to have in earlier dreams of being in races in which he tricked his competitors in some manner and magically won the race but felt empty once he did. Now, he could see this figure as representing all the ways in which he had tried to control life rather than live it—to infuse vitality into a self deadened by dissociative isolation from full participation in the world.

As he approached the final months of treatment, the main insight of the dream was that this part of him *remains* important, even as he is terminating. He must never be "cured" of being that self or he will lose the creative energy that connects him to his own past—what is "behind" him that he can now own as a genuine past rather than enact as a substitute for the present. Because he is no longer as "possessed" by that self, he more and more feels its presence as an essential part of him that will "keep him moving"—a source of "forward" energy. But he knows he cannot afford to let it get ahead of him—ahead of his desire to live life by being in it, and he knows he must still keep an eye on his own capacity to "let it win," or he will lose his relatedness to the immediacy of life itself and will go back to his old feeling that life has not yet begun.

REFERENCES

Bosnak, R. (1996), *Tracks in the Wilderness of Dreaming.* New York: Delacorte Press.

Bromberg, P. M. (1998), Staying the same while changing: Reflections on clinical judgment. In: *Standing in the Spaces: Essays on Clinical Process, Trauma and Dissociation.* Hillsdale, NJ: Analytic Press, 1998, pp. 291–307.

——— (1999), Playing with boundaries. *Contemp. Psychoanal.,* 35:54–66.

——— (2000), Potholes on the royal road: Or is it an abyss? *Contemp. Psychoanal.,* 36:5–28.

Freud, S. (1900), The Interpretation of Dreams. *Standard Edition,* 4&5. London: Hogarth Press, 1953.

——— (1908), Creative writers and day-dreaming. *Standard Edition,* 9:141–153. London: Hogarth Press, 1959.

Korzybski, A. (1954), *Time-binding: The General Theory.* Lakeville, CT: Institute of General Semantics.

Levenson, E. A. (1988), The pursuit of the particular. *Contemp. Psychoanal.,* 24:1–16.

Mouchaux, C. de (1978), Dreaming and the organizing function of the ego. *Internat. J. Psycho-Anal.,* 59:443–453.

Reik, T. (1936), *Surprise and the Psycho-Analyst.* London: Kegan Paul, Trench, Trubner.

Sullivan, H. S. (1954), *The Psychiatric Interview.* New York: W. W. Norton.

Tauber, E. S., & Green, M. R. (1959), *Prelogical Experience.* New York: Basic Books.

Winnicott, D. W. (1967), The location of cultural experience. In: *Playing and Reality.* New York: Basic Books, 1971, pp. 95–103.

——— (1971), Dreaming, fantasying, and living: A case-history describing a primary dissociation. In: *Playing and Reality.* New York: Basic Books, 1971, pp. 26–37.

10

Daydreams: Another Royal Road

Marianne Goldberger

I am glad to be invited to walk on the royal road, because it gives me the chance to describe a somewhat different path, a less traveled road, daydreams, which also ends at the same destination as dreams: the unconscious. More specifically, I'll talk about a particular *kind* of day-dream, which I call a transference daydream because it involves a patient's thoughts and feelings about the analyst. Such daydreams can be created outside analytic sessions, or elaborated right there in an analytic hour. When they happen during an hour, one has a special opportunity to observe in detail an individual's defenses at work. Day-dreams, just like night dreams, can be studied as compromise formations. My emphasis is on the defense aspect of the compromise which automatically involves superego functions as well. Superego demands motivate self-critical and editorial functions.

I am borrowing the words *critical* and *editorial* from Martin Stein's 1989 paper, in which he used the words *critic* and *editor* to refer to the process of secondary revision of dreams. In a way, they apply even better to daydreams, since they are produced with a certain amount of volition, and thus cannot be as easily disowned. (People experience a dream while sleeping as something that just ''happened to them.'') Naturally, people edit their daydreams in any case, but when they have to be spoken out loud in the presence of an analyst, the tendency to edit is even stronger.

I am going to use illustrations of daydreams occurring during analysis to demonstrate how they can enhance our understanding of a patient's defenses, and therefore enhance the patient's chances of gaining access to the material protected by those defenses. I will focus on the criticisms and editing that go on as the daydream is being created. The ego's editing process is more accessible in daydreams than in dreams during sleep, because daydreams are much more under the patient's conscious control. At the same time, all clinicians are aware that patients are usually more hesitant to tell their daydreams, as compared to night dreams. Most people feel more responsible for daydreams. Thus the ego's defensive function can be revealed by carefully following a patient's difficulties in relating a daydream.

I want to digress briefly to compare daydreams and night dreams. Everyone knows that analysts have always been fascinated by dreams. In fact, people in general have always been fascinated by their dreams. Our patients are usually eager to tell us their night dreams. (there are exceptions of course, such as when the content is frightening or offensive to the dreamer). When stuck in a silence, patients sometimes express the wish that they had a dream to tell. It's a prepackaged production from the night and patients assume that analysts love dreams. People often have a little distance from a dream, some sense that, as I said before, it is something that just happened *to* them. With daydreams, by contrast, there is usually a strong sense of agency, and a strong feeling of privacy about them. The very fact of having daydreams often feels childlike and so patients may well feel embarrassed by them, especially if they are of the Walter Mitty type; that is, dreams of glory. Daydreams are closer to the analytic surface; patients are aware of this when they say that daydreams feel very personal. Note that people often tell their night dreams freely in social situations, but would not ordinarily do this with daydreams.

Some analysts may think that night dreams provide access to the unconscious because they occur in a different state of consciousness. But daydreams at times have more immediacy, as I shall try to demonstrate. Some patients are able to become increasingly comfortable with their own capacity to make up stories during an analytic hour, and can then make playful use of their imaginations.

Before I give specific illustrations, it may be helpful to contemplate the following paradigm. A patient comes late for an analytic hour, and starts talking about the analyst having looked annoyed when he came in. Actually, he is almost never late, and he goes on to describe the events that led to his lateness today. He doesn't think there was any "unconscious" motive making him late, but he speculates about some possibilities. Then his thoughts go back to the real adversities encountered en route today, emphasizing that they made him late despite the ample time he had given himself. The analyst comments that he sounds as if he is defending himself against an unspoken accusation. The patient agrees, and again mentions the annoyed expression he saw on the analyst's face. The analyst wonders if perhaps he has some ideas about *what* might be annoying about his lateness. After protesting that he "knows" this is probably not true, the patient speculates that since the analyst herself is almost always on time, punctuality must be important to her, and therefore she might think he doesn't take his analysis seriously enough if he is late. He says, "It's not so much that you dislike being kept waiting; it's the implied insult that's irritating, that it'll seem as if I don't think you're important enough."

That's the paradigm. Fantasies about the analyst, such as that one, can be viewed as daydreams which are invented right there during the analytic session itself, and have the potential for further elaboration. The paradigm hints at the fact that patients often are not even aware of *having* a daydream.

My first illustration comes from the analysis of Dr. A, a biochemist, who had an obsessional character with marked isolation of affect. Her inhibitions were particularly apparent in her fears of any manifestation of aggression. Here I need to describe my former Washington office. A freestanding three-car garage had been converted into an office, which was reached by an alleyway parallel to but half a block behind the one on which the front of my residence was located. It was situated in such a way that some patients remained unsure about which of two houses (on the front) belonged to the office. In the course of Dr. A's analysis some construction work, including several days of bulldozer activity, was done in the back yard which patients passed en route to the office parking area. So the construction was unavoidably conspicuous.

Dr. A began having a daydream that I was building a swimming pool, and she had considerable difficulty telling me about it. One reason for the difficulty was her awareness that her thoughts were accompanied by a sense of annoyance, and the idea that I was building it with her money. She was troubled that her feelings were distinctly "not nice," since her sense of worth was heavily dependent on thinking of herself as a nice person. After some analytic work on this issue, she was able to become aware of her resentment that I might earn more money than she. For some time, the pool issue remained on the level of thoughts of this kind, usually experienced as intrusive and alien.

One day, during an analytic session, she was a little surprised to find herself picturing people playing in and around a pool. As soon as she realized that this daydream had to do with my pool, she slowed down and then fell silent. She had become silent because of the annoyed feeling toward me that always made her uneasy. Although she knew better intellectually, she felt that I would dislike her if she expressed direct criticism of me. All the people in her family, her mother in particular, were touchy about criticism. The next day, the pool fantasy recurred, this time with children in it, playing and using a diving board. She fell silent, and toward the end of the hour said that her thoughts had taken "such a horrible turn" and were so "unspeakable" that she could not bring herself to tell me.

In the next session she did not remember the daydream until halfway into the hour. She forced herself to tell me her rejected thought, believing that this was expected in analysis, but accompanied her confession by repeated assertions that this was the most terrible thing she could possibly tell me. She said she had thought about those children around the pool as my children, and after insisting that she did not even know if I had any children, she said, "And I pictured that one of them got killed by diving into the pool." After a pause she continued, "And that isn't even the worst of it. The thought that passed through my mind that I can't stand to tell you is: it serves her right! That's the worst thing anybody can say to a mother. That means that I'm wanting one of your children to die. I can't stand it that I'm a person who's capable of even *thinking* such a thing.''

This session was actually a turning point in the analysis. Dr. A had told the daydream only under duress; she forced herself to say it out loud. This meant that she still maintained a certain defensive distance from the thoughts even as she said them—she disavowed them in a particular way. Her insistence on the vileness of her thoughts meant that she was still honoring her strong prohibitions against aggression. As long as she was in pain she demonstrated to herself and to me that she knew these thoughts were wrong, that she was suffering as a result of thinking them, and that she would try not to allow this to happen again. The intensity of the coercive tone with which she forced herself to talk about these thoughts made it clear to me that more analysis of her inability to ''own'' her aggression was necessary before she would be able to integrate the murderous content of the daydream.

The imperative need to keep her archaic prohibitions unchanged began to be understood when she experienced her fears that I would be extremely hurt by her striking me on a highly vulnerable spot, and that I would abandon her by removing myself from her emotionally. Her fantasies about the ''worst things one could say to a mother'' led to a new awareness of her capacity to entertain cruel thoughts, at the same time as she realized how thoroughly she had learned to inhibit such a capacity. It was during this period of analysis that for the first time she made meaningful connections with the era after her younger brother was born.

My second example also comes from when I was living in Washington. I worked with an analytic patient from an affluent and elegant diplomatic family, who said she almost never had thoughts about me. Since she was a sophisticated reader, she was aware that analysis had a lot to do with transference, but she said I was simply never on her mind. ''And besides,'' she said, ''I don't know anything about you.'' After several years of analysis, it became clear that she feared saying anything that would suggest that she was superior to me. With trepidation she admitted that she had noted what I was wearing at the beginning of every session, but had never commented, since it was ''none of [her] business.'' It took some time before she could tell me that her hesitation stemmed from her feeling that her clothes were much more fashionable and of better quality than mine.

A couple of years after she'd begun to talk about clothes, she was able to tell me that she sometimes had thoughts about the linen napkin covering the pillow of my analytic couch. That napkin somehow gave her an unpleasant feeling; she knew she did not want to talk about it, but had no idea why. This remained a puzzle until she revealed her distress about the fact that I did not live in a more elegant neighborhood, like the one where she lived. Now she realized that she had a persistent picture of me as "downscale," an idea that troubled her so much that she was hardly able to admit it to herself. She thought of me as the main source of income for my family and this meant I would have little money left for myself. That's how she explained why my clothes were not nicer. Then she connected her downscale view of me with the linen napkins, but could not say any more. I wondered about her initial hesitation to tell me her feelings about the napkins, but she had only the vague feeling of wanting to avoid the subject.

After many months of analytic work dealing with her considerable fears about saying anything that might be hurtful to me, she ultimately remembered that during her childhood, refugees had come peddling at her family's backdoor, showing a suitcase filled with linens from the old country. She had not thought of this memory since she was a child (though it had been consciously available), and she could not bear to connect that memory to me.

This patient's fixed daydream about me as downscale served important defensive purposes. It kept out of awareness any competitive feelings toward me, and allowed her feelings of sympathy for me to remain in the foreground. Only after the daydream was finally explored, could she entertain the possibility that there were areas in which she was more capable. She spoke cautiously about her superior sense of color and fabric. Although our ages were identical, she had always imagined that I was younger. Now she was able to mention, and then later enjoy, the fact that she had maintained a more youthful figure than I.

This example illustrates the occult aspect of daydreams. As the various elaborations about my being downscale slowly emerged, we realized that the picture of downscale had been present for a long time. Actually, it had become a rather fixed fantasy, a daydream. Only when a small bit of the fantasy came out of obscurity, could the rest of the daydream be brought into focus. An analyst needs to be sensitive to noticing the small bit of a daydream lying around, so to speak, and pick it up, so that the rest of the daydream that is still occult can be brought to the patient's attention. This makes daydreams less scarce in analytic material.

My next example comes from a colleague who has kindly allowed me to use detailed process notes from his analysis of an anxious and depressed woman writer in her twenties. The patient had been talking about her upset after a telephone conversation with her sister the day before. Her sister had brushed her off, saying this wasn't a good time to talk, and the patient felt she really had to talk to her about a particular issue. She said, "There's no use in playing this phone game that we always get into, and getting hurt and angry and guilty, all the same things over and over again without talking about the issue itself. It's hard for me to talk to her about this because I'm so neurotic and such a *spaz* and Lisa is really laid back, and I'm scared she's gonna say 'there's no problem.' "

After a long pause, the analyst inquired about the silence. The patient shrugged the matter off, saying "I don't know . . . It's not really important . . . I just don't wanna get into it . . . it's something I want to say to *Lisa* so why should I say it to *you*?"

The analyst said, "Maybe you're making it unimportant because you don't want to say it in front of me," and the patient said, "Well, I relate differently to Lisa from the way I relate to you."

Silence again. Then she went on.

> Okay, I'll just tell you and then it'll be over, and we don't need to discuss it. I thought about what I'd say to Lisa when I do call her again. This is what I'd say to her [and here's the daydream]: "I'm sorry I'm this way, such a spaz. I'm sorry I'm so neurotic and so hyper, but there's this thing that bothers me and I know it's not your fault, it's all me. I wanna talk to you so it won't happen any more, so we won't have a problem when we talk on the phone."
>
> Now I wanna call her, but the reason I didn't tell you is that I don't want you to think I'm a wimp. I talked to you about what I claim to be valid feelings, and then I diminish them when I plan my talk to Lisa. I want you to take me seriously. You see, that's why I didn't want to tell you because I was afraid you wouldn't take me seriously and then you'd be disapproving. [Pause] I wanna please you, I want to be a good patient,

> quote unquote, so I wanna do the good patient things, which is to stick with what I talked about in analysis. You stick with it, have some integrity.

Then the analyst said, ''If you do it differently you think I'm not going to like it. Apparently I want you to do it just how we talked about it.''

> Yeah, you'll look down on me. You'll say, ''Oh, you're so good in analysis but when you get out in the real world you suck.'' Also I'm disappointing you . . . you're thinking you're helping me, and then when I go backwards it's a disappointment, I'm letting you down. Don't you consider this your job? Don't you want to be successful at your job? [Pause] I have two things in my analysis I have to do—I have to come in with something interesting to say, hopefully a dream, and I have to go away improved in some way.

The analyst again, ''A dream is interesting but a daydream about what you plan to say to Lisa isn't.'' The patient responded:

> Well, daydreams are boring, they don't mean anything. Night dreams . . . well, I like my visual images. I think of myself as a creative dreamer, and I always find a lot to talk about in my dreams that I didn't know about, and also whenever I say I had a dream last night you perk right up. You don't care about daydreams. What's important about daydreams? They're deliberate . . . they sort of reflect what I say to you . . . but in this case it didn't . . . I mean this daydream that I just had was inspired by our talk, so I thought it was just exactly what we'd been talking about, until you actually made me say it, and then I realized that it *wasn't* what we'd talked about, it was different, it was a new version that was less scary to use; it was modified.

Now the analyst said, ''It's the new version you didn't want to say, because I don't want you to make new versions.'' The patient said:

> Yeah, I should stick to what you say; you're the analyst, you know more than I do. [Pause] Sometimes, if we discuss something about Jay [the patient's boyfriend] and then I talk to him, I say what we talked about, rather than being spontaneous. You know, I'll think back, now what did we say. 'Cause I know it's right . . . [Pause] Actually, I guess I was kind of lying then, too, I do modify it for Jay. [Laughing] Now that I think

> about it, I totally modify it for him. I water it down. Yeah, you and I talk about X and what I talk to other people about is watered down X.

This vignette illustrates several aspects of the use of daydreams in analysis. Initially, the patient was ready to delete the daydreams altogether, a common occurrence. And as I already said, sometimes patients don't realize they're actually having a daydream; only through the process of analysis do they become aware of their frequency. Once the patient was able to tell the daydream, her need for revision became clearer. The ever-present tendency to edit gave access to the patient's hesitations in speaking, and of course the analysis of those defenses yielded more information—about the transference, in particular.

In this example, the patient initially was aware only of her reluctance to tell her daydream. But as she told it, she realized she was troubled by having to reveal to her analyst that she'd edited it, because this made her think she'd revealed a weakness. She was certain this weakness would make the analyst lose respect for her. Exploration of her concern actually led to the expression of another daydream, and this other daydream was about the analyst's expectations of her. It had characteristics that one often sees in such transference daydreams; that is, some elements had already been formed at an earlier time, but were only now brought into the analysis, and, if the defense analysis has been adequate, spontaneous elaboration is possible.

Looking at the first daydream we can learn something about the patient's defenses. She said to her sister, "I know it's not your fault, it's all me." We see the aggression turned on herself. Another way of warding off aggression was demonstrated when she said she'd "watered down" the original version, taken all the sting out of it. Similarly, in the transference the patient was convinced that the analyst would approve of her only if she bowed to his authority, and renounced assertions of her own.

My last example comes from the supervised analysis of a man in his thirties, the oldest of several children born in quick succession, who came to analysis because of his severe sexual inhibitions. He was referred through a psychoanalytic clinic and was aware from the outset that his analyst was a candidate in training. During the third year of analysis, his analyst became pregnant, and although he'd previously been very hesitant to give voice to any thoughts or curiosity about her, at this point he was increasingly able to talk about his fantasies about her.

The sequence I'd like to describe contains old daydreams about the analyst, never spoken about before, as well as a new daydream which was spawned during an analytic hour. After analysis of defenses against verbalization of such daydreams, which have been preconscious or conscious all along, the patient also feels freer to have new, spontaneous elaborations.

When the patient first talked about the analyst's pregnancy, his upset feelings were dominated by envy, expressed primarily in terms of the analyst "having her life in order," in contrast to himself. He was concerned about her being away when the baby came, and even more concerned that she might be away for a long time, perhaps permanently. During this period he was starting to earn more money through freelancing. On one occasion he was elaborating on his difficulties charging by the hour for his freelance work. He realized he was reluctant to charge for all hours he had worked for fear that his client would leave him. The material seemed to parallel so closely the situation of his analytic fee that the analyst suggested such a connection. The patient had not been aware of this but he understood and was made uneasy by it. He soon mused, "What makes a person announce what they're usually paid . . . " consciously referring to his freelance fee. The analyst reminded him that during the consultation she had told him what her usual fee was. She suggested that he might have had thoughts about this subject at that earlier time, but had not spoken about them, and he might be close to recalling these thoughts now.

During the next analytic hour, the patient said he had been wondering why the analyst brought up the fee since he himself had not been aware of the fee issue. He said, "You don't usually just bring up something I haven't talked about at all." He then described a number of fantasies. He thought first that the analyst wondered how he handled his money, and why he apportioned money as he did. He thought that she was "just curious," not critical or intrusive. He emphasized that he uses his freelance income for "extras" and does not count it as part of his regular income. He also fantasied reasons why the analyst might need money, and said, "You've a right to say, 'What about me?' " (The analyst had recently moved into a new office.) Then he confessed that he'd often wondered about the reason she charged him a low fee. Maybe in the beginning she took him for educational reasons, but now that she was out of her student phase, surely she'd drop patients like him. Perhaps he should come only twice a week, and step aside for high-fee patients.

Then he talked about when the analyst had told him she was pregnant. He was pretty sure she'd told him only because she'd had to, that she would have avoided it if she could. He said he felt the analyst was angry about this, and then he became silent. He did not know what more to say. After the analyst addressed his difficulty in elaborating his picture of her being angry, the patient went on. The analyst had never answered his rare personal questions about her, but tried to analyze them, so he *now* said he had concluded that she strongly prefers to be anonymous. As he entered the office today his brief glance at her face had made him think that perhaps she was angry. Now he felt sure that this was the case, and that the reason was that she'd been forced to tell more about herself than she wanted to.

He returned to his image of her preferring to keep her pregnancy hidden from him. His thoughts now went to his mother's secretive ways. He had previously described his mother's furtive manner in regard to her affair with the man who was later to become his stepfather. He described in greater detail than before the forceful ways he felt she indicated that his curiosity was entirely unacceptable. He also mentioned that at the same time his mother would leave visible traces of her lover's presence in the house.

This example illustrates that interpreting the defense in a daydream may allow the patient to remember more details and even a whole forgotten segment of the daydream about the lowered fee. It also demonstrates how a patient's increasing ability to elaborate a transference daydream may facilitate understanding inhibitions, as well as the genetic origins of those inhibitions. This patient spontaneously made the connection to the genetic origins, and began to be able at last to be curious about the analyst.

In conclusion, I have shown that patients are commonly reluctant, even afraid, to reveal daydreams about their analysts. A frequent fear is that they may sound foolish, especially since the fantasies may not correspond with reality. Most patients require some time to discuss their embarrassment about saying something that might be "way off" about their analysts, before they're willing to mention their speculations out loud. After all, transference daydreams are inventions about the analyst. If we create an analytic atmosphere in which these inventions about the analyst are taken as a unique source of information, transference daydreams become more available.

The analysis of defense allows a patient to make the unattended background into a daydream. And I use the term *unattended background* to refer to thoughts available to consciousness but not put into words; that's why they're partly occult. Remember Fenichel's (1941) famous advice about interpretation: He pointed out that an intervention is at the right level if the preconscious derivative can be recognized as such by the patient, *merely by turning his attention to it*. That makes the manifest daydream story available to the patient. The occult portion is still warded off by defenses to the extent that forbidden impulses are contained in the story. (By the way, I've found that referring to these fantasies as ''stories'' is less threatening than calling them daydreams.) It's only by pointing out the inhibitions that limit more invention that the rest of the occult part can emerge. Only as the defense imagery of daydreams is analyzed, images of the analyst gradually shift from a restrictive authority to an object of sexual and aggressive drives, that is, the unconscious impulse.

REFERENCES

Fenichel, O. (1941), *Problems of Psychoanalytic Technique*. New York: Psychoanalytic Quarterly Press.

Stein, M. H. (1989), How dreams are told: Secondary revision—critic, editor, plagiarist. *J. Amer. Psychoanal. Assn.*, 37:65–88.

11

Disguised Imperatives: Dreams and the Dance of Basic Motivation

Mervyn M. Peskin

As Freud retrospectively noted in 1933 (pp. 7–30), the theory of dreams had been his true bearing in the confusing endeavor of arriving at an understanding of the unconscious workings of the mind. Unconscious instinctual wishes of childhood as they relate to current problems are the motivation for dreams. However, they are adaptively disguised and distorted and the disguise is disguised to the dreamer. Deception and self-deception in regard to basic motivation are integral to the dream and to the working of the mind. This I believe is the essence of what I retained of my original readings of *The Interpretation of Dreams* (1900).

Having studied earlier hominid evolution, in particular the remarkable expansion in volume and complexity of the hominid–human brain, I was impressed with this formulation. Darwinian fitness depends profoundly on social success in our species. The vastly more intricate levels to which social competitive exchange have been ratcheted up is one likely significant cause of the rapid increase in brain complexity and size. Moreover, sophisticated intimacy indicates a significant role for disguise in the playing out of motivations that are fundamental to the evolutionary success of the individual. A century ahead of current developments, Freud had attempted to incorporate a concept of innate motivation, contributing to the vicissitudes of early development, into a functioning model of the brain. He was the first to describe the powerful resistance that he came to understand inevitably opposed and disguised these motivations. As I have said elsewhere, I still believe that the pleasure–unpleasure principle is basic to the working of motivation; and as all psychological phenomena are correlated with neurophysiological phenomena, energy discharge *may* possibly be correlated with pleasure-unpleasure. However, a basic energy discharge principle, or any other neurophysiological correlate, is not part of a psychological elaboration of motivation (Peskin, 1997, 2001). Therefore instincts, or *innate specialized mechanisms* as they are currently called, should be considered from a purely psychological perspective without regard to any postulated energic correlates. As a psychoanalyst, I, like every analyst, have had the opportunity for a unique in-depth perspective on human motivation. Basic wishes from current life and from different stages of development, associated with different senses and different object representations, orchestrated and accompanied by emotions from joy to terror, displace, substitute, join, and conflict in a final integrated dance of motivation, much of which is unconscious. It is this unique perspective that offers us profound therapeutic possibilities and gives our data great potential value as part of neuroscience.

In retrospect, my clinical work with dreams shows a shift, perhaps common, from an expectation that they were specially revealing of the unconscious to a greater appreciation of the ubiquity of disguise in their formation. Very significantly this disguise is not only defensive, it also serves the covert achievement of goals or wishes. Together with a better awareness of the intricacies of transference-countertransference, from which the communication of a dream in psychoanalysis can never be free, I have grown skeptical of the idea that dreams are a special path, a royal road, or that there is any royal road, in the difficult endeavor of understanding the mind. I believe I do have a compass, but it is not the interpretation of dreams, as valuable as that often is. It is rather the psychoanalytic theory of the mind itself, whose elaboration was pioneered by Freud and in which the interpretation of dreams was his *via regia,* his magnificent route, as I would translate it, to his original understanding of the unconscious.

My work with dreams has naturally been influenced by clinical experience and by certain teachers who have themselves interpreted Freud and in some cases revised him. Prominent among these are the ideas of Brenner (1982) in regard to compromise formation and defense. The dream, I believe, is a compromise formation, much of which is unconscious, between wishes, defense, and self-punitive trends, in which the greatest amount of gratification is achieved consonant with the minimum degree of unpleasure. The unpleasure is of two types, anxiety, if the impending fulfillment of a wish is associated with a future fantasized danger, and depression or shame, if the fulfillment of a wish is associated with a danger which is fantasized to already have been incurred. This compromise formation (dream) inevitably interrelates with others. Most significantly for clinical work it interrelates with transference–countertransference fantasies and enactments. Thus there is considerable variation and complexity in the significance and role of dreams in psychoanalytic work.

There is of course one aspect of the dream that does distinguish it. Freed of ongoing external perceptions during sleep the mind is peculiarly occupied with its own desires at a time when higher cognitive functions (prefrontal cortical activity) are diminished. Taking a brief theoretical discursion, it is interesting to consider the question, Why then are failures of disguise so much the exception in dreams? Why do we not see more naked, undefended motivation? I would offer the following answer. From an evolutionary perspective, there is evidence that dreaming is an adaptation. The neuroelectrical correlates of dreaming are seen in every mammalian species studied. If so, it has likely been selected because it conferred an adaptive advantage. Psychoanalytic evidence suggests that in our species this advantage consists in the running through, or exercising, of basic motivational programs as they relate to mental representations of current experiences and current problems. However, defense and disguise are themselves coadaptive to motivation, both as a restraint and as an aid to achievement. Naked motivation is rarely adaptive. It is a crude modus operandus, tolerated, albeit briefly, only in childhood, and too unsophisticated for the complexities of family and social life, including the patient–analyst relationship. Thus dreams in which disguise is lacking would almost invariably be failures in an adaptive exercise. I would suggest that they include not only anxiety dreams but dreams in which other strong unpleasurable affects break through. I will start with the example of a dream in which depression and humiliation associated with the fulfillment in fantasy of certain wishes are prominent affects.

Mrs. A, in her thirties, a talented, emotionally tortured artist, emaciated and tense, prone to depression and rages, complained that after a promising start, in which she had excited the interest of many people, her career was "going nowhere." She had agonized over starting psychoanalysis, six months before, with much approaching and avoiding. She was conflicted over showing herself and her work and any attempt to gain insight into her motivations was especially fraught for her. I learned that she was involved in a sadomasochistic struggle with an overindulgent, underempathic maternal figure, whom she described as a "Behemoth, you never knew where you were with her." Mrs. A repeatedly developed intense attachments to people who unconsciously represented this figure, only to withdraw in anguish, accusing them of belittling behavior toward her. Often they broke off with her, saying she was too difficult to deal with. Prominent among these were certain homosexual women and Mrs. A was extremely upset at the idea she was "lesbian." She presented her husband as both domineering and someone who looked after her. The marriage was stormy and there were no children. Her father had died when she was a teenager. He was experienced as remote, somewhat self-involved, but gentle; no match for the behemoth, Mrs. A's mother. In her conscious thoughts I was predominantly experienced as gentle, though she was extremely wary of me. In a Friday session, after telling me yet again about the dismissive, humiliating behavior of a charismatic, well-known woman colleague who had taken an interest in her, I pointed out that, as on past occasions, she had at first been drawn to, hopeful, and excited by this woman, before once again being repelled by her. Knowing Mrs. A's volatility, I felt a certain apprehension in drawing her attention to this pattern. Sure enough she angrily disagreed. This woman was well known, well connected, and had a lot to teach. It was quite natural to seek her out and to be enraged by her dismissive behavior. Mrs. A left the session upset, which, given her balkiness at starting analysis, left me concerned.

However, after the weekend she reported the following dream. She is talking to F, a large, big-breasted woman acquaintance. The dream continues, and I quote: "I have to get away from her—across a bridge. My father is there sitting in his light blue sports car. He looks straight ahead. Then I am back close to F. She comes inside me and I have an orgasm." The dream left Mrs. A very depressed and she still felt humiliated. However, greatly animated, she emphasized that the orgasm was horrible, it felt like being electrocuted and that F was fat and physically disgusting. She then associated to her father in the dream. He had owned a fancy car like that. He seemed unresponsive, dead. She then returned to F, how rude and negating F was of her and her work. I asked if she thought her dream related to her feeling provoked by what I said on Friday about her being initially excited by the new woman. She said she was upset and confused by me but immediately went on to talk about her need for connections and proper mothering. Her mother had blown hot and cold, overindulgent and doting, or in a rage. She was all over you. It was humiliating to talk of her.

Unusually, Mrs. A was very late for the next session. She apologized repeatedly but asked with the same animation as the day before, did I think she "wasn't going to show?" The woman colleague had called to see how she was and they had spent an enjoyable and very helpful time together. She had lost track of how late it was. I interpreted that contact with this powerful woman was so important and pleasurable to her that it made her lose track of time and forget about me. She apologized again, and "really hoped that" I wasn't upset. She felt so good to be with this colleague. In a following session she associated to how she could feel elated, as if she were ballooning, when one of these "maternal" women paid close attention to her and praised her, but that she could then easily be deflated by them. It was like a rollercoaster. She felt she was a "plaything in their hands."

I believe this dream did fulfill in fantasy certain childhood nurturing and sexual wishes related to being filled up, which were accompanied by orgasm. However, they were highly conflicted and they constituted only one part of the compromise making up the dream. First, Mrs. A was made much more anxious by the sexual wishes than the nurturing ones, though both were important and both aroused anxiety. In both dream and associations she defensively used the nurturing wishes to disguise the sexual wishes and treated the amalgam thus created as if it were purely nurturant (F is big breasted and is disgusting not sexually arousing, and in her associations Mrs. A now acknowledges that she needs mothering). This is an example of reaction formation (disgusting not arousing) and one wish having defensive function against another (nurturant defending against sexual). Their fulfillment was associated both with pleasure and with unpleasure. She felt humiliated and depressed at being deflated and belittled (i.e., becoming mother's plaything at the same time as she is gratified by mother). Depression and humiliation were the predominant affects of the dream. The orgasm was intense but not pleasurable. The dream also incorporated more current transferential issues. Unconsciously experiencing me as the overstimulating maternal figure, the dream is a reaction to my interpretation.

At the same time she became strangely animated, excited, in associating to this dream which I experienced as quite dramatic. It represents an attempt in fantasy and in the transference to arouse her impassive, dead father. But her wishes to excite and connect with him are punished in fantasy by the dangerous, enticing mother, whom she cannot pull herself away from. She is electrocuted, punished, gratified, and deflated at the same time. The fulfillment in fantasy of the wish to be totally gratified as mother's plaything predominated, though consciously she predominantly experienced this dream and the accompanying orgasm as deflating and depressing. Lastly, there are aggressive wishes to be the overstimulating sadistic figure, "with whom one never knows where one is," which I experienced to some degree countertransferentially in response to the dream and her behavior in the transference, of which the dream was a part. I experienced apprehension at her anger, fear she would leave, followed by surprise and interest in the dramatic dream, then anxiety at her not showing up, then pleasure at our progress. These aggressive wishes and the wishes to arouse which were to prove important in our work, were not conscious to Mrs. A. They play little part in the manifest content of the dream where they are disguised by other very important conflicts involving the nurturing and sexual wishes. Thus this revealing dream is a compromise between nurturing and sexual wishes and other, aggressive wishes, and the gratification, unpleasure, punishment, and defense associated with them. Her enactments in the transference and the conflicts disturbing her life can be recognized as made up of similar compromises. Mrs. A subsequently developed a sexual fantasy of being put over a man's knee and spanked. While this remained humiliating she was aroused by it and took pleasure in the accompanying orgasm. Thus in this new compromise formation wishes to be babied, sexually stimulated, and punished are still involved, with the one crucial difference that the dominant person doing this was not a woman but a man.

My next example is of the use of two dreams involved in the complex compromises of a developing transference. Mr. B, an unmarried, successful professional man in his thirties, came for treatment on account of impotence and feelings of insecurity, after he was confronted by a girl friend with whom he had been impotent that he "had a problem and better do something about it!" Formerly he had rationalized his potency problems, blaming women for being too aggressive or too critical. He had grown up in an Eastern European communist country, the child of an unhappy marriage. His mother, an ardent communist, was beautiful, domineering, and scornful of his much older father, who was tired and sickly. Mr. B revealed that he felt himself to be weaker and less robust than other men and had to rely on what he called "clever and sometimes dirty tricks" to keep ahead. He constantly felt insecure as a child and still felt that way. He remembered that his mother had been critical of him and would threaten to give him away to gypsy women, who were dirty but sexy. They practiced black magic which terrified him. He had great fears of infection involving his crowded home and the many illnesses he witnessed including an illness of his mother's when he was 7. He longed to get away and fantasized traveling to open, faraway places, like beaches. Fantasies of his psychoanalysis as a journey, both back to his childhood and away from it, had emerged in which dreams played an important part. I was experienced both as a wished for, feared, and envied male guide, and in a KGB–mother transference, as an investigator building a dossier on his defects.

In the second year of his analysis, as he put it, "a fantasy came true." On a trip to South America he met a woman on the beach. She was beautiful, passionate, and playful. She was divorcing her ne'er do well husband and had accepted Mr. B's invitation to visit him in New

York. He was overjoyed. He felt better, doubted he would need to stay in treatment, reported no dreams, was derisive about what I had to say, and missed sessions. However, her approaching arrival was not only stirring triumph and joy. He was growing anxious as well. Like the sexy gypsy women, he now told me, she believed in the occult and that they had met in a previous life, and like his mother she could express fury and scorn at her husband.

After talking of these anxieties he reported a dream: "I am a child riding on a tram. My father is sitting opposite." As it is about to leave, a last passenger boards and sits next to him—a woman dressed in black, dirty and disheveled, she looks like a punk but quite sexy. "This woman leans over and tongue kisses my father; he is embarrassed but gets into it. She comes across to start with me. I am angry and push her away and wake up with a scream." He associated further to his mother's illness. She had been hospitalized with a severe "brain infection." He had been terrified of losing her and getting a stepmother, a word which he told me translated literally in his native language meant evil mother. His mother had returned from the hospital with her head completely shaven and was constantly irritable. He was afraid of being infected by her. I said he made it sound as if he had lost his mother and she had been replaced by an evil mother. Mr. B was very moved, sad. He then observed that it was very unusual for him to dream of his father. I said that I felt telling me the dream was a way of asking for my help after shutting me out. Perhaps, I suggested, he was letting me into his life again like he had let his father into his dream. He was impressed with this interpretation saying I had some "good tricks too."

But in the next session he produced another, two-part dream. He is to go on an expedition in central Asia. His equipment isn't ready. He is invited to have tea with some people but grows impatient and decides to leave anyway. In the second part he meets two cute girls and a weird guy on a bicycle, wearing a black sleeveless vest and a black cape with red-orange in it—like a Hare Krishna. He is queer; a circus performer. The girls admired him and Mr. B was envious. He went on to say that he had recently read of the reopening of the Karakoram route, Marco Polo's route. As a boy he had been fascinated by Marco Polo. He supposed that having tea referred to me—what insipid Englishmen spend their time doing. I wondered whether Marco Polo, an explorer and guide, also referred to me; at least he had my initials. Mr. B laughed, he had read about an English cyclist riding the whole route. I said that needing my help and being so impressed with my interpretation yesterday, he needed to put me down as a ludicrous figure with trivial powers lest he become too admiring like the girls in the dream.

Soon after he revealed that when insecure after rejection by women he masturbated with homosexual fantasies of being strengthened by men. However, intense competition also plays a part in forming the dream. He wishes to set off before me and before he is ready (i.e., to leave psychoanalysis), which was to become an intermittent threat of his. Setting off first is both an attempt to outdo me and also has a defensive function against his passive wishes. Furthermore, the Hare Krishna aspect (and my being dressed in black like the woman in the previous dream) were not only derogating. Hare Krishnas can seduce people and steal them away, like the gypsy women. He also had the fantasy that if he were loved by an idealized, magical woman he would be superior to other men. However, when faced with actually performing sexually with such a woman, in reality and not in fantasy, he felt insecure. His wish for magical reinforcement from a man, in order to stand up to the woman sexually and not be rejected and infected by her, gained force. This accounted for his behavior leading up to the dream. His wishes for love from the magical woman were satisfied; he did not need me, and I was derided like his father. As she approached his bed her demonic side accentuated in fantasy, and he needed help.

The first dream is a compromise between his sexual wishes, his fears of the powerful woman, and the defensive wish for a man's protection. The dream itself is an opening he gives me to help him. But my wished for help arouses fear and envy, he is too impressed. He responds with the second dream whose formation is a compromise of wishes for help, gratification in being helped, the fear and envy aroused by these wishes, and the defensive denigration and displaced admiration, which reduces the fear and envy and disguises the wishes for my help. There are also important competitive wishes, which in this dream play mostly a defensive role, though they are also gratifying.

Now a symposium on the use of dreams will tend to select for useful dreams. At least that has been true in my case. It should be noted, however, that there are many times where dreams are less directly useful in regard to their content and it is their deployment in unconscious strategies involving the analyst that is more significant. Such was the case with a patient who had many dreams which I thought were valuable and tried for some time to interpret. But the most useful interpretation turned out to be that she was feeding me, beguiling me, and keeping me at bay with the flow of dreams. This interpretation led not to more useful dreams or more useful associations but to her stopping this production of dreams, and talking with anxiety of why she needed to behave this way. A dream may contain a precious revelation or constitute a deceptive decoy or evasion.

In conclusion, what I hope to have shown is that although I do not believe that dreams are a unique road to an understanding of unconscious conflict and compromise, they are important compromise formations valuable in interpreting the intricate, shifting tides of motivation, which Freud, using dreams as his lodestar, was the first to navigate.

REFERENCES

Brenner, C. (1982), *The Mind in Conflict.* New York: International Universities Press.

Freud, S. (1900), The Interpretation of Dreams. *Standard Edition,* 4 & 5. London: Hogarth Press, 1953.

——— (1933), New Introductory Lectures on Psycho-Analysis. *Standard Edition,* 22:1–182. London: Hogarth Press, 1964.

Peskin, M. M. (1997), Drive theory revisited. *Psychoanal. Quart.,* 66:377–402.

——— (2001), Back to basics—The psychoanalytic conceptualization of motivation. *Psychoanal. Inq.,* 21:658–674.

Discussion

Chair, Ruth Imber
Discussants, Philip M. Bromberg, Marianne Goldberger, Mervyn M. Peskin, and Audience Members

Marianne Goldberger: When I was in training the idea was common that it was questionable whether patients could be analyzed if they didn't dream. I don't know how many people subscribe to that any more: I certainly would not subscribe to it, and sometimes analysis results in people dreaming. I had one patient where I recommended analysis, and she said, "I can't do analysis because I have no memories and I never dream." She became the most prolific dreamer, really creative dramas. I think that old dictum probably has disappeared by now. So the question arises, Why not ask the patient to make up a dream? Several people have mentioned to me that when doing child therapy—they were only asking children to make up stories, so why not ask the adults to make them up? I think it is a very pertinent question and there is nothing wrong with doing it, you just do it a little more subtly with an adult than with a kid. With a child I might say,

"If you want to make up a story about that, I'll be your secretary." And then they often are happy to do that. But there are adult ways of saying the exact same thing. I wouldn't say make up a story, but I certainly would say something that sounded suggestive, "Can you say something more about that?" That's the same thing.

In my view, there isn't much difference between fantasy and daydreams, they are on a continuum. My thoughts about the lack of difference emerged when I was asked to write a paper about daydreams and I found it a clinically useful way to think about the material. Martin Stein, in honor of whom I wrote that paper, disagreed with me when discussing the paper. He said that one should use the word *daydreams* only for those fantasies that were the most planned, elaborated, with detailed situations. Another reason to focus on daydreams was the analytic adage that patients don't often tell you their daydreams. For many people they are more private than dreams, and this might be an issue of technique. If you think of fantasies and daydreams as being on a continuum, you might be more aware of their potential existence and facilitate patients mentioning them.

Ruth Imber: This is what confuses me because patients are always telling us fantasies, but they are only telling us fantasies. You are telling us that they don't comfortably share daydreams. So there is some difference that you are trying to get at.

Marianne Goldberger: I think it also has to do with labeling. Some patients are immediately threatened if you say, "Do you have any fantasies about that?" "Me have fantasies? Am I crazy?"—to the unsophisticated. It is not so unusual that the idea of fantasy is frightening, as if you are slightly off if you fantasize. Especially children, "You do too much fantasying." So, I think fantasy also can be threatening for certain people. For other people, of course, they are aware it is a very creative activity.

Philip Bromberg: I'm the one non-Freudian on the panel. I look at it a little differently. I kind of look at daydreams as an intermediate place between fantasy and imagination. The distinction, which is always most interesting to me, is the distinction between fantasy and imagination, the ability to conceal oneself in a given situation in which we are who we are now, rather having to be a different person who you can't really see as yourself. The latter is closer to what I see in fantasy. I think as an analysis progresses one of the touchstones of the work's being beneficial is that a patient is more and more willing to make a transition between fantasizing about something and imagining it. I see the ability to daydream as sort of transitional space. A person has to make a choice between whether this situation could in fact exist as a real model or still requires some more change. There was another part of this question which also interested me, the idea of inviting a person to daydream. The way I work makes it very easy to invite somebody to daydream, because I am always speaking to whatever aspect of self that exists. There is much less conflict around having to own something and thinking that one's self really blends into another. In a sense I am inviting that part of the self which isn't at the moment present to be there in the session with its voice, and it has to do with a daydream but in fact it is really the same principle that I was describing in the way I was working with the patient in the paper that I presented.

Mervyn Peskin: Commenting on what Philip Bromberg just said. He would see fantasizing, daydreaming, and night dreaming as different self states, and I could resonate with that clinically, although I wouldn't conceptualize it as self states. I would see an important role for motivation and defense. I may ask a patient "What comes to mind?" and the more unpleasure, anxiety, shame they experience the more they will be unable to have a fantasy or reveal a daydream.

For instance, I had a patient who was very reluctant to talk about me let alone fantasize. The first time she did so was after I was late answering my buzzer one day. She angrily asked, "What happened to you? Where were you? I was worried about you. I thought you were lying on the floor stabbed, dead, robbed—and I was jabbing that buzzer the whole time!" We eventually got to her wishes to jab me and let me have it. As I understand it, the reason she was able to elaborate her thoughts (fantasy) about me being jabbed to death on this occasion was because she felt I had done something hurtful to her. She was a victim and therefore less guilty. Her wishes to hurt me, for a host of reasons, could be expressed in the fantasy. Maybe this could be conceptualized as different self states but I would still see a crucial role for motivation and defense.

But a daydream would be something that the patient creates and coddles as it were, has pleasure in and nurtures. You have to own a daydream in a way you do not own a fantasy which can be random. I still believe defense is involved in these different forms of mental production.

Ruth Imber: I am going to go in another direction now. Taking off from a question that was originally directed to Mervyn Peskin, what is the meaning and how do you work with patients reporting orgasms in dreams? One of the things that I was struck with in terms of the three presentations is that Philip Bromberg, being the non-Freudian, seems to focus least on the body. Marianne has the patient with the clothes, which I think starts to move through the body. Mervyn, of course, has full-blown sex. Philip Bromberg certainly gets to very important issues, aggression and competition, with this patient, but I am wondering whether there are differences in how the three view what is being defended against or represented in dreams. Whether in a basic way you think you can get to more bodied, embodied, experiences through dreams, more childlike, you know. In theory we talk about childhood wishes and all that, but I mean, literally, can you then talk with the patient more about the body? Would Philip Bromberg use a dream to do that? Or would he keep it on the level of competition in a more disembodied way?

Philip Bromberg: Maybe I wasn't clear enough in the way I explained what I was trying to do in the approach that I was taking to dreams. It's all about the body. In enabling somebody to get back into a dream, as a space in which they existed and can exist again in the session, it is all about the body and sensory experiences. It includes trying to enable them to get back into the body in which they were in the dream and feel intimate physically, so that they can actually feel things like temperature, the degree something was happening. They feel it personally as a total psychosomatic experience, and the more questions that I ask that have to do with their connection to the experience that is going on in the dream, the more physical it becomes, the more it brings affective experience into the dream in a live way. So that the associative process begins through the physical experience of the dream itself, rather than through thoughts about the dream. So it's totally physical.

Mervyn Peskin: And I would say in regard to the first patient I spoke about, that it isn't all about the body. This patient did tend to have dreams with orgasm, which dreams changed in nature and content. But what developed in working with these dreams and the conflicts involved was that she was able to develop strong, mutually supportive, invigorating relationships with other women in her life both as friends and professionally. She was physically emaciated to begin with, she could not take in psychologically and bodily from anyone, unless she was intruded upon in fantasy. She put on weight. She is an attractive woman. Her career improved, because of these nurturant and exciting relationships that she is now able to better maintain with these other women and men in her life, who have been professionally very valuable and useful to her.

So the analysis of something drastically sexual, if you will, had everything to do with lessening her suffering and self-imposed emotional starvation and she has blossomed in ways that aren't strictly concerned with the body at all, though you can see and understand the role of her body in the compromise formations involved in her symptoms and her improvement.

Ruth Imber: Do you think that you privilege reports of sexual experience?

Mervyn Peskin: No, I don't think so. I chose this case and this material, because I thought it was very interesting and illustrative of how I work with dreams. There is also a contemporary danger of underprivileging sexual material. One other element that I thought was very interesting was that the physiological experience of orgasm, which is normally associated with pleasure, was as part of this patient's conflicts, an unpleasurable, electrocutionlike experience. This shows just how important psychological conflict can be in determining what is experienced as pleasure.

Marianne Goldberger: I think the issue of self states is extremely important and I realize that part of the communication has to do with what language we use. If we take that woman who was upset about the swimming pool, and translate what I said, that she has an extremely high investment in being nice. So let's say she could not bear being someone who would have nasty thoughts; that's a different state. And what I mean by "own" is actually saying, that's why I think state is a very good way of thinking about it, if she could experience herself as someone who could also be nasty sometimes, she would not need to disavow that part of herself and that different state.

Philip Bromberg: This too bears on a question that was asked before that I didn't comment on, What about patients who don't dream? I have found that very frequently, patients who don't dream, as we work, begin to dream the more I talk to them in self-state language. I'm not saying to them, "You feel this" or "You also feel that," so that they have to hold two incompatible ways of doing it in the same consciousness, and they can't. If I talk to them saying, "There's a part of you that is feeling different from what you are feeling now," it is as though that part of them sort of wakes up and says, "Oh, you know about me." And the first indication that this is happening is often in a dream, which is the last thing you are going to expect from that patient, because that patient is not a dreamer.

Ruth Imber: Another question that came up in a discussion involves whether Philip Bromberg, and Marianne Goldberger, and Mervyn Peskin would work differently in terms of confronting or interpreting defenses as they appear in dreams. My sense is that Philip Bromberg does not like to have to use either confrontation or interpretation, if possible. He prefers to create an atmosphere of safety and letting things unfold, whereas I think the other two panelists would be more active in showing the defenses and trying to reduce them.

Mervyn Peskin: This gives me an opportunity to say something that working as a compromise-formation clinician, I think is important to get across. I think that people who work with conflict or compromise-formation theory try to be clear about what they are doing. I certainly tried to be clear and focused in my presentation, at least as much as time allowed. However, sharpness of clinical detail does not equate to sharpness of technique. I believe this dream was evoked by my saying to my patient that she had first been excited and filled with hope by her colleague before feeling so put off by her. I was saying something she needed to hear, and maybe there is a confrontation in that. With the other patient, when I said, "perhaps Marco Polo also refers to me," I was helping him to see something he had not been aware of, but was there a confrontation in the perjorative sense in either case? The word *confrontation* sometimes worries me when it is brought up in these contexts.

Marianne Goldberger: I was going to say that the analysis of defense is exactly about safety. I think we are quite together, just maybe the language is different. If I say something about defense to a patient, I am saying, "You don't feel safe here." It is all about safety. You don't need defenses if you feel safe. Of course, you can never feel entirely safe.

Philip Bromberg: With me the issue of defense is very complicated because working from a self-state point of view, I don't see defense in the central way that a conflict theorist is going to see defense, because I don't see the issue of conflict in the same way that conflict theorists see the issue of conflict. I see conflict as something that develops in the course of the analysis, not something that simply gets analyzed in the course of analysis. I see that the capacity for conflict is something that tends to develop so that after an ability to experience conflict develops in a certain area then there is much more in evidence in my mind in the work for what traditionally is looked at as a defense against the conflict. It is quite possible then to be able to interpret in a much more traditional way, but until that happens, the word *defense* simply gets in the way for me because it is not so much a defensive process as it is an inability of different parts of the self to be able to coexist in the same state of consciousness. You could look at it as, I suppose, one part of the self being the favorite against another to keep it out. But it is not terribly useful, I feel, to look at it that way because it violates the integrity of each part of the self. So if you can address each separately, not one as a defense against the other, you would be able to more and more get a dialogue between them that is much more complex than one being a defense against the other.

Marianne Goldberger: I agree with you entirely about the dialogue becoming explicit, but I have to take issue with what you are saying about the conflict beginning in the analysis. You have mentioned an experience that I am sure all of us have had, with your 2-year-old in the other room where you can't see him, saying, "No, no," and you know you'd better get in there because that kid is up to something, though he is already conflicted about it.

Mervyn Peskin: I would also agree with what Marianne Goldberger has just said. Regarding Phil Bromberg's remarks on complexity, I would note that there is no shortage of complexity when you work with compromise formation and defense. When he carefully works with the manner different self states relate and the reasons they are held apart, I would see the gentleness as part of all good technique and the dynamics between self states as significantly defensive. I would conceptualize them that way and try to be as gentle as he tries to be.

Ruth Imber: On a different topic. This was directed to Phil Bromberg but I think that the questioner would probably be interested in everyone's reaction if they have one. How do you view flashbacks, most common in posttraumatic stress disorder and also in fugue states in the spectrum of dissociation?

Philip Bromberg: I view them in a way that is not so different from the way I was describing this patient that I presented in a dream called "Snapshots," referring to snapshots that were not in an album. I see them as real experiences of some events that have a level of negative affect that was so entirely high that it could not be processed cognitively into narrative memory. So that the visual experience remains unprocessed in terms of meaning to the person. So what you get is something we are all familiar with, which is a person who has experienced trauma and ends up knowing that something happened to them but they can't say it with any degree of self-validity because there is no internal self-narrative that holds that experience as part of it. So the work becomes a kind of helping the person to process the experience, and sometimes it can be done without including your relationship to the patient with it, although that can be necessary. The example that I gave was with someone who was ready to do this in a relationship with me, but very often somebody is not ready and the best advice is to try and stay out of the mix and help them process the memory without intruding yourself into it. It's a kind of a gathering of experiences that have no narrative meaning. If you really talk about it together, you have to be thinking about what your patient is saying, and responding in a way that is going to let them see not only that you get what the experience is, that you have them in your mind, but your mind is actively engaged with it. So that they then have a representation of the other person who is thinking about what is going on in their mind. Anyway, it is what Peter Fonagy called the relevance of mentalization. But it's a process that gets to be very central in the process of trauma, and this includes flashbacks. I have done a lot of work in adult onset trauma, so it is much more central to me than to others over there.

Audience Member: I don't follow Phil Bromberg's last exposition on trauma. I am asking something that occurred to me before the last question. I am thinking about multiple personality. I know that's a loose term, but there it is. I'd like to ask the panel to discuss or define its relationship here to daydreams, to what they called imagination, and the difference between imagination and fantasy. Because to me, multiple personality is like renting a series of film scripts. Each fragment, each personality, seems to have its own script. I think it is kind of fascinating in view of this panel to see how you would see it.

Marianne Goldberger: Well, in one way you are right back to Papa Freud who talked about dreams as representing ourselves perhaps in every piece of the dream. It wouldn't even have to be a human being, and when I wrote that paper about dreams (1989) that you referred to, I talked about dreams as being a multiple personality experience in which maybe for the first time a person experiences the self in a different way. So in that way a dream can make room for imagination where one might not otherwise be able to do that. I think perhaps that's why people are attracted to dreams because we are everywhere in every dream if we are able to experience it that way.

Philip Bromberg: I was hoping that I could get away with not having to respond to the question about multiple personalities. The reason is I'm afraid that if I respond I will give the impression that somehow the way I work is closely allied to working with multiple personality, because I have such a commitment to dissociative processes. I feel the issue of multiple personality itself is so complicated that I could say different things about it. I do think that working analytically with someone who has a dissociative identity disorder is quite possible and often can be successful if you are doing more or less with the same attention to self states that I have been advocating in routine psychoanalytic process. Though in working with a real multiple it introduces some additional factors in management that make it at times look like it is not analytic. Regardless of whether the patient happened to be defined as having a multiple personality, it has to do with enabling the patient to get closer and closer to the actual experience that they live with in that state in its own terms.

Like Ruth Imber's question about the body—when I asked my patient to focus on visual images, sounds, and physical sensations and he said, ''It's funny, I can feel what a hot day it is.'' Now that's in part because I didn't ask a question, ''What kind of a day was it?'' I asked ''What kind of a day is it?'' And that is simply one example of the way I would try to focus the experience into another. And he did it. He said, ''I can feel what a hot day it is, there is steam coming off the concrete.'' Now, I know that the word *concrete* is a wonderful moment because it verifies my theme. I said, ''What is it like to be running a race on such a hot day?'' And he said, ''It feels great.'' So he is describing his experience in the moment of where he is in that dream. He said, ''The heat's not getting to me, but I can see the face of the guy behind me and he is feeling the heat.'' So, it's an experience in which he is gathering into himself the actual event that takes place in the dream and when it gets connected to what's taken place between the two of us, there is no doubt in his mind that the experience is authentically him, so that there is much less likelihood of his dissociating again.

Audience Member: Do you have any thoughts one way or the other about patients, particularly patients who can only be seen once or possibly twice a week, writing down dreams? Patients often ask whether they should write them down. I know people have different thoughts about that technique.

Marianne Goldberger: I think that this is like a lot of precepts in analysis. You know when it is obviously being used in a way that is not helping the analytic dyad get closer to what is going on. Why make a rule about it? Sometimes, somebody who is extremely motivated writes down dreams, and Fenichel says, "The patient determines the subject of the hour." And I must say that I don't see any need to change that.

Mervyn Peskin: I would agree to that in regard to rules. As they say in the fight movies, the only rule is that there are no rules. Sometimes it can be highly productive when a patient is motivated to write down a dream. But the writing down has a meaning and that meaning will depend on what is motivating the patient and why they are writing down the dream. In this regard let me say that though dreams can be very helpful, as we have heard throughout this panel, there are times when they are best understood as decoys. I recall a patient, a prolific dreamer, whose further progress in analysis was associated with her stopping to produce her elaborate dreams, which were being used to fend me off and beguile me, and her starting to talk about why she needed to behave this way.

Philip Bromberg: For me, if a patient comes in with a dream that's written down, I want to know whose dream it is. Who had the dream? And sometimes the patient comes in with the dream and they have no associations with the dream. So that makes it obvious that the person who is bringing in the dream is not the person who dreamed it, so you see who dreamed it and bring the dreamer in. There are certain patients who write their dreams down frequently and it is almost like an individual way of communicating from a part of yourself that wasn't ready to be in the session; it's like writing a letter, so it matters to be able to talk about the writer.

REFERENCE

Goldberger, M. (1989), On the analysis of defenses in dreams. *Psychoanal. Quart.,* 58:396–417.

Part III
Commentary and Rejoinder

Chair, Owen Renik

Commentary

Sydney Pulver

The papers in this volume represent a variety of viewpoints, including the relationists, the researchers, Mahlerians, Kleinians, evolutionary theorists, Anna Freudians classical analysts, and conflict theorists. I will focus on the clinical aspects of the presentations. My basic thesis will be that, although our panelists come from different psychoanalytic schools, they all work with dreams in much the same way. With two exceptions, they seem to share the view that thinking takes place out of the realm of consciousness, that people have feelings they don't know about and that they do not wish to know about, and that they keep themselves from knowing about those feelings in order to prevent unpleasant affects from being aroused; that is, they use defenses. Most of the panelists seem to share the conviction that our job in psychoanalysis is to help our patients to understand what feelings they are trying to remain unaware of, and to understand the ways in which they protect themselves from this awareness and the reasons why they do so.

Given this general agreement as to approach, it should be worthwhile to direct some questions to the two panelists who seem to approach things somewhat differently. I am not suggesting that James

Fosshage does not feel that there is an unconscious or that patients don't use defenses, but merely that his approach to dreams as illustrated by the material he presented, seems to reflect, not the conflict theory used by most of our panelists, but rather a theory of deficit or developmental arrest.

James Fosshage's theory of the therapeutic process seems to be a developmental one. The young man he described was just beginning to come into touch with some of the warm feelings that he had about Fosshage. In his dream, someone else was moving into the basement of Fosshage's house, and the patient was saying complimentary things about his analyst. James Fosshage described this as a developmental achievement, something which the patient couldn't do before because he had never learned to feel that kind of feeling. Fosshage implies that the therapeutic process is essentially a kind of learning process, that his patient, through a corrective emotional experience, gradually developed the ability to feel warmly toward and intimate with him. It was, as Edna O'Shaughnessy noted, as if nothing unconscious was occurring. I think most of the other panelists would view this young man in different terms. They would say that for some reason, his feelings toward Dr. Fosshage were troublesome, and that he needed to repress them. They would further say that, in the course of therapy, he had come to understand some of his anxieties about these feelings and was therefore more free in feeling and expressing them. My question then for James Fosshage is: Does he in fact view this young man's problem as purely a developmental arrest, or does he view it (as I suspect most of the other panelists would) as conflict laden?

If we turn now to the way that our panelists work with the dream, two themes emerge. First, they all get associations to the dream and second, they are all interested in the transference, in what is going on between the patient and themselves.

Several issues related to associations arose. Perhaps the most interesting is the question, How do you get people to associate? Some of our panelists simply asked their patients what came to their mind about specific dream elements. In some situations, they simply waited and patients began to associate by themselves. We can presume that early on in the treatment many patients were asked for associations and some learned that this is the way to understand dreams. Some of them, of course, might have been those wonderful people who associate spontaneously, "I dreamt about a blond woman. My mother is blond you know." All of the panelists, whether they asked for associations or not, treated the material in the sessions, both before the dream and after the dream, as if they were associations to the dream itself.

It is interesting to try to understand why therapists asked for associations to specific elements at the particular time that they did. Much of the time, it seemed to be a hunch. Something in the dream struck the analyst, and for reasons which they probably would not be able to put into words, led them to think that associations would be useful in further explaining things. Examples of this type of hunch would be Edward Nersessian and the stony testicles and Paul Lippmann and the red nose. Aside from hunches, our panelists were clearly led to ask for associations if it seemed that there was a relationship of the dream element in some way to the analyst. Here, there was a tendency not just to ask for associations, but to make a kind of interpretation: "Do you think that might be connected in some way with me?" Analysts asked for associations to elements in the dream which had a bizarre or unusual quality, and to those elements which seemed to reflect strong affect. Elsa First focused on the affect itself, as did several of the others, as, for example, Edward Nersessian and the green dream, in which the affect of danger was striking. It was this affect that led Nersessian to ask for associations.

An aspect of the dream which intrigued panelists was the patient's experience of the dream. They investigated this experience in different ways. James Fosshage asked his patient to put himself into the dream. Others asked their patient to revivify or to relive the dream experience. This approach is a variant of the more general attempt to get more detail about the dream itself. In the earlier discussion, someone asked whether it would not be as effective to simply ask a patient to make up stories about anything as it would be to ask them to recount dreams. This particular question reminded me of the impression I often have that there is very little in current psychoanalysis that was not foreshadowed by the founders. Many years ago Ferenczi (1920) used the forced fantasy technique, which was precisely this same thing: telling people to put themselves in a certain situation, have a fantasy about it, and tell the analyst what it feels like to relive that experience. Although this does yield useful content, the panelists agreed that it does not replace dreams and their associations, and that there is in fact something special about dreams. James Fosshage talked about "filling out," inquiring about the experience of the dream in more detail. This is a therapeutic technique used in general, not just in working with dreams. People avoid knowing things by speaking in generalities, by being vague. In such situations, which occur frequently, it is very useful to ask for the details: "Tell me specifically what happened. Tell me the details." The exploration of defensive vagueness applies to the dream experience as well. Areas of dream detail can be precise and sharp, but other areas can be very vague. When they are, we want to ask for the details.

To recapitulate, the general approach to working with dreams used by most of the panelists included:

1. Getting associations.
2. Emphasizing the importance of the dream experience.
3. Exploring the transference. It's really unnecessary to say very much about this. It is the backbone of psychoanalysis, whether there is a dream or whether there isn't a dream. We are always trying to understand what is going on between us and the patient.
4. Exploring defenses. Not everyone called them defenses, but everyone was very alert to the ways in which their patients tried to avoid dealing with underlying feelings. Marianne Goldberger emphasizes defenses in a way which is very similar to the close process analysis used by Paul Gray (1973). Their approach to the dream of Marianne Goldberger's patient would have been very similar. She looked for points in the recounting of the dream where the patient was having difficulty, and pointed out that difficulty. She further pointed out the way in which the difficulty manifested itself and perhaps the reason for it. Defense interpretation, like any interpretation, can be done in a sarcastic, critical, nasty way. Patients can be told that they are resisting, or other destructive interpretations made. This may have been an artifact of the old caricature of classical analytic technique. I hope we are today more aware of patients' narcissistic sensibilities. We point out ways that people are staying away from things in terms and in a manner that they can use, not in a way that will be offensive.

Let us go now to styles of interpretation, one's manner of understanding things and getting them across. A striking aspect of the panels was the large variety of styles manifested by the panelists. The variety did not, in my mind, correlate at all (or at best very little) with the particular psychoanalytic school that the panelists came from. It correlated instead with their individual personality characteristics. Perhaps the style was also influenced by what was going on with the individual patient. Edward Nersessian advocates parsimony, and it may be that is his particular individual style. He is not particularly verbose. I characterized Edna O'Shaughnessy, for example, as "gentle, but persistent." Here we have an example of how individual personality characteristics triumph over the demands of the school of psychoanalytic thought to which the therapist belongs. Edna O'Shaughnessy's school, the Kleinian school, is not noted for defense analysis. If anything, it has the reputation of cutting quickly deep into the id. Edna O'Shaughnessy, on the other hand, basically did defense analysis. She pointed out a number of different ways that the patient was staying away from certain feelings. To some degree, this reflects a recent change in Kleinian style, but I think it mostly reflects Edna O'Shaughnessy.

Another theme which arose this morning was that of metaphorical interpretation of dreams. Do we look at a dream and try to understand it as a metaphor, or do we take each of the dream elements, get associations, and pick out trends from these associations. These are two quite different approaches to understanding dreams, and everybody in this panel used both of them. Everyone paid attention to the manifest dream (pace Freud) and frequently used it as an allegory, but no one neglected associations and everyone used them in their interpretations.

Finally, I would point out that many of the apparent theoretical conflicts among the panelists, such as the use of the manifest dream versus the latent dream, were, in fact, when you look at what they actually did with the dream, merely semantic quibbles. I would suggest that as a whole our panelists all approached dreams in very similar ways, psychoanalytic schools notwithstanding.

REFERENCES

Ferenczi, S. (1920), The further development of an active therapy in psychoanalysis. In: *Further Contributions to the Theory and Practice of*

Psycho-Analysis, compiled J. Rickman; tr. J. Suttie. New York: Boni & Liveright, 1927, pp. 198–216.

Gray, P. (1973), Psychoanalytic technique and the ego's capacity for viewing intrapsychic activity. *J. Amer. Psychoanal. Assn.,* 21:474–494.

Commentary

Howard Shevrin

Although Freud's theory of dreaming has been alluded to in most of the papers, perhaps in greatest detail in Ellman's paper (Chapter 2), generally only one or another aspect of the theory has been cited, depending on its relevance to the particular point at issue. At the risk of being too schematic I would like first to give a quick overview of the theory, which I will use as a point of reference for my comments on the various papers.

In a masterful review chapter, Freud (1900) started by rejecting theories of dreaming that treated dreams as the mind's effluvium or waste product, a position revived by Crick and Mitchison (1983) most recently, and thus Freud rejected the position that dreams were without intrinsic meaning or significance, a position taken by Hobson (1988). Freud also rejected theories that treated dreams as having generic meanings such as might be interpreted by using a dream book, which I might add, are still in circulation, and similarly he rejected theories that interpreted dreams as oracular messages which had some one meaning that had to be divined.

In place of these explanations he proposed a complex set of propositions, which for the first time explained dreams as the immediate product of certain complex mental processes that in turn were related to other mental processes embedded in individual life experiences and the history of the dreamer. A dream could not be fully understood without knowing both the nature of the mental processes producing it and the relevant particulars of the dreamer's current and past life. Thus his theory required both stipulating the nature of those mental processes producing the dream and obtaining the dreamer's associations to the dream; only in this way could one arrive at some understanding of the dream.

There are two basic presuppositions underlying all of Freud's theorizing which apply equally to dreams as to any other mental product: The assumption of a psychological unconscious and the assumption that this psychological unconscious causes changes in conscious experience and action. Once we understand how these causes operate we can then infer the nature of what is going on unconsciously. Otherwise put, the unconscious is seldom ever transparent, and even when it appears to be transparent, as described in Gillman's instructive paper (chapter 7) about dreams in which the analyst appears undisguised, we are still dealing with transformations of unconscious influences.

I would like to stress the importance of these two presuppositions in Freud's theorizing, because it is the basis for his distinction between the latent and manifest dream. If you discard this distinction, then you are also discarding his first basic assumption that consciousness cannot be understood without postulating the existence of unconscious processes. He further postulated that the unconscious processes at work causing the conscious dreams were of a different nature from those generally at work in the waking state. They followed primary process rules in which the principle of identity was violated so that one dream element could be two different things (or people) at the same time, or two different places at the same time, and in which the asymmetric directionality of time could be violated so that chronology could be reversed or two events occurring at different times be made to happen at the same time. In addition to condensation and timelessness he further identified displacement, representability, symbolization, and secondary elaboration or revision as the other unconscious mechanisms which produced the conscious or manifest dream. Language also suffered a sea change. Words, for example, in his terminology were treated as "things" and could lose their referential function as counters in meaning. By "thing" one can read that they are treated purely phonetically or graphemically, so that words totally different in meaning could be run together either in speech or as written. The sum result of all these mental operations resulted in a conscious dream that to the waking mind would appear bizarre, irrational, and a collage of seemingly unrelated and impossible combinations but whose underlying meaning could only become clear through understanding the operation of these unconscious causes and obtaining the dreamer's associations.

He further theorized that these unconscious primary process mechanisms, constituting what he called the dream work, operated upon thoughts, feelings, memories and desires, much as defenses such as repression, reaction formation, and projection operated upon unconscious thoughts, feelings, memories and desires during the waking state. The person was the same person whether asleep or awake, but because of what he considered to be the regression in mental functioning brought about by sleep, the nature of these defensive operations changed. This regression, marked by a weakening of repression, allowed otherwise repressed desires and wishes potentially greater access to consciousness.

The last important piece of Freud's dream theory had to do with the role of motivation in the form of wishes derived from instinctual demands. In perhaps his most fundamental and controversial formulation of how the mind works, he postulated that these wishes were always striving to reestablish a condition of previous gratification by the shortest possible avenue which results in the hallucination of gratification. This strong push, however, runs into problems because this immediate gratification creates dangers in the form of loss of love, loss of the object, castration, and loss of self-regard. More circuitous routes are found that utilize the primary process mechanisms of the dream work so that some modicum of wish fulfillment is achieved without encountering the dangers to be avoided. There are further considerations involving psychic energy, which I would need to spend too much time to explicate fully; I will only say that the notion of cathexis central to the concept of psychic energy, which functions as the impetus, or initiating cause, setting all this complicated mental machinery in motion, has a counterpart in cognitive psychology where it is called activation. Elsewhere I have tried to spell out the functional parallels between the concept of cathexis and activation (Shevrin, 1997). Parenthetically, I will note that the philosopher of science Quine (1957) has observed that no science can do without something like an energy concept if it wishes to explain phenomena.

This complex and imposing edifice of theory, which also undergirds Freud's theory of neurosis and development, cannot easily be picked apart, accepting this aspect and rejecting that, without the whole edifice collapsing. The theory is also very much in need of testing on a variety of levels, psychological, clinical, and neurophysiological. It is, of course, true that one need not work with this theory at all, which applies to several of the papers I will comment on later.

Two of the papers, Blechner's (chapter 1) and Ellman's (chapter 2), present interesting hypotheses concerning the ways in which several important aspects of Freud's dream theory can be tested through brain physiology and anatomy. Ellman cites his research on what many would believe is one of the more esoteric of Freud's concepts—drive strength. He has demonstrated that there is an inverse relationship between drive gratification and the need to dream. Ellman's findings not only support the important role of motivation in dreams, which has also been supported more recently by Solms's neuropsychological lesion studies (2000), but links such support to the REM sleep state. If these findings are replicated, a most important piece of Freud's dream theory receives independent support—the role of motivation and motivational strength as dream instigators.

Blechner hypothesizes that dream condensations may draw upon two different brain mechanisms, one for perceptual recognition and one for individual identity. If this hypothesis can be supported it would provide a neuroscience explanation of one primary process mechanism—condensation. I have one reservation about this explanation, based in part on clinical experience. Often condensations are simply fusions of two different people. In a recent dream, one of my patients identified a dream figure as a condensation of her dance instructor and a younger image of her father drawn from a family photograph (note how the principle of identity is violated). But I have also encountered condensations of the kind described by Blechner. Perhaps then there are different kinds of condensation with concomitantly different neurophysiological instantiations.

"Blechner's second hypothesis is to me of great interest. He states that the specifics of bizarre dream experiences may clarify what are the different stages of perceptual processing" (p. 39). Charles Fisher formulated a similar hypothesis on the basis of his pioneering subliminal studies in which he found that images obtained following subliminal stimulus exposures often incorporated piecemeal perceptual features of the exposed stimuli in odd combinations in addition to whole objects (Fisher, 1957; see also Shevrin, 2003). We now know that the visual system is comprised of some thirty discrete perceptual feature analyzers, which need to be "bound" together before a unified object is perceived. The dream work may draw upon these perceptual fragments and enlist them for its own needs, producing in this way various displacements and rebuslike formations.

Blechner also calls attention to a potential difficulty in Freud's dream theory concerning the point at which sensory or perceptual information is available to dream formation, which for Freud could only occur at the time of dreaming. Again it was Fisher who pointed out, on the basis of his subliminal investigations, that primary process transformations were at work in the recovery of subliminally registered stimuli into daytime images (Shevrin, 2003). These images, along with many other preconscious registrations, were subject to the same primary process transformations as dream thoughts and thus might provide some of the dream content. In a manner of speaking, dreaming begins behind our eyes during the daytime and only becomes conscious as dreams during sleep.

As further evidence for the relationship of primary process mechanisms to dreaming, I would like to cite briefly a sleep–dream subliminal study I conducted with Fisher (Shevrin and Fisher, 1967). Borrowing directly from Freud's theory that dreams were constructed on the same principles as a rebus, I had devised a rebus stimulus—a picture of a pen and a knee forming the word *penny.* The subliminal effects of this stimulus could be measured in several different ways relating to Freud's conception of primary and secondary process mentation. On a primary process basis, one could look for penny and its associates, like nickel, dime, money. On a secondary process basis, one could look for associates of pen such as ink and paper, and for associates of knee, such as leg and bent. One could also look for clang associates of pen such as *pen*nant and o*pen*, and clang associates of knee such as *ne*ither and a*ny*. Note how the rebus and clang associations treat words, not as referential counters in meaning, but as concrete sounds that can be combined to form a new entity, much in the way in which a condensation forms. Words, in Freud's terminology, were being treated as "things."

The rebus stimulus was presented subliminally before subjects retired to sleep. They were awakened following REM periods and stage 2 non-REM periods. Our hypothesis was that the primary process transformations would be present following REM awakenings, and the secondary process transformations following non-REM awakenings. This is exactly what we found. What I would like to stress is that the subliminal stimulus was operationally unconscious and remained so, only appearing later in transformed ways. Fiss, Klein, and Bokert (1966) found similarly that TAT stories obtained right after REM awakenings were characterized by more bizarre, primary process stories than after non-REM awakenings. These studies provide evidence that the mind simply works differently during dreaming sleep than during nondreaming sleep. Moreover, the nature of the difference appears to accord with Freud's conception of primary and secondary process mentation.

The evidence from the Ellman, Solms, Shevrin, and Fisher, and Fiss, Klein, and Bokert studies supports Freud's dream theory in two particularly important ways: (1) the importance of motivation and drive strength as dream instigators, (2) the importance of primary process transformations of unconscious latent contents. Any clinical use of dreams should keep this evidence in mind.

When we now turn to a consideration of the largely clinical papers, we encounter a diversity of approaches and theories, each presented ably and claiming to have arrived at a valid understanding of the dream in question. As I read the papers I wondered how to make theoretical sense of these different approaches and how to decide which might in fact be correct. I would like to use two criteria for evaluating this diversity of approaches: (1) In what way is the approach in accord with or departs from Freud's theory and with what consequences? (2) To what extent is the approach in accord with whatever evidence we have about the nature of dreaming drawn from other sources, such as the kind of sleep–dream research previously cited.

Two authors, Fosshage (chapter 3) and Bromberg (chapter 9) and to a lesser extent, Blechner (chapter 1), wish to emphasize the importance of the dream as a manifestly coherent if difficult to understand representation of important internal states. For Fosshage, the dream is a metaphor that is capable of being "read off." He explicitly discards the distinction between latent and manifest content and along with them the need for dreamwork, primary and secondary process mechanisms, and motivational or drive strength. In short, he rejects the essentials of Freud's dream theory. He appears to gain a relatively easy entrée into what seem to be important state representations, which in Freudian theory would be accounted for by the work of secondary revision and would thus not be at the heart of the dream's meaning. Here we have a potentially testable hypothesis.

But I believe Fosshage also loses a great deal theoretically, which he may not in fact be ready to accept. As I tried to show in my brief account of Freud's dream theory, the distinction between latent and manifest is the dream form of a basic presupposition concerning the relationship between conscious and unconscious processes. Get rid of the distinction between latent and manifest and you also get rid of that distinction. There is thus no role for unconscious processes. The dream metaphor arises directly into consciousness. The "elusiveness" of the dream metaphor is caused by such factors as poor dream recall and lack of clarity in the dreaming process itself. But he also identifies as factors, difficulty in understanding the meaning of images from a waking perspective, and difficulty in making sense when juxtaposing two different states, waking and sleeping. With these two factors in mind, he appears to be saying that something different happens in dreams from waking life. Perhaps Fosshage has dealt with this elsewhere, but, in order to have a viable theory, he would need to specify what those differences between waking and sleeping states were, and how they are different from Freud's ideas. He would also have to deal with the evidence previously cited that motivation and drive strength are intimately involved with dreaming, and that one difference between waking and sleep mentation appears to follow the primary process rules which do not produce a coherent dream narrative.

Bromberg's view (chapter 9) that dissociated states of the self surface in dreams, which again can be read off from the manifest content, presents a more complicated position. Insofar as the states are dissociated, some mechanism must be posited that produces the dissociation. Presumably, once dissociated, the state of the self exists in some unconscious condition and there is something about the sleep state that undoes this dissociation. Thus Bromberg would need to specify these additional processes in order to make his theory work. As with Fosshage, he would also need to account in some way for the findings that motivation and motivational strength play an important role in dream formation, and that at least some of the dream mechanisms appear to follow primary process rules.

If Fosshage and Bromberg can be said to have a concept of unconscious processes, it is of a dispositional rather interactive nature. For Freud, unconscious processes are in constant interaction with conscious processes. The latent unconscious dream thoughts are driven by underlying motives to become conscious or be enacted. For Fosshage and Bromberg, at best the unconscious is a dispositional alternate state waiting to become conscious when a change in state from waking to sleep allows it to happen. Once conscious its meaning is available. Very little in additional data is necessary. There is thus no need to postulate defensive alteration of dream content, underlying conflict, and certainly no distinction between latent and manifest. In effect, the edifice of Freudian theory cannot withstand this drastic an overhaul. Their views constitute a different conception about how the mind works. Whether it is better or truer remains to be seen. As previously noted, their understanding of dreams would not find it easy to account for the role of motivation, or the nature of primary process mechanisms.

Several authors rely on a rebuslike treatment of dreams insofar as their interpretations often hinge on seemingly trivial dream features such as the raw, red noses in Lippmann's dream. Blechner takes a position intermediate between that of Fosshage (chapter 3) and Nersessian (chapter 4), Goldberger (chapter 10), and Peskin (chapter 11), on the role of manifest themes and concrete details. He maintains that the analysis of the concrete details should fill out and support the manifest theme, and that if they do not then something is wrong in the interpretive process. As it stands, this is offered as an assertion or intuition without any support. From the standpoint of Freudian dream theory there is no reason to believe that secondary revision would need to be consistent with the associations to specific dream elements. Here we have another hypothesis that could in principle be put to the test.

As best as I could determine, Nersessian, Peskin, and Goldberger appear to base their work with dreams primarily on Freud's dream theory. Goldberger demonstrates that the same processes may be at work in daydreams, although at times I was hard put to distinguish what she meant by a daydream as opposed to larger category of fantasies. Her work with daydreams is consistent with the position taken by Fisher (Shevrin, 2003) that some waking mentation can be quite dreamlike in its mechanisms and formation. Peskin stresses deception and self-deception as motivations developed under evolutionary pressure for resorting to disguise. Nersessian suggests that too much attention to the transference implications of dreams may blind us to potentially rich material and he gives several convincing examples to illustrate his point.

Finally, I would like to say a word or two about Paul Lippmann's paper (chapter 8). He describes himself as the offspring of two very different traditions: the clinical interpersonal tradition in New York City, and the Rapaport (chapter 7) *The Interpretation of Dreams* (Freud, 1900) seminar tradition at Austen Riggs. How his analytic DNA must have boiled and corkscrewed with that mixture! But in a more serious vein, these are two of the traditions very much in evidence in this symposium. Lippmann takes a reflective stand with respect to each. He observes trenchantly that the ''vanity of modern psychoanalysis, particularly in the increasingly dominant relational form, is seen in the belief that we have achieved significant progress and have come a long way in our theory and in our technique over the last one hundred years. I think this assumption can be argued'' (p. 183). Although he grants that maybe ''it could all make sense, if one had the desire and patience to apply Rapaportian learning to Freudian creation (our secular version of the relationship of Talmud to Torah, from which much of the spirit of psychoanalysis arose)'' (p. 182). He offers a sentiment with which I agree, and makes a fitting close to my discussion, ''I believe it important not to assume we are better at our work than were the originators.''

REFERENCES

Crick, F., & Mitchison, G. (1983), The function of dreaming sleep. *Nature,* 304(5922):111–114.

Fisher, C. (1957), A study of the preliminary stages of the construction of dreams and images. *J. Amer. Psychoanal. Assn.,* 5:5–60.

Fiss, H., Klein, G. S., & Bokert, E. (1966), Waking fantasies following interruption of two types of sleep. *Arch. Gen. Psychiatry,* 14(5):543–551.

Freud, S. (1900), *The Interpretation of Dreams.* London: Hogarth Press, 1953.

Hobson, J. A. (1988), *The Dreaming Brain.* New York: Basic Books.

Quine, W. (1957), The scope and language of science. *Brit. J. Philos. Sc.,* 8:1–17.

Shevrin, H. (1997), Psychoanalysis is the patient: High in feeling, low in energy. *J. Amer. Psychoanal. Assn.,* 45(3):841–864.

——— Ed. (2003), *Subliminal Explorations of Perceptions, Dreams, and Fantasies: The Pioneering Contributions of Charles Fisher.* Madison, CT: International Universities Press.

——— Fisher, C. (1967), Changes in the effects of a waking subliminal stimulus as a function of dreaming and non-dreaming sleep. *J. Abnorm. Psychol.,* 72(4):362–368.

Solms, M. (2000), Dreaming and REM sleep are controlled by different brain mechanisms. *Behav. & Brain Sc.,* (Spec. Iss.), 23 (6): 843–850, 1040–1081, 1083–1121.

——— (2003), Dreaming and REM sleep are controlled by different brain mechanisms. In: *Sleep and Dreaming: Scientific Advances and Reconsiderations,* ed. E. F. Pace-Schott, M. Solms, M. Blagrove, & S. Harnad. New York: Cambridge University Press, pp. 51–58.

Rejoinder

Dialogue with Commentators, Presenters, and Audience Members

Owen Renik: Thanks to both Sydney Pulver and Howard Shevrin for getting the ball rolling in such a nice way. Jim Fosshage in his presentation emphasized a wish to collapse the distinction between manifest and latent content and Philip Bromberg spoke about the importance of dealing with separate self states that are held apart in consciousness. Now Sydney Pulver has asked both of them whether in fact they work with a concept of the unconscious and with essentially a dynamic unconscious, a concept of the unconscious held in place by some defensive process, and Howard Shevrin has put it from a slightly different angle: Do they subscribe to the presupposition psychologically causative, rather than dispositional unconscious, or are they actually subscribing to a presupposition of a different kind of dispositional unconscious?

James Fosshage: These are huge questions. It is interesting that I felt that the commentators were very well chosen because Sydney Pulver is doing synthetic thinking, bringing us together, and it was an excellent discussion. Howard Shevrin was accentuating differences and looking more analytically again at the differences, and I think we clearly all have both trends within us; namely, we would like to come together in some way but also we would like to point out the differences as well. In terms of the question, let me approach it first as regards the unconscious and then go to Sydney Pulver's points. I can pull the two together. I don't tend to see the unconscious and refer to the unconscious, I think that we are talking about levels of awareness. I talk about unconscious mentation or conscious mentation. I think that does have a significant impact which I can't go into in detail at the moment.

The other point, I am not sure that I agree with Howard Shevrin's difference as he positioned it. I think that clearly there are defensive processes that go on, and go on unconsciously, that are not relatable to consciousness, there is no question about that. What I have been questioning is the assumption in terms of dreams, the ubiquitous operation of defensive functioning in the formation of dreams. I don't think that's accurate, and I think that's an essential difference between some of us on the panel. I feel that it is very tricky how defenses operate in dreams. Sometimes I think that they are directly observable in dreams, sometimes I feel you can only tell if you compare the context of the dream to the waking context. And in those ways I do not think that defensive functioning necessarily results in the disguise or translation of images as the classical model would have it. But defenses clearly operate. I think it makes a great deal of difference in terms of how we see dreams and how ubiquitous we feel the defenses are, and also if it results in translation of dream imagery, which positions us as analysts as not being able to trust the dream imagery as directly revelatory. That's a major difference, I feel.

The unconscious: It also differs amongst us on the panel—what is unconscious? More fundamentally it goes back to motivational models of the classical theory in terms of assuming that dual drive theory (libido and aggression) are the essential motivations. If you assume that or the Kleinian emphasis on aggression, or if you assume the object relational primary strivings toward attachment, or the self psychological view of motivation as centered on the development and consolidation of the self, maintenance of the self, or developmental strivings, those are fundamentally different motivations. The ripple effect of these different motivations is what we are seeing in terms of how we understand dreams, and those operate often unconsciously or can also be conscious at the same time. But how we understand human beings is very different based upon those motivational principles, and I think that is where we get very different ideas about the unconscious and what is unconscious.

Sydney Pulver's point about what was defended off: I feel what was defended against by my patient was any feeling of trust of me. He was defending or protecting himself against trusting. His attitude, his conscious attitude, what was in the foreground, was distrust. You can certainly see that as defensive if you will. Certainly I would talk about it as protected. Philip Bromberg might talk about it as a separate self state, I certainly would talk about it as a self state too, but I do think the patient was fending off trust, and the trusting was emerging for the first time more fully within the dream, directly in the dream.

Now if you emphasize defenses you would not believe that dream. The tilt would be, well he's defending against his distrust and the distrust in the waking reality or how he experiences me in the waking reality is distrusting, that would be seen as reality. This is where Philip Bromberg and I would agree. I see two separate states of mind in the dream. In fact, the patient was trusting me and I took that, "the message is the message," as we have talked about it, it was directly revelatory in the dream. So, where we position ourselves as analysts is crucially important in terms of understanding.

In terms of technique which Sydney Pulver was addressing, asking for associations is a very different clinical process that has a very different feel from asking patients to get into that dream experience, however we do it, in order to elaborate and connect with that affective experience within the dream. Now that is a very different experience. It's not as if they are mutually exclusive and as if you can't get to asking for associations to the dream experience, it depends upon the patient and the process, but it tends to move somewhat differently and I think that's where there is a difference.

Philip Bromberg: At a recent American Psychoanalytic Conference, I was on a panel that had to do with the changing nature of the unconscious in clinical practice. At that time I spelled out in detail what my view was of the unconscious and how it differs from the view held by Freudian conflict theory. Howard Shevrin's questions with regard to my work. They are relevant questions, even though they are framed by an implication that my view, because it constitutes a different conception about how the mind works, is on shaky ground simply because, as he puts it, "the edifice of Freudian theory cannot withstand this drastic an overhaul." There are no small number of analysts, however, who believe a drastic overhaul of Freudian theory is in fact long overdue, and the question of whether it can withstand it is mainly a matter of whether it is flexible enough to acknowledge some fundamental flaws. I do indeed work from a different view of the mind and a different view of unconscious processes, a view that sees both dissociation and conflict as central to all mental functioning, normal and pathological. It is a view that is intrinsically psychodynamic (as well as structural) but psychodynamic in a way that conflict theorists have trouble with. Howard Shevrin calls my view of the unconscious *dispositional.* I never heard the word before, but if by the word he means nondynamic, he needs to find a new word.

A conflict theorist cannot really grasp the internal consistency of my perspective without understanding how I see the mind and the way it is structured, which in turn leads to how I see personality growth and personality change, and, clinically to how I talk to my patients and why I do what I do in the way I do it. If a conflict theorist doesn't really grasp my view of the mind, his temptation is to take the easy route and try to see it as just another way of talking about conflict and repression. He can then attempt to squeeze my perspective into the template of conflict theory as long as he doesn't think about it too closely.

Ed Levenson: When I read James Fosshage's paper (chapter 3) and some of his ideas about dreams, I always felt that we were going down the same road for about three-quarters of the way and then we separated. For example, there is the issue of the translation or the representation of the images in the dream. He insisted that is different from the classical ideas, and I just wanted to say that is not so. Most of chapter 6 of *The Interpretation of Dreams* on dream work has to do with the issue of representation, and one of the tasks of the dream is to translate the thoughts into images, primarily visual images. That is not only based on defense, but is also based on the capacity of the mind in sleep and the restrictions that are applied to it at that time.

Mervyn Peskin: Replying to James Fosshage and talking as someone who is closer to the conflict model, when he said that a defense analyst would not agree that the patient wanted to trust him, would see this as some disguise or that there was something that was untrue about it, I don't fully agree with that. I would agree that the patient did want to trust him but think that there was more to it. I would not see trust as the terminus, as the end of the line in regard to motivation. What is the benefit of trust? Why do we trust each other? Trust is enormously valuable and adaptive, but why? I would not call trust a basic motivation. There are agendas we have with each other and trust is necessary in order to fulfill a more basic set of wishes, some of which are selfish and therefore need to be disguised.

Mark Blechner: This idea of the *dispositional unconscious* is new to me. I don't want to have to choose between the two. With either, I think we are falling into the trap of thinking of the unconscious as a "place" or "thing" in the mind, instead of an adjective describing a quality of mentation. Thus, we often say "the unconscious," but we rarely say "the conscious." This way of speaking has profound implications, because it implies a structure of the mind or brain that holds certain kinds of ideas.

Edna O'Shaughnessy: I am really in a state of befuddlement here. I have been struck by how very different we are and how complicated our differences are, both in technique and in terminology, and also how some of this overlaps. There are bits of congruency that I seem to see and other divergences that seem to me to take us very far apart. The dream that has come back is James Fosshage's dream. I speak as a British Kleinian. The patient brings in a dream in which he is telling somebody else that the analyst is not a charlatan, he's a trustworthy fellow and really, if I remember it right, advising him to move into the basement. Now, I would be starting to think in terms of splitting, that there is one part of the patient that is staying outside of this, which Fosshage inquired about, "So do you think that . . . ?" "No," he says, "I am still feeling very doubtful and anxious about you." I would start to be thinking that there is going to be one bit of the patient watching from outside what's going on, in quite a mistrustful, anxious way. And there is another bit of the patient that is moving in, moving into the basement. And I would try to inquire, what the symbolic meaning of that is: What is the basement? And being of a Kleinian persuasion, I'd be wondering about projective identification, is he projecting himself into the basement, whatever that's going to mean, is he getting identified with Dr. Fosshage's house, because he plainly thinks the analyst is not a charlatan. So, is he bringing something of his split way of dealing with a very anxiety-arousing situation? I would be wanting further exploration with the patient about what is this moving-in kind of relationship? It struck me as so very different. There are, of course, such important ways in which we are all the same in that we all have patients on the receiving end of our clinical work.

Audience Member: We are all really talking about the health in patients. We speak about the unconscious most of the time as if it is a place, a thing, rather than a force. One of the things that I am impressed with in my work with patients is that I have to have confidence in them. For me to have confidence in them I have to know that they have healthy forces within them. Many times, the first time someone seems to have healthy forces is within the dream. I haven't heard much about the healthy forces in dreaming. Many times I connect dreaming with feeling and the main connection is it's natural, and part of the importance of dreaming and feeling and connecting them, it shows us we are alive. The second thing is it gives us a great clue as to what is happening inside of us. It's like the child in us. And the third thing is really in the feeling part. We all want to develop confidence, which is a feeling, not a thing. What the dream does for us is that it gives us support, it tells us that there are reasons for what we do and that there is more to us than what we see on the surface. So that is why I connected dreaming and feeling. They just have to go together in that sense. Most of this I got from Karen Horney. Her feeling about healthy unconscious forces made a big difference to me.

Owen Renik: I think you can detect some familiar controversies lurking behind the discussion. There are controversies about meaning being created or discovered, and therefore how that bears on the explorations of dreams; controversies about the pathologization versus the nonpathologization of that which is outside awareness; questions of the analyst's authority in relation to this investigation.

Howard Shevrin: I would like to make a comment on what James Fosshage said and also what Philip Bromberg had to say. I think that in particular what Philip Bromberg was saying in the context of his own thinking, that is, the model that he uses, that we were reaching some understanding of the nature of the difference. But let me if I can clarify that one step more, in the light of what James Fosshage was saying about that dream. Now, I also recall at a certain point in the discussion of the panel, which Edward Nersessian and James Fosshage were on together, that Edward asked him at one point something about the relationship between his conscious view of himself and what was revealed in the dream? And in particular where does anxiety enter the picture? I think that was part of the question.

And I was very interested in James Fosshage's answer. What I understood him to be saying was that there was essentially a dissociated aspect of his patient's mind which was trusting. But to allow that part of himself to gain ascendence, which means not only consciousness but to actually influence his behavior and his relationship with his analyst, that's what was causing anxiety. Fosshage's answer to what was causing anxiety was that here you had a self-system, if you like, or an aspect of the individual, or a certain important dimension of his mind, which had been organized and functioning for a long period of time, and the anxiety derived from the fact that he would have to change that. He would have to change this positional organization of his way of relating himself to his analyst and that's what made it hard for him and created the anxiety about allowing himself to become aware of his desire, or as James Fosshage said, his motivation, or his need, to trust.

This borrows from a dispositional view of the unconscious and something also about the organization of that dispositional unconscious which has an automatic matrix to it. It does not interact in the way in which the Freudian presuppositions describe, and Edna O'Shaughnessy just gave an excellent example of the way she would work with that very same dream. These are interesting and important differences and they can't be adjudicated within the clinical situation.

They are the basis, the presuppositions that each of us works with as clinicians. They organize our work. The adjudication of these differences has to come from other sources. Now, this is not going to be easy, nor are many of us necessarily interested in doing that, but this is a very important point to me and I wanted to make that clear. There are these differences and no one should surrender their presuppositions until they have to.

James Fosshage: I understand better what Howard Shevrin had meant and I would agree with it up to a point. Certainly, you can talk about these attitudes and dispositions, I talk about attitudes organizing patterns, but the distinction still feels a little troublesome and problematic because I would ask the question still—you are right, part of the anxiety is due to the fact that the distrusting adaptation, what he has developed, provides a certain cohesiveness, or self-cohesion, which any change is going to bring about, some anxiety. Any potential change will bring about anxiety; that's what you are referring to as disposition. However, I would ask the patient too, and I would be right here, not only in the comment about Edna O'Shaughnessy, that asks the question about what are your fantasies, what would you expect if you trusted me, as portrayed in this dream? Do I believe in fantasies? Of course I believe in fantasies. We differ probably in how we conceptualize the origin of fantasies—the degree to which they are intrapsychically generated or they are generated out of processing relational experiences.

Now, Edna O'Shaughnessy's portrayal of the clinical situation was very meaningful, and what is striking to me is that she believed that dream as being directly revelatory of one aspect of the patient, and in that sense you did not translate or try to get underneath the manifest to some latent meaning. She believed it as directly revelatory, and I would very much agree with that. I would agree that these are two aspects of the patient, and I certainly agree to explore what the basement means. So I found that very interesting material.

Audience Member: I am not sure this fits with directly revelatory or hidden meaning, and I'm not sure how this fits with dispositional versus dynamic unconscious, but I hope it does and I hope it's clarifying. My first thought is that it is not always clear what are the good forces and what are the bad forces. In Philip Bromberg's dream, the self was first this transference person, and then there is the person who is the untrusting part of the self, the person who couldn't take the heat, and then became the good part of the self. So the dream has to be explored in many ways for those transformations to occur, and after that Philip Bromberg's comment that what we are doing is finding a place in the dream and hoping that the dreamer would find a place in the dream, that feels like what is going on in the session and in the transference. I have a question on James Fosshage's polarization of the dissociations: You don't know where they lead, that they can lead to other depths, such as depths of affects, which were also re-creations of experience, so following associations is a little foggy.

Robert Gillman: I believe in the dynamic unconscious, but I find myself very much in agreement with James Fosshage who says we should trust some of the manifest content, and if you listen to most analysts today of a classical bent you see that they pay a great deal of attention to the manifest content and its story. They pay a great deal of attention to the object relations expressed, to the trust that is shown in it, and it seems to me that from the very beginning of my analytic training we heard, for example, about a termination dream, and if you look at the literature about termination dreams, so much of it is based on the manifest content. I don't think that the difference between us has to do with our believing in the manifest content, but our various levels of content. We need to find more of the dreamer in the dreamer, we need to find out all the aspects of why the dreamer created that dream, directed the dream, who are the cast of characters, and so on; that's in the associations. So the associations enrich the dream but they don't throw out the manifest.

Paul Lippmann: There is a person at this symposium who has just written a wonderful book on the world of alternative healing, and he is thinking of writing a book on dreams. If he comes away from this meeting with the sense that there *is* no psychoanalytic view of dreams, I think he would have come away understanding the true state of affairs. We are in a state of flux. There is an enormous amount of motion between us. Dreams have been a mystery from the beginning of time; we haven't figured them out yet, thank God. As soon as we figure them out, you can be sure that the world economy will find a way of making a buck off it.

Freud wrote, "It's a pity that one cannot make a living, for instance, on dream interpretation" (Masson, 1985, p. 266). It's in that letter when he gave up his neurotica to Fleiss, when he said he no longer believed in the seduction theory. And it is hard. The HMO people, if you tell them that what you are doing with the patient and what you want to do is you are listening to dreams and you have a particular view of the unconscious or a different view of the unconscious, it doesn't matter. This particular world is not interested in our interest in dreams and maybe that is to the good.

The motion between us is seen, for example, in the fact that there are four people here on the panel who are faculty at the White Institute, with very different points of view about the unconscious and about dreams. The classical people are extremely, increasingly interested in the goings on between the two people in the room. I cut my eye teeth on what's going on between the two people in the room. Right now I'm profoundly interested in the deepest intrapsychic goings on within the one person in the room, a one-person psychology and an interpersonalist. We have a Jungian who is a member of the Stockbridge Dream Society. I can't get him to talk about Jungian points of view. He is so busy talking about transference, countertransference, and attachment theory.

The world of dream interpretation is a vast one and it would be well for us every once in a while to get past our particular arguments about which model is at stake and to open our minds to the world of dream interpretation. Ben Kilbourne (1981), for example, who is moving to Stockbridge and will join the Stockbridge Dream Society, has written wonderful papers about the Moroccan view of dreams. Anthropologists would take our psychoanalytic view, apply it to the indigenous people, and see whether their dreams confirmed our theories. Well, what Ben did was to take dreams from *The Interpretation of Dreams,* one of Freud's patient's dreams, and bring them to Moroccan dream interpreters and ask them what their view of this dream is. It's a wonderful paper that has been published in the journal *Dreaming.*

It is very hard to stay with dreams. Even our associational method sometimes takes us away from dreams. In a naturalist approach to dreams, if we just look at dreams and see what they do before creating meaning out of them, whether in an analytic session or a therapy session, they change the set. Dreams come in from left field. We could be talking for two weeks, two months, about a particular problem with one's mother, and all of a sudden one is riding a green horse in a blue field somewhere. Out of left field. Now, many of us get very busy and then try to reintroduce that outfield experience into day experience, and for some patients that is very important to do. But as James Hillman and others have said, maybe it is important to follow the dream where it takes us. The change in set gives us an opportunity to let the unconscious, if you will, dictate the terms of the discussion. It is a very brave and exciting thing to do. When a dream comes out of left field, although we know we are in termination, or even if we want to talk about the last bill they didn't pay, the dream says, "No, go that way." To follow it takes courage and some clinical understanding and a lot of experience, but that's a very important kind of thing to do.

Owen Renik: Howard Shevrin said something very important that is a kind of a bookend to Paul Lippmann's point about the great world of dreams and not being so married to any point of view that we are not open to its vast richness. Nevertheless there are specific and consequential differences among the panelists about their understanding of and approach to dreams, and those differences relate to fundamental assumptions about the mind and the way the mind works, and what the term *unconscious* means, and those differences will be of consequence in the way psychoanalysis is practiced. But Howard Shevrin makes the point that it is not possible to adjudicate those differences within the clinical situation because people can proceed consistently from very different assumptions, and so I think he was saying the difficult process scientifically that lies ahead of us is to devise systematic research that does attempt to adjudicate these differences. There is the possibility though that if the differences are consequential and lead to more or less effective psychotherapy, that the marketplace will also have something to say about the different efficacies of the fundamental assumptions, though that's a complicated subject in and of itself.

Paul Lippmann has opened the discussion up for us and I would like to move on to a neuroscience question: Is any pleasure center of the brain also an aggression center? Are these two parts of our basic survival system?

Steven Ellman: Let me first discuss an earlier point Paul Lippmann made in talking about some of the differences, because he brought up something that is slightly different from what Howard Shevrin said, that these differences can't be adjudicated within the clinical situation. I think it depends on how one studies the clinical situation. It's true it may be difficult to give up one's basic premises, but there might be some theories that can predict to both kinds of clinical situations, or to a number of clinical situations. So that to think that you can't do it within the clinical situation seems to me to be an assumption that I wouldn't join. I think it depends on how one constructs their theory.

I would also like to add a complication to the theoretical point of view, which is to say that there are some people who regard themselves as Freudian, as I do, who are not classical analysts. There is a book, *The Contemporary Freudians* (the senior editor was my wife, I was the last editor on the book)—in one of the chapters I talked about self and object Freudians. The reason that I bring that up now is that at some points in the treatment situation, some of us might look very much like Philip Bromberg, particularly in terms of getting to a point where we think transference can be interpretable and we are really trying to get to some type of criteria for what we mean by ''interpretable transference.'' Not that the patient is unanalyzable, but rather that we have to understand better the conditions under which various kinds of interpretations can be tolerated and utilized. But sometimes when we reach this position, which is not a static position, we then look much more like classical analysts, at least for a period of time, and then recognize that what I have called ''analytic trust'' breaks down under some conditions and cycles reappear. This is similar to a way that, in a different context, Edna O'Shaughnessy described in terms of defensive cycles.

I think the same thing is true about dreams. A dream can be treated in one way at a particular time in the treatment, as sort of an external event, but as one begins to understand the patient's dream life, it really gives you a feeling (since I believe in a dynamic unconscious) of very interesting things that you didn't see as a part of yourself that you now begin to experience more as part of yourself. I will go quickly to what I said about pleasure centers. I said that wherever in the brain one can elicit aggression, and there are places where you can put in an electrode and get aggressive behavior (e.g., you can get mouse killing in the rat), you can elicit that kind of thing, those same areas are pleasure centers. That is, if you allow the animal to press the bar to obtain that stimulation it will do various kinds of work for it and find it pleasurable. So that in this model, aggression isn't necessarily a destructive force, although it can be, but it is part of survival mechanisms. Well, when I brought this up I was thinking in line with an extension of Freudian thought, to try to talk about the dream occurring—one of the reasons we looked at REM sleep in the beginning was because we thought REM sleep was a natural state which we thought Freud was sort of alluding to. It was a state where the brain was very activated, and we thought it might be a candidate for what Freud called "drive." So from my perspective the dream contains the elements of the dynamic unconscious, which involves certainly the idea of survival of the self, in terms of a certain theory of Freud's at a particular time. But survival of the self in this model involves various kinds of basic biological bodily events, that involve aggression and a elaboration of what Freud tried to describe in psychosexuality.

Melvin Lansky: I would just like to go back to what Paul Lippmann said. The idea of staying close to the dream is very important. We have talked about how eclectic we all are, and yet in fact none of us is technically a Jungian. I am glad he brought up James Hillman, who does talk very much about staying close to the material of the dream. When I teach my dream interpretation courses I always recommend to my students that when a patient tells you a dream, you write it down verbatim, and the reason for that is that it is very hard to hold onto dreams, to the details of them. We tend to regularize them. It's actually an interesting study of your countertransference if you look at your patient's dream text and then you see what you remember of them via the dream and how you transform it over time.

Audience Member: Otto Isakower used to say in his dream class: "Shriven es farbutten." "Writing is forbidden." And his reasoning was that if you write down the dream you are turning it too much into a verbal product. You are getting away from the image aspect of the dream. So for almost the same reason he was giving the opposite instruction. Apparently he also said that he would not say to a patient, "What are your thoughts about that?" He would say, "Let's look at the dream together.'' The idea was to stay close to this visual aspect of it. So, I'm not saying that there is one right way to do it, but the whole idea of keeping that as a goal, to stay close to the experience in the dream, is very important.

Steven Ellman: One of the things that I tried to go over was the two different points of view in the Kris Study Group. One group talked about the exceptional position of the dream, and the other group, which essentially was Charles Brenner's group, said that the dream has no exceptional position and that one should look at this as simply one more association with compromise formations and things like that. So that the idea of staying close to the dream as opposed to anything else, I think Brenner would say (and here I would agree with him) one would stay close to all experiences in the analytic situation. If you start to pick a word or pick something like this then there might be a transference–countertransference sequence that would be very difficult to look at. Nevertheless, I still think the dream is an exceptional event that conveys things in a way that nothing else can. To that extent I wouldn't agree with Brenner, though I see the danger that he is alluding to.

Marianne Goldberger: I don't know what Charles Brenner would say, but I wanted to go back to basics: What is the dream? I think of the analytic clinical situation as when the patient comes to the hour and tells me the dream. There are several other quote–unquote dreams, we haven't talked about that. Something that happens while you are asleep, something that you may or may not remember when you first wake. A lot of patients tell you: ''This is not what I remembered when I first woke up, I just remember a little bit, just before the hour, and now I find that I want/don't want to tell you.'' So there is always a gloss. The dream includes the gloss and the situation in the hour. Do other people think that the dream is all those other things? And then, what is the dream? I don't think there is a dream, except in the clinical situation.

Arnold Rothstein: I just wanted to comment on my understanding of Brenner's position. I think it is misunderstood. It is not so much that he doesn't think dreams and analysis of dreams are very valuable, but my understanding of his position is that the concept of technical neutrality is superordinate. If you value dreams particularly, then you are moving out of the technically neutral position, which has particularly profound shaping implications as a communication within the transference. So that if you write down the patient's dreams, you are, in your activity, making a communication to the patient which engenders performance, gifts, deviance, compliance, transference activity. So to protect against that transference–countertransference activity, which is always very valent in analysis, it is important not to overvalue any form of data. Because of the privileged history of the position of dreams in Freud's self-analysis most analysts, despite what they say theoretically, like dreams. So the concept of technical neutrality Brenner emphasizes helps colleagues maintain a position where they don't influence the transference too much.

Mervyn Peskin: Having presented a compromise–formation perspective on dreams (see chapter 11) I would like to add to what Arnold Rothstein just said in regard to a dream being a compromise formation that can be extraordinarily valuable in understanding the unconscious, that a dream can also function largely as a decoy. Like any other compromise formation it can be helpful in understanding the unconscious but because of the historical emphasis mentioned, sometimes too much can be expected of dreams in regard to revealing the unconscious, thus enhancing their ability to be used as decoys or subterfuges in the analytic relationship.

Owen Renik: There is a potential convergence among certain of these concepts. If, for example, as Steve Ellman suggests, as do others in the neural sciences, dreams are a printout of our efforts to rehearse survival strategies and process survival related information during the REM states, and if that is guided by the basic tropisms of the organism to avoid pain and to seek pleasure, that is obviously very consistent with the notion of the dream as a compromise formation, which answers in part Marianne Goldberger's question: "What is the dream?" Compromise is a compromise among various motivational principles with which the dreamer has to deal. It represents an attitude toward the dream by the way that it tends to take it analytically as a constructive effort at self-help and guards against the kind of presumption that

I think Jim Fosshage is interested in avoiding by the abuse of the manifest–latent dichotomy. There are converging lines of thought among the panelists.

Steven Ellman: My only source for Brenner was what he has written and he came up to me after the talk and said, "That was my position." Part of the Kris Study Group report said that the dream had no exceptional position, is quite specific, and is like any other fantasy, daydream, it had the same regressive elements. I asked him quite specifically, "Is that your position, Dr. Brenner?" and he said, "Yeah." So I certainly agree that neutrality is what he is talking about, but I think the Kris Group also presented a position on the dream which it seems to me is just empirically incorrect.

Ruth Imber: I don't think most of the Freudians think of the patient dreaming (the act of dreaming, not the reporting of the dream, not even perhaps the memory of the dream, but the actual experience of the dreaming) as a way of staying in touch and communicating to others, frequently the analyst. I guess there are times when unwittingly, that's the way I am sometimes viewing the dream that a patient tells me, that even during the dreaming in some way there is some attempt to maintain contact and communicate with me.

Edward Nersessian: I think I should say that I had the privilege when I was younger of working with Brenner for many years and I have some idea of his position, which I have come to disagree with over the years. Brenner is right in his clinical recommendation, which is don't drop everything else when a patient reports a dream. However, it is true that the dream is an exceptional event, different from daydreams and different from day events, and that not to pay it real attention usually over the years gets accompanied by a loss of talent about interpreting dreams, and a know-how about interpreting dreams and an understanding of things such as certain symbolism and translation into imagery of thought, that you have to keep yourself involved in it to be able to do it. And unless you pay more attention to the dream you lose the ability to really understand dreams. I also think Brenner's position is very much part of his and Arlow's wish to remove the topographic theory from our psychoanalytic theory. I don't think that was a completely good idea, I think some aspects of the topographic theory are in fact now revealing themselves as very useful and very important to us.

Arnold Richards: Just a brief point in reply to Ruth Imber. Martin Bergmann, a Freudian, wrote a paper on the communicative functions on the dream, so if I believe in that paper I am a relationalist also.

James Fosshage: We heard varying thoughts from the neuroscientists here, Mark Solms, Steve Ellman, and Mervyn Peskin, from an evolutionary standpoint, about the participation of the higher cortical areas of the brain and the higher brain functions in terms of dream formation. This is a very controversial issue and it is an issue that has not been solved in terms of neuroscience. There is a lot of research being done on REM, for instance, and the impact of REM in terms of increasing learning. There is a tremendous amount of research in that area and there is also a lot of research in terms of dream content where researchers have concluded that the principal function of dreaming is problem-solving efforts, which certainly involves higher cortical levels of the brain.

Neuroscientists are also guided by particular models as they are doing their research. What is striking to me is how those who hold a classical model, their neuroscientific findings tend to tilt in a certain direction and those who don't may move in a different direction, so their models are constantly influencing that research as well. I mention for instance Jonathan Winson, who wrote a book called *The Brain and the Psyche.* From an evolutionary standpoint he concluded, "That the task of associating recent events to past memories and evolving neural substrates to guide future behavior was caused when the animal was asleep. That is the fundamental purpose of dreaming is processing information and developing neural substrates, in order to guide behavior. It serves a primary adaptive function". Jonathan Winson came up to me at one point and said that my particular psychoanalytic model happened to correspond to his findings. Within neuroscience we need to go back and forth between what we know as clinicians and what the neuroscientists are finding as well.

Philip Bromberg: I want to make a comment about the issue of staying close to the dream because in a central way, that's what my paper was all about. When I talk about staying close to the dream, what I'm referring to is a process of working with the dream that allows the "dreamer" to exist experientially as a physical reality rather than a self state the patient talks about. Marianne Goldberger's point, I think, is relevant to this: What is the dream? Is it an experienced event—a reality in which the patient exists when he is asleep, or is it a story he brings to the session and reports? I think this is a critical issue because it addresses the fact that memory is a construction. Over the years I've become increasingly appreciative of the power contained in bringing the dreamer into the session through helping a patient to reenter his dream space. Even though some patients are able to do this better than others, staying as close as possible to the dream as an event that is reexperienced rather than told, allows the use of dreams to become alive affectively rather than just be plausible cognitively.

Howard Shevrin: In connection with the point that Steve Ellman was making: Can anything be tested within the clinical situation? I tried to give that some thought as I was listening to the various presentations. There is one that was actually mentioned by Paul Lippmann in response to Bob Gillman's paper about the appearance of the analyst in the dream and that really this is a disguise and it occurs 10 percent of the time in his collection of dreams from his patients (Shevrin and Eiser, 2003). Paul Lippmann was saying that he thinks that his percentage is a bit lower than that and he wondered whether a relational approach, which gives the patient an opportunity to say more about the analyst in the course of clinical exchange, might in fact reduce the incidence of dreams about the analyst. He made the hypothesis, and I think I am right in this, that they would be of inverse relationship, in other words. The more the patient had an opportunity to voice thoughts, feelings, reactions in the relational exchange with the analyst, the less need there would be to dream about the analyst in a undisguised way. That to me sounds like an eminently testable hypothesis. Now the hooker is that whichever way the results would go would be interpreted by proponents of a particular model as being within it. We will find out something interesting to be sure, but it will not be conclusive.

Owen was reminding us of the threat rehearsal theory of the function of dreams. One of the articles that I have been reviewing for commentary for *Behavior and Brain Sciences,* is from a professor of philosophy from Finland by the name of Revonsuo (2003), who indeed maintains this position and provides an enormous amount of empirical evidence, mainly from questionnaires when people are asked about their dreams, that indeed people dream most of the time not about wishes but about threats, anxiety arousing situations. I have a lot of problems with this from a conceptual standpoint, but then he said that in fact his theory is that this dream mechanism, this function of dreaming, developed 100,000 years ago, when our ancestors were presented daily with far more threats than we are now, threats from hairy mammoths and things of that kind. Nevertheless then he said how can we get some idea about what it was like back then 100,000 years ago? He said let's go to the Amazonian Indians who had very little contact with the world beyond the individual tribe. Anthropologists have visited them and written down their dreams. He gave an example of fourteen dreams. Let me give you a couple of these examples which he felt refuted the wish-fulfillment theory of dreams and supported his evolutionary view of threat rehearsal in dreams. One dream: ''I was having sex with my neighbor's wife and her husband attacked me.'' That's a threat dream, okay? ''I found myself interested in approaching this young girl and my wife got very angry at me.'' And I can give you several other examples like that.

Then dreams are used to consolidate learning, which is another very important consideration as a function of dreams. Another one of the papers by Vertes and Eastman (2003) dealt with this. They reviewed the entire literature in the field, voluminously, tediously, and I had to read the whole thing. The outcome of this review was that no judgment could be arrived at. There were as many studies that demonstrated there was no consolidation of learning. So, the jury is out so far as whether dreams have the consolidating function.

There is also the hypothesis that dreams give the dreamer the opportunity to relate the present to the past. There is only one problem with that, present and past are confused. That's one of the things that happens in dreams, a part of the primary process; chronology is often violated. Things that are in one sequence are reversed in their sequence, or two events that happened at different times coincide. Well, how can one learn to connect the past with the present under those circumstances, when the mechanisms of the primary process tend to dictate that past and present are confounded? If we relied on the dream to do that for us, we would have disappeared a long time ago.

Owen Renik: I am interested in the phenomenon of patients who sleep and sometimes dream during the analytic hour. I would be interested in any experiences you have had and theories about it. Also, an obvious and practical point, the more resistant the patient, the more exceptional is the place of the dream, regardless of theoretical point of view.

Robert Gillman: I have had patients who sleep and dream and I thought: "Now I am going to get the real thing." And I don't think it was REM sleep. I think these patients had kind of hallucinatory or brain experiences that were not particularly verbalizable or comprehensible and I was very disappointed. That's my experience.

Ellen Rees: I had one experience with a patient who actually spent nine months in a long analysis falling asleep and dreaming on the couch. I would agree that probably the characteristic of the dream would be a non-REM dream to the point that I would wonder with Marianne Goldberger whether or not you could equate them as a form of almost a transference fantasy daydream, but he was genuinely asleep. Now, the functioning of the dreaming that I came to understand in this particular patient, I don't know whether I would generalize it, is that this was a patient who used narrative fiction as an encapsulated form of expressing transference for defensive purposes. I think that he found the dream sufficiently distanced that he could begin to represent erotic transference phenomena for the first time only by representing it as a dream or in the form of a dream. However, it raised in my mind something that Philip Bromberg is raising too, that that state of mind was necessary, and that he genuinely over time seemed to have no form of access to a blatant transference fantasy that was represented in fictional form, which then came in dream form. So I think it was an emergence of a state.

Philip Bromberg: As Ellen was talking I was thinking about a patient of mine that I had written about in 1984, a paper which Arnold Richards knows about because we share an interest in the Isakower phenomenon. My patient actually experienced the Isakower phenomenon on the couch during an analytic session. He didn't fall asleep, but was in fact in a light trance state. Having never experienced this before, I didn't know what was happening or how to think about it. Visually, he could have been seen as sleeping because he had his eyes closed and was breathing deeply, but he was in fact in a hypnogogic state, part of which occurs in a twilight consciousness that is neither wakefulness nor sleep, but a state of tension between the two. As such, it allows for a transitional experience to take place where the person is able to play with imagery in a way not possible while awake. The fact that it happened during a session is particularly fascinating and makes me wonder whether many of the experiences that analysts have with patients who look like they fell asleep on the couch are with patients who are not actually asleep, but in trance states.

Sydney Pulver: It seems to me that in a state of napping or momentarily falling asleep, a number of different phenomena can happen. First of all Schilder showed long ago that in hypnogogic states, as you are about to go to sleep, you develop a kind of visual imagery which is a visual, symbolic transformation of what you happen to be thinking about. If there is a certain problem on your mind that is knotty, you may develop a mental image of somebody tying a knot, or what have you. It's a simple symbol. But on the other hand, from my own personal experience as an inveterate napper, I love to nap, and I can tell you I may nap for ten minutes and in that ten minutes I am sure that I don't have REM sleep. I don't know how I know, but theoretically I am not supposed to. But I dream dreams which I have not been able to distinguish from regular nighttime dreams. They just seem to be the same thing, content-wise, experience-wise. So, a number of different phenomena can happen in there.

Paul Lippmann: One of my analysts once fell asleep during my session when I was on the couch, and it was disturbing to say the least, but we had an opportunity later to talk about what his dreams were while he was sleeping. They weren't really dreams, they were a kind of hypnogogic experience, and we worked very hard to relate his kind of hypnogogic experience to some of what I was talking about and feeling about and I am happy to report that we found absolutely no correlation whatsoever. What was on his mind was what was on his mind. If you let yourself be aware of hypnogogic experience sometimes it's absolutely the strangest kind of stuff that doesn't follow neatly from what was just on your mind.

I want to thank very much the organizers of the meeting for allowing and encouraging people from different institutes to come together and talk together about something as remarkable as dreams and for the different journals to give us this opportunity—a rare treat. And I wanted to read something which comes from Anthony Shafton, *Dream Reader* (1995). Well, he took the theme of the twenty-four dream interpreters in the Talmud and he went further. He wanted to take the twenty-four different interpretations of a single motif and the dream motif he chose was the dream of flying, and this is what he wrote. These are the kinds of things he found this one dream experience could be interpreted as:

> (1) Vestibular stimulation from turning in bed. (2) Labyrinthitis or mid-brain disease. (3) Pre-coronary personality. (4) An ancestral vestige of life in the sea or in the trees. (5) A memory trace of childhood games of movement, being tossed about. (6) Infantile grandiosity. (7) A symbol of death because ghost and angels fly. (8) Desire to escape from anxiety, responsibility, parents, the limits of nature, the analysis. (9) A will to dominate others. (10) A dread of contamination by others. (11) High self-esteem or sense of personal power. (12) Optimism or stimulation for success. (13) Freedom. (14) Rising above difficulties. (15) Being ungrounded. (16) A warning of overstuffing one's self in waking life. (17) Feeling good, high. (18) Not feeling good. (19) Genital erotism, romantic erotism, sexual liberation. (20) Kundalini power, often preceding out of body experience. (21) Really flying in an astral body. (22) A prelude to lucid dreaming. (23) Spirituality. (24) A sense of fun or playfulness [p. 24].

If we add to these the question of how did you feel, it could be I felt terrible, I felt wonderful, a dream image is a most complex thing.

Robert Gillman: I want to add number twenty-five. When my son was a few months old, I was carrying him across the room and I said, "Hey, I just started analysis, and I said that's like my flying dream! That feeling of being carried across the room." And I never had that flying dream again.

Edward Nersessian: I just want to say about the sleeping dream, in my experience I had one case where this happened often but the patient was a physician who was on call and would nevertheless try to come to the hour and would not have slept for sometimes twenty-six hours and would fall asleep. When he would wake up and I would say, ''What were you thinking?'' he would fall back to sleep again. But in other circumstances my experience usually has been that this occurs in a state of resistance and the patient doesn't really sleep but dozes off for very brief moments, and when you ask them to describe their thoughts, what you get is a description of the process of the transformation of thought into visual imagery. And those are several phenomena when you ask about them, the gradual transformation of thought into imagery that you get, and I have never been able to analyze them.

Mervyn Peskin: The second patient I presented (see chapter 11) toward the end of his analysis would fall asleep in sessions. Sometimes he would sleep for twenty or thirty minutes but wake up pretty much on time. Sometimes I had to waken him. I did regard this as sleeping as at times he would snore and seem disoriented on awakening. Often he would sleep for three or four minutes and in a fragmented fashion report dreams he had immediately on falling asleep. Though they were often quite rich affectively, seemed to be dealing with well-known themes, and were often intriguing, I agree with what was said in that I was unable to make much headway with these ''in session'' dreams. They related to termination and were dominated by resistance to what he was feeling. Though he was close to me I could not reach him at those times. However, in regard to compromise formation, at the same time his sleeping in my presence so close to me was an act of great trust replete with other wishes. He was using the couch as a refuge and a place to be sheltered by me before he left, as he had used his analysis earlier. It was both a distancing and a staying close.

Audience Participant: Since you are all talking about how patients who sleep and dream on the couch don't really provide much that is workable, I thought by contrast that the question earlier in the day about flashbacks got short shrift. Rather than this kind of sleeping, flashbacks are very unusual phenomena that are the closest thing we have to dreaming in the waking state. Marianne Goldberger, for example, made clear in her paper (chapter 10) that daydreams are not all that different in a certain way from fantasy and reverie. But flashbacks share with nocturnal dreams the quality of being experienced with hallucinatory vividness and coming unbidden. My own experience is that unlike the kind of material we are discussing now about patients who doze on the couch, that flashbacks give us the opportunity, since they do occur in the waking state, to wonder why they are occurring and potentially throw light on why and how dreams occur and whether it is possible to approach flashbacks like dreams, and what working with flashbacks tells us about working with dreams. I would like to hear from people who have any experience with working with patients who have had flashbacks and whether they have been able to approach them analytically, unlike the material we are now discussing.

James Fosshage: I certainly have had experiences with patients who have had flashbacks, but typically they are dealing with traumatic material. But certainly the unbidden aspect for it and the spontaneous aspect are very similar. But it has to do with traumatic material and of course dreams are much broader, dealing with all sorts of material. We always have spontaneous fantasies and this is what Marianne Goldberger was getting at in terms of fantasies and daydreams. Or *waking dreams* is another term that we have talked about which of course corresponds but is a far larger rubric than flashbacks.

Audience Member: I have worked with many war veterans, but the first time I encountered the phenomenon of flashback was with a World War II veteran who had the experience before we were using the term *flashback.* He presented it as a waking hallucination. It was the following: He was in his fighter plane, in command of his wing, over the English Channel where they had just scored a direct hit on a German submarine and some of the German sailors were floundering around in the water. He had just radioed headquarters to find out what he could do about rescuing them and instead he was ordered to remain there with his squadron to make sure that no rescue could take place. He carried out his orders, but he experienced it as an unimaginable conflict. And this flashback came up repeatedly in his treatment during times of great conflict.

Sydney Pulver: We were talking about Marianne Goldberger and it made me think of a question that I wanted to ask her about her presentation, in a way it relates to the various phenomena that we have. Marianne, you were asked afterwards about the difference between fantasy and daydream, and I wanted to ask you something a little further. You talked a lot about your patient's daydreams, but as you described what they actually were, they sounded, at times, more like just thoughts. In other words, not visual images but just an idea. I'm wondering if that's what they were and, to go a little bit further, would it make any clinical difference? I wonder if anybody thinks it would make any difference. Let's suppose I were your patient, and I was walking into your office, and I think, "You know I bet she is building a swimming pool with my money." No visual imagery, I just think of it. If we contrast that to my walking by and having a mental image of a swimming pool and then a little fantasy about children being there. So the basic question is: Do you think it matters which is which? Does it have any clinical impact?

Marianne Goldberger: That's a good question. I am not sure I can answer it, except of course it makes a difference in the vividness of the patient's visual, mental, verbal, and affective experience. Anything that increases vividness, I feel, I think everybody would agree, makes a difference. You said some of the things I described are thoughts, and you are quite right. When I was working on the subject I realized that very often what starts as a thought can end up as a longer elaboration. No, I don't have any investment in calling that a daydream, rather than a fantasy. Those are fantasies. When defenses are low they get more detailed. You know, some people have much more elaborate daydreams, writers, imaginative people. But I don't know if you should call those daydreams—they have an extended fantasy and then some go write a short story.

Howard Shevrin: Well, I think this does return us to a very important issue, which has cropped up from time to time in the course of our discussion, most recently when Paul Lippmann was talking about the need to pay attention to the manifest dream. I don't think I would take any exception to that. However, and this gets us back to the fundamental distinction I've been trying to convey between the dispositional and interactive unconscious, is that a particular mental product may look the same but may be the result of a very different underlying process. In other words, you can have a thought about yourself and a swimming pool, you can have a daydream, and you can have a dream, and the content may seem in fact similar. There may be differences in vividness, for example. But the critical thing is that the way in which that product, if you like, was delivered into consciousness was different.

In fact I do have some research bearing on that. I would like to present the conclusion of the research and summarize it. This is a study which I did with Charles Fisher, and I mention that because Charles Fisher was one of the leading research lights at Mount Sinai. But the outcome of the research, and it was a sleep–dream study, was that when people were awakened from REM sleep, they produced content that was much more primary process in nature than when they were awakened from non-REM sleep. So although there are different kinds of mentation, although things that occur during the night can all be called dreams because they happen during the night, they can be the outcome of a very different process, depending on other prevailing conditions, like whatever goes on in REM sleep versus non-REM sleep. I think that Steve Ellman's research speaks to that. But I would generalize this point and say that there is manifest content and there is manifest content. Some things may arise from one kind of unconscious process, and some things may arise that look the same from a very different unconscious process. The only way you can find that out in the clinical situation is through the free-associative process. So I think that to simply say pay attention to manifest content does not answer the question, how did it get there?

Paul Lippmann: As both Wittgenstein and Grünbaum, more recently, and many others have said, one of the problems with the free-associative method is that if you start with anything, with a nonsense syllable, in three or four steps you will arrive at some core preoccupation of the person. We don't need a dream, or a manifest dream, to set off that process. People will eventually get to what's on their mind. I think that both Wittgenstein and Grünbaum are using that argument. It's not entirely a well-buttressed argument, but it still presents a problem to me.

Audience Member: I think there you touch on an empirical question that can in fact be answered. All of us who have been talking about dreams, the one thing that we agree on is how multifaceted, how many sided they are, as compared let's say to a thought or a conjecture, or simply remembering something. They seem to have a multiplicity of inherent meanings, as compared to other mental products. I think Grünbaum and Wittgenstein are wrong, therefore, and I think that dreams do have a privileged place insofar as they give us access to many different avenues, which other mental products do not gain us access to as readily.

Owen Renik: We are bouncing back and forth from point to point but I did want to say that I had the same experience as Jim Fosshage in working with flashbacks, that they are workable, but I think you said that flashbacks deal with trauma whereas nocturnal dreams deal with a variety of material, which suggests the possibility that all dreams are about trauma. That is to say, trauma defined as the organism having been given an experience which it finds it still has to do further work on in order to peaceably manage and adapt to it, and it is just in these extreme instances that the "trauma" is dramatic and vivid in an unmistakable way, whereas the quieter trauma, the traumas that are the occasion for dreams every night are less obvious to us. Although when we investigate the daily residue we are lucky enough to be able to identify that we have the feeling that there are actually, in some small ways, experiences that need to be worked on. So maybe the connection teaches us something about trauma as well as about dreaming.

Marianne Goldberger: We all feel that dreams are very important, that's a universal feeling of homo sapiens. That doesn't mean that we as analysts know theoretically that it is necessarily true, except that our patients react to them very much. I don't think we can achieve much by saying, "I think it's important." What the patient says is important.

Audience Member: The distinction that some people are making between REM dreams and non-REM dreams, is that clinically useful? And if so, in what way? How does that fit in with the whole body of dream research starting in the midsixties? Are there certain kinds of mentations in dreams and what does that mean?

Howard Shevrin: Maybe Steve Ellman can say something about it too. But first of all, from a pragmatic standpoint, of course, as analysts we don't know from what state the particular dream is reported. The patient experiences it as something that happened during the night and calls it a dream. My guess would be that on the basis of the research that I have just tried to cite, as well as from other research, that there is in fact a difference in the mental process involved in the REM dream as compared to the non-REM dream, and I would say that more likely those dreams that prove more useful in the analytic situation are REM dreams rather than non-REM dreams. How we would ever work out a research protocol to determine that I don't know. Except that—I have a vague memory of this, going back quite a few years into the seventies—Greg Greenberg up in Boston undertook some research along these lines that had to do with the fact that the patient reported most often the last dream before awakening in the morning, which is a REM dream. But whether one can discriminate within the analytic situation those dreams that are products of REM versus non-REM sleep, that's another question. And that point I don't know how it could be done, except along the ways I was just describing, taking into account the kind of work that has been done, which seems to indicate, although there is controversy about this, that REM mentation is different from non-REM, and I would say simply by shorthand that it is more primary process than is the case for the non-REM. So perhaps those dreams that present themselves as more bizarre, more disjointed, less revised if you like, maybe even appear less metaphorical in nature, might in fact be the product of REM sleep. Those that are more fragmented and less organized would be the product of non-REM sleep. I think that both are of interest to analysts, clearly, but they would I think result in a different aspect of what goes on, if you like, unconsciously. This would be my concern.

James Fosshage: My understanding in terms of the REM and non-REM research is that REM as Howard Shevrin has suggested typically involves imagistic mentation, it is more predominantly imagistic mentation, although there is typically some participation of universal oriented or secondary process. In non-REM it is more secondary process and it tends to be more similar to a replay of a daily event or something we have to do; for example, we have to mow the lawn tomorrow. There is quite a bit of research concerning the differences and there is some research which suggests that for those therapy situations in which there is a focus on REM dreams as compared to those that focus on non-REM dreams, the former patients tend to stay in treatment longer. I think one of the clinical implications that is so important is that dreams vary as to the level of significance. That is very important because we didn't have that in terms of the traditional model within psychoanalysis. We were taught that all dreams were equally important and it was up to the analyst to get to the right meaning. But there is a good deal of research that shows this non-REM/REM differentiation suggests that there are differences in significance.

Mark Blechner: First of all, Foulkes has found that 20 percent of non-REM dreams are indistinguishable from REM dreams. So I don't think that we can ever say just from hearing a dream for sure whether it is a REM or non-REM. Also, Mort Reiser commented about how I had told him that something I had discovered was really discovered by Dostoevsky. He was referring to a paper I wrote in 1983 about dreams in borderline and schizophrenic patients. I thought I had made the discovery that a lot of the dreams that such patients brought in the beginning of treatment tended to sound not like dreams but just almost like a kind of ordinary communication about what happened. But what they were telling me in their waking communications was more chaotic. I did discover since then that Dostoevsky noted that in *Crime and Punishment* and so did a number of other people before me. But another possibility that has been suggested about that phenomenon is that in fact patients who are psychotic or borderline may be remembering or reporting more non-REM dreams. And at least clinically I found that those dreams very often tell me something very simple and direct that the patient wasn't telling me in any other way, so they can also be very useful, even if they are not bizarre, especially in such patients.

Owen Renik: I just want to comment that I am astonished by the energy not only of the panel but of the audience. I can only feel that it is trickle down from the remarkable energy of Arnold Richards who has made this whole thing possible and I don't think that there is anyone else who could have done it. So thank you.

Arnold Richards: Thank you all and I just want to say a word or two. I think it has been a terrific meeting, I am very pleased. This meeting is the most organizationally diverse meeting, I think, in psychoanalysis. And even though we don't have the experimental means to adjudicate these differences, I think that what we have to do until we do that, we have to be together, and talk to each other, and share our clinical work. Thank you very much.

REFERENCES

Blechner, M. J. (1983), Changes in the dreams of borderline patients: *Contemp. Psychoanal.,* 19:845–498.

Kilbourne, B. (1981), Aspects of the handling of symbols in Moroccan dream interpretation. *The Psychoanalytic Study of Society,* 9:1–14.

Masson, J. M., Ed. (1985), *The Complete Letters of Sigmund Freud to Wilhelm Fliess, 1887–1904.* Cambridge, MA: Harvard University Press.

Revonsuo, A. (2003), The reinterpretation of dreams: An evolutionary hypothesis of the function of dreaming. In: *Sleep and Dreaming: Scientific Advances and Reconsiderations,* ed. E. F. Pace-Schott, M. Solms, M. Blagrove, & S. Harnad. New York: Cambridge University Press, pp. 85–111.

Shafton, A. (1995), *Dream Reader.* Albany, NY: State University of New York Press.

Shevrin, H. & Eiser, A. S. (2003), Continued vitality of the Freudian theory of dreaming. In: *Sleep and Dreaming: Scientific Advances and Reconsiderations,* ed. E. F. Pace-Schott, M. Solms, M. Blagrove, & S. Harnad. New York: Cambridge University Press, pp. 216–218.

Winson, J. (1985), *Brain and Psyche: The Biology of the Unconscious.* Garden City, NY: Anchor.

Vertes, R. P., & Eastman, K. E. (2003), The case against memory consolidation in REM sleep. In: *Sleep and Dreaming: Scientific Advances and Reconsiderations,* ed. E. F. Pace-Schott, M. Solms, M. Blagrove, & S. Harnad. New York: Cambridge University Press, pp. 75–84.

Name Index

Subject Index

D